Media, Mobilization and the Umbrella Movement

The Umbrella Movement in Hong Kong caught the world's attention and imagination at the end of 2014. The 79-day occupation campaign took on some of the characteristics of the recent wave of large-scale protest movements around the world, including the prominent roles played by the media – both conventional and digital – in the mobilization and communication processes of the movement.

This edited volume, *Media, Mobilization and the Umbrella Movement*, brings together nine contributions which examine various aspects of the media-movement nexus, including the power of televised images to mobilize people, the role of social media in the insurgent public sphere, young activists' social media strategies, media influence on citizens' understanding of civil disobedience, the government's response to digital media tactics, public discourses about the rule of law, and local and foreign media coverage of the movement. This high-quality collection will enhance understanding of the Umbrella Movement, and also facilitate and trigger more research and dialogue comparing the Umbrella Movement with other similar protest movements around the world.

This book was originally published as a special issue of the *Chinese Journal of Communication*.

Francis L. F. Lee is a Professor in the School of Journalism and Communication at The Chinese University of Hong Kong. He is lead author of *Media, Social Mobilization, and Mass Protests in Post-colonial Hong Kong* (2011) and author of *Talk Radio, the Mainstream Press, and Public Opinion in Hong Kong* (2014).

Media, Mobilization and the Umbrella Movement

Edited by
Francis L. F. Lee

LONDON AND NEW YORK

First published 2017
by Routledge

2 Park Square, Milton Park, Abingdon, Oxfordshire OX14 4RN
52 Vanderbilt Avenue, New York, NY 10017

Routledge is an imprint of the Taylor & Francis Group, an informa business

First issued in paperback 2018

Copyright © 2017 The Centre for Chinese Media and Comparative Communication Research, the Chinese University of Hong Kong

All rights reserved. No part of this book may be reprinted or reproduced or utilised in any form or by any electronic, mechanical, or other means, now known or hereafter invented, including photocopying and recording, or in any information storage or retrieval system, without permission in writing from the publishers.

Notice:
Product or corporate names may be trademarks or registered trademarks, and are used only for identification and explanation without intent to infringe.

British Library Cataloguing in Publication Data
A catalogue record for this book is available from the British Library

ISBN 13: 978-1-138-22309-7 (hbk)
ISBN 13: 978-0-367-07472-2 (pbk)

Typeset in Times New Roman
by RefineCatch Limited, Bungay, Suffolk

Publisher's Note
The publisher accepts responsibility for any inconsistencies that may have arisen during the conversion of this book from journal articles to book chapters, namely the possible inclusion of journal terminology.

Disclaimer
Every effort has been made to contact copyright holders for their permission to reprint material in this book. The publishers would be grateful to hear from any copyright holder who is not here acknowledged and will undertake to rectify any errors or omissions in future editions of this book.

Contents

Citation Information	vii
Notes on Contributors	ix
Introduction: Media Communication and the Umbrella Movement *Francis L. F. Lee*	1
1. Mobilization by images: TV screen and mediated instant grievances in the Umbrella Movement *Gary Tang*	6
2. Social media and Umbrella Movement: insurgent public sphere in formation *Paul S. N. Lee, Clement Y. K. So and Louis Leung*	24
3. Media and information praxis of young activists in the Umbrella Movement *Alice Y. L. Lee and Ka Wan Ting*	44
4. Social movement as civic education: communication activities and understanding of civil disobedience in the Umbrella Movement *Francis L. F. Lee*	61
5. A legal realist view on citizen actions in Hong Kong's umbrella movement *John Nguyet Erni*	80
6. Contested news values and media performance during the Umbrella Movement *Chi Kit Chan*	88
7. Business as usual: the UK national daily press and the Occupy Central movement *Colin Sparks*	97
8. The coming colonization of Hong Kong cyberspace: government responses to the use of new technologies by the umbrella movement *Lokman Tsui*	115
9. Yellow or blue ribbons: analysing discourses in conflict in the televized government-student meeting during the Occupy Movement in Hong Kong *Yiqi Liu*	124
Index	137

Citation Information

The chapters in this book were originally published in the *Chinese Journal of Communication*, volume 8, issue 4 (December 2015). When citing this material, please use the original page numbering for each article, as follows:

Introduction
Media Communication and the Umbrella Movement: introduction to the special issue
Francis L. F. Lee
Chinese Journal of Communication, volume 8, issue 4 (December 2015) pp. 333–337

Chapter 1
Mobilization by images: TV screen and mediated instant grievances in the Umbrella Movement
Gary Tang
Chinese Journal of Communication, volume 8, issue 4 (December 2015) pp. 338–355

Chapter 2
Social media and Umbrella Movement: insurgent public sphere in formation
Paul S. N. Lee, Clement Y. K. So and Louis Leung
Chinese Journal of Communication, volume 8, issue 4 (December 2015) pp. 356–375

Chapter 3
Media and information praxis of young activists in the Umbrella Movement
Alice Y. L. Lee and Ka Wan Ting
Chinese Journal of Communication, volume 8, issue 4 (December 2015) pp. 376–392

Chapter 4
Social movement as civic education: communication activities and understanding of civil disobedience in the Umbrella Movement
Francis L. F. Lee
Chinese Journal of Communication, volume 8, issue 4 (December 2015) pp. 393–411

Chapter 5
A legal realist view on citizen actions in Hong Kong's umbrella movement
John Nguyet Erni
Chinese Journal of Communication, volume 8, issue 4 (December 2015) pp. 412–419

CITATION INFORMATION

Chapter 6
Contested news values and media performance during the Umbrella Movement
Chi Kit Chan
Chinese Journal of Communication, volume 8, issue 4 (December 2015) pp. 420–428

Chapter 7
Business as usual: the UK national daily press and the Occupy Central movement
Colin Sparks
Chinese Journal of Communication, volume 8, issue 4 (December 2015) pp. 429–446

Chapter 8
The coming colonization of Hong Kong cyberspace: government responses to the use of new technologies by the umbrella movement
Lokman Tsui
Chinese Journal of Communication, volume 8, issue 4 (December 2015) pp. 447–455

Chapter 9
Yellow or blue ribbons: analysing discourses in conflict in the televized government-student meeting during the Occupy Movement in Hong Kong
Yiqi Liu
Chinese Journal of Communication, volume 8, issue 4 (December 2015) pp. 456–467

For any permission-related enquiries please visit:
http://www.tandfonline.com/page/help/permissions

Notes on Contributors

Chi Kit Chan is Assistant Professor in the Department of Journalism and Communication, Hang Seng Management College, Hong Kong, China. His research interests include journalism, media sociology, risk communication, and cultural identity.

John Nguyet Erni is Chair Professor in Humanities and Head of the Department of Humanities and Creative Writing at Hong Kong Baptist University. He is an elected fellow and member of the Executive of the Hong Kong Academy of the Humanities. His recent books include *Understanding South Asian Minorities in Hong Kong* (with Lisa Leung, 2014) and *Cultural Studies of Rights: Critical Articulations* (2011).

Alice Y. L. Lee is Head of the Department of Journalism, Hong Kong Baptist University. Her research interests include online news media, media education, media and information literacy (MIL), Net Generation, and knowledge society. She is the vice-chairperson of the Hong Kong Association of Media Education.

Francis L. F. Lee is a Professor and Head of the Graduate Division at the School of Journalism and Communication, The Chinese University of Hong Kong.

Paul S. N. Lee is a Professor in the School of Journalism and Communication at The Chinese University of Hong Kong. He received his PhD from the University of Michigan, USA. His research interests include international communication, telecoms policy, new media, and media analysis.

Louis Leung is a Professor in the School of Journalism and Communication at The Chinese University of Hong Kong. He currently serves as Director of Centre for Communication and Public Opinion Survey, and is founder and Director of the MSc in New Media program since 2000. His research interests focus on the uses and effects of new media. He holds a PhD in Communication from The University of Texas at Austin, USA.

Yiqi Liu received her PhD from the Faculty of Education, The University of Hong Kong. Her research interests include critical discourse analysis, language and gender, and content and language integrated learning (CLIL).

Clement Y. K. So is a Professor in the School of Journalism and Communication and Associate Dean (Student Affairs) of the Faculty of Social Science at The Chinese University of Hong Kong. He serves as a board member of the Hong Kong News-Expo and secretary general of the Hong Kong Journalism Education Foundation. His major research interests include Hong Kong press, news sociology, citation analysis, and development in the field of communication.

NOTES ON CONTRIBUTORS

Colin Sparks is Professor of Media Studies and Director of the Centre for Media and Communication Research in the School of Communication at Hong Kong Baptist University. Before moving to Hong Kong he worked for many years at the University of Westminster in London, where he was Professor of Media Studies and Director of the Communication and Media Research Institute (CAMRI). He is a founding member of the Editorial Board of *Media, Culture and Society*.

Gary Tang (PhD, 2016) is currently a Post-Doctoral Fellow in the the School of Journalism and Communication at The Chinese University of Hong Kong. His research interests include political communication, social media, and public discourse.

Ka Wan Ting is a broadcast journalism graduate from the Department of Journalism at the Hong Kong Baptist University. She is enthusiastic about studying the development of the Hong Kong media. She has been assisting in research on the bomb generation (the post-90s) and their social engagement in Hong Kong, with particular reference to their utilization of social media.

Lokman Tsui is an Assistant Professor in the School of Journalism and Communication at The Chinese University of Hong Kong. Before joining the School, he was the head of free expression for Google in Asia and the Pacific. He received his PhD from the Annenberg School for Communication at the University of Pennsylvania, USA.

Introduction

Media Communication and the Umbrella Movement

Francis L. F. Lee

The Chinese University of Hong Kong, Hong Kong

The relationship between the media and social movements has attracted a huge and growing amount of attention from communication scholars and social scientists in the wake of recent social protests across the world, most notably the Arab Spring, the Spanish Indignados, and Occupy Wall Street. These protest campaigns exhibited several common and often unconventional characteristics. They employed the occupation of public space as the main form of collective action and simultaneously involved a wide range of actions taken by individuals and small groups. The actions were often unplanned, and the participation of individuals was spontaneous. Nevertheless, the protests scaled up very quickly. They had a decentralized formation, and social movement organizations did not play a strong leadership role. Digital media technologies constituted an important platform for participants to coordinate among themselves and mobilize each other. These movements have become the objects of empirical research and innovative theorization, with Castells' (2012) conceptualization of networked social movements and Bennett and Segerberg's (2013) explication of the logic of connective action being arguably the most influential accounts to date.

Against this background, in late 2014 the Umbrella Movement in Hong Kong caught the attention and the imagination of the world. Let's begin with a brief note about the movement's origin. The Chinese government had promised that in 2017, Hong Kong could vote for the chief executive of its government in a popular election. However, the Chinese government wanted to ensure that no subversive politician would be elected as the chief executive of Hong Kong. It also seemed to be concerned that other cities in the mainland would strive for the same right if unconstrained popular elections were institutionalized in Hong Kong. Commentators had long suspected that China would set up electoral procedures and frameworks such that only the candidates that it approved could stand for election. Thus, in January 2013 pro-democracy academics and politicians began discussing plans for Occupy Central, which was conceived as a civil disobedience campaign to force the Chinese government to make concessions regarding democratization.

The Chinese government stood firm, however. On 31 August 2014, the National People's Congress announced the electoral framework in which candidates would need to obtain support from more than half of the members of the nomination committee in order to stand in the popular election. Because China would place tight control on the formation of the nomination committee, this framework would effectively allow China to rule out the candidates it disliked. In response, the proponents of Occupy Central announced that the campaign would proceed. In late September, a series of concurrent events turned the planned Occupy Central into the unplanned Umbrella Movement (Table 1 provides a

Table 1. Timeline of events from 31 August to 29 September 2014.

Date	Event
31 August	The National People's Congress (NPC) decided on the framework for the election of the chief executive of the Hong Kong Special Administrative Region Government in 2017. The decision stipulated that only two to three candidates should be allowed, each candidate needs to be supported by more than half of the nomination committee to become eligible, and the basic formation of the nomination committee would remain unchanged. In response, the proponents of Occupy Central and pro-democracy citizens rallied in Tamar Park, which is next to the Government Headquarters (GH). Benny Tai, the initiator of Occupy Central, announced that the planned campaign would go ahead.
11 September	Chan Kin-man, another initiator of the Occupy Central campaign, hinted in a radio program that the occupation would begin on 1 October.
22 September	The Hong Kong Federation of Students (HKFS), the city's university student union, began a one-week class boycott protesting against NPC's decision. Protest rallies and "civic lectures" were organized in front of and around the GH.
26 September	The one-week class boycott ended. Student leaders continued the protest in front of the GH. Late at night, students rushed into a closed area in front of the east wing of the GH, which used to be an open area where protest rallies were held in previous years. Conflict between the police and the protesters ensued, and several student leaders were arrested.
27 September	Protests in front of the GH continued as more people, especially youngsters, joined the protests and demanded the release of the student leaders.
28 September	In response to calls to begin Occupy Central earlier than planned because of the student protests, Benny Tai announced the beginning of Occupy Central at 1:00 a.m. In the morning, tens of thousands of citizens went to Admiralty, the district where the GH is located, to support the movement. The police closed off the area and prevented citizens from joining the protesters in front of the GH. In the afternoon, the huge crowd of citizens breached the police defense line, inadvertently starting the occupation of the main roads in the Admiralty district.
28 September evening	At around 6:00 pm, the police fired tear gas in an attempt to disperse the crowd. The attempt failed, and more people congregated in the street. The police continued into the night to use tear gas in the attempt to disperse the crowd. Some protesters, in the attempt to prevent a successful eviction by the police, started to occupy several other districts in Hong Kong. Within 24 hours, occupied sites appeared in at least four major districts in the city. Occupy Central – an action that was supposedly planned with clear lines of command and leadership – thus evolved into a more decentralized occupation campaign, which the leading groups could not fully control. The international media dubbed the occupation the Umbrella Revolution based on the images of protesters protecting themselves with umbrellas against the pepper spray and tear gas used by the police. Local activists appropriated the term and changed it to the Umbrella Movement, emphasizing that the action was not aimed at overthrowing the Chinese government.

timeline of the events in September 2014). The occupation began on 28 September and lasted until 15 December, when police evicted the last occupation site.

On one hand, the Umbrella Movement shared some characteristics of the recent wave of occupation protests around the world. The Umbrella Movement involved the construction of a space of autonomy (Castells, 2012), which was constituted by the combination of urban physical space and cyberspace, and the participation of individuals was seemingly spontaneous. Similar to Bennett and Segerberg's (2013) characterization of the logic of connective action, "I Demand Genuine Popular Election" – a core slogan used throughout the movement – could be regarded as the "personal action frame" under which individuals participated in the campaign in their own ways. Furthermore, the digital media undoubtedly played important roles in the communication, organization, and coordination that took place among the occupiers. Participation in the movement was self-actualizing and expressive: occupiers grew vegetables and flowers, practiced public arts, erected the Lennon Wall, built temporary temples, churches, self-study areas, and mobile classrooms, set up resource sharing centers, and so forth. The occupiers not only protested but also helped develop the occupied areas into a special lifeworld according to their vision of the ideal community.

On the other hand, the Umbrella Movement was not the ideal typical networked social movement or connective action, and it was not entirely spontaneous. While no one could predict the exact manifestation of the movement, the idea of an occupation campaign had been promoted for nearly two years. The movement exhibited a strong tendency towards decentralization, but it was not entirely "leaderless". The proponents of Occupy Central and two major student groups were continually viewed as the leaders of the movement, even though it was also clear that many participants did not trust them. More importantly, the movement arguably needed "leaders", or at least "representatives", because, unlike Occupy Wall Street, the Umbrella Movement had clear policy goals, and therefore needed to enter into interactions and negotiations that were in line with these goals. Moreover, although the digital media played important roles in mobilization and in on-site coordination and communication, the role of the mainstream mass media in conveying information and images—especially the shocking images of the use of tear gas by the police—was equally, if not more, crucial to the fast acceleration of the movement on 28 September.

The Umbrella Movement arose in a specific social and political context. Social protest is not rare in Hong Kong. On 1 July 2003, half a million citizens joined a protest against the then imminent national security legislation and the government's performance in general. The protest became a watershed, "critical event" altering the political dynamics in the city, while also contributing to people's sense of collective efficacy and energizing the social movement sector in Hong Kong (Lee & Chan, 2011). Since then, the number of protests and rallies in the city has continued to rise, and numerous local scholars have provided analyses of the growth of social mobilization (e.g., Lee & Chan, 2013; Ma, 2011; So, 2011). There has also been much analysis of the role of the digital media and the rise of online-based citizen self-mobilization in Hong Kong (e.g., Chan & Lee, 2015).

The challenge for scholars who try to understand the Umbrella Movement is to be able to see the Umbrella Movement as a part of an emerging "family" of movements around the world without losing sight of its local specificities. In other words, the challenge is to gain a contextualized understanding of the Umbrella Movement without overemphasizing its uniqueness, which would render impossible the dialogue and comparison with other cases of social protest.

Certainly, neither this short introduction nor the articles in this special issue can offer a well-developed and comprehensive account of the Umbrella Movement. The reason that the *Chinese Journal of Communication* has compiled this special issue, "Media Communication andthe Umbrella Movement," is to promote the discussion and analyses of the roles of the media and communication in the occupation campaign. This special issue includes four research articles and five commentary essays. We did not request that the authors speak from the same perspective; we did not even require that the authors use the same terms for the movement. The authors of the articles and essays included in this issue used the names Occupy Movement, Occupy Central, and Umbrella Movement to refer to the same object of analysis. All the articles and essays in this issue aim to present initial analyses and thoughts about various aspects of the movement.

The issue begins with Gary K.Y. Tang's article on the role of television in mobilizing people to join the movement. Drawing upon the notions of public screen and image events in the social movement literature and based on data derived from a survey of protesters in the Umbrella Movement, Tang argued that live broadcast images of tear gas flying over the cityscape in Hong Kong created "mediated instant grievances" among the watching public, leading more people to participate in the protest. Tang's arguments and evidence thus point to the role of conventional mass media in the formation of large-scale movements in Hong Kong, a theme well recognized in studies about large-scale movements in Hong Kong (e.g., Lee & Chan, 2011; Chan & Lee, 2015) but often receiving only subsidiary and simplistic treatment in accounts of occupation movements in other societies

Paul Lee, Clement So, and Louis Leung analyze the significance of digital media technologies in the Umbrella Movement by articulating the notion of the insurgent public sphere. Because digital media have provided the platforms for the growth of online alternative media, they have allowed citizens to connect with social activists and critical journalists in Hong Kong. The digital media thus contribute to the formation and sustaining of the counter-public in society. This empirical analysis shows that the reliance on social media for news is indeed related significantly and consistently to the support for the Umbrella Movement and to critical attitudes toward the police and the Hong Kong and Chinese governments.

Alice Lee and Ka Wan Ting's article analysed the communication strategies and media practices of young activists. Through focus group discussions, in-depth interviews, and the analysis of social media content, the study reveals how Scholarism, a prominent young activist group constituted mainly by high school students, built interpersonal networks, disseminated information, and mobilized actions through the skillful use of social media. However, Lee and Ting's analysis also emphasized the young activists' ability to interact with and attract the attention of the mainstream news media. They contended that the young activists can be considered as "agents of mediatization" adapted at the media and information power game associated with new modes of movement mobilization.

Francis Lee's article focuses on the events that preceded the Umbrella Movement. He argues that the debates surrounding Occupy Central since early 2013 constituted a critical discourse moment in which activists attempted to legitimize a new form of protest actions. Lee's data analysis shows that Hong Kong people's understanding of civil disobedience increased from 2013 to 2014. While the concept of civil disobedience was widely debated in the mainstream media, related ideas and messages were defused through digital media, and social media use related significantly to the understanding of the concept at the individual level. Lee argued that, although the Umbrella Movement took up an unplanned form, ideas of civil disobedience articulated throughout the Occupy Central campaign influenced the dynamics and the ending of the movement.

In addition to the four research articles, we invited authors to contribute commentary essays to enrich the discussion and analysis of the movement. John Erni's essay offers a critical discussion of how the idea of the rule of law was articulated by the power holders in ways that undermined the justifiability of civil disobedience. Erni argues for a legal realist's perspective, which recognizes the necessary political and moral bases of legal reasoning and hence the possible justifiability of disobedience through the appeal to a higher law.

In his essay, Chi Kit Chan discussed the performance of the mainstream news media in Hong Kong during the Umbrella Movement, paying particular attention to debates surrounding the media's (lack of) "objectivity." His discussion pointed to the problematized character of news objectivity in contemporary Hong Kong, and yet he also noted the continual relevance of the concept in media criticisms even among the alternative media practitioners. Colin Sparks discussed the British press's coverage of the Umbrella Movement. He noted that the British press, with the exception of several elite newspapers, did not pay continuous, high levels of attention to the events in Hong Kong. The British press also did not exhibit a strong pro-movement attitude in their coverage, arguably partly due to China's economic and strategic significance to Britain.

Lokman Tsui wrote about the role of the digital media in the Umbrella Movement from a perspective that highlighted the concerns of surveillance, censorship, rumormongering, manipulation of public opinion, and counter-framing by the power holders and their supporters. The essay is an eloquent reminder of the threats that could undermine the utility of the digital media as the technological basis of the space of autonomy, as well as the need to protect the open Internet from colonization by a political power. Lastly, Yiqi Liu provided a linguist's look into the televised "dialogue" between the student leaders and top government officials during the Umbrella Movement. The essay argues that the two sides' discourses constituted a contrast between delocalized nationalism (favored by the officials) and local isolationism (favored by the student leaders). It contends that neither approach is entirely suitable for Hong Kong, and more genuinely dialogic encounters between the two sides are needed.

We believe that the articles and essays included in this special issue not only enhance our understanding of the Umbrella Movement but also make specific contributions to the literature on social movements, new media, and political communication. We hope that this set of articles and essays provides a series of snapshots that allow readers to see the similarities and differences between the Umbrella Movement and other movements around the world. We also hope that this special issue will engender further analyses and studies.

Disclosure statement

No potential conflict of interest was reported by the author.

References

Bennett, W. L., & Segerberg, A. (2013). *The logic of connective action*. New York, NY: Cambridge University Press.
Castells, M. (2012). *Networks of outrage and hope*. Cambridge: Polity.
Chan, J. M., & Lee, F. L. F. (2015). Media, communication and social mobilization in contemporary Hong Kong. In G. Rawnsley & M. Y. Rawnsley (Eds.), *The Routledge Handbook of Chinese Media* (pp. 145 of Ch London: Routledge.
Lee, F. L. F., & Chan, J. M. (2011). *Media, social mobilization, and mass protests in post-colonial Hong Kong*. London: Routledge.
Lee, F. L. F., & Chan, J. M. (2013). Exploring the social movement society in Hong Kong: development of contentious collective actions. In S. K. Cheung, K. C. Leung, & K. M. Chan (Eds.), *Hong Kong, discourse, media* (pp. 243–263). Hong Kong: Oxford University Press. [In Chinese]
Ma, N. (2011). Value changes and legitimacy crisis in post-industrial Hong Kong. *Asian Survey, 51*(4), 683–712.
So, A. (2011). The development of post-modernist social movements in the Hong Kong Special Administrative Region. In J. Broadbent & V. Brockman (Eds.), *East Asian social movements* (pp. 365–378). New York: Springer.

Mobilization by images: TV screen and mediated instant grievances in the Umbrella Movement

Gary Tang

School of Journalism and Communication, The Chinese University of Hong Kong, Hong Kong

> This article discusses the effects of the televised images of the use of tear gas on people participating in the Umbrella Movement. Although the role of the Internet and social media in political mobilization has been widely discussed, the importance of television cannot be overlooked. This article argues that the widely transmitted broadcasts of live images of the police firing tear gas into the protesting crowd generated "mediated instant grievances" in a substantial sector of the viewing public, thus contributing to the size and scale of the Umbrella Movement. The study reported here provides evidence for this argument by analyzing the results of a survey of protesters that were on site during the early stage of the movement (N = 969). The study sought to determine whether and how the television images were related to the participants' political attitudes, reasons for participation, and views of self-mobilized actions. The findings showed that, in particular, mediated instant grievances motivated the participation of the "amateur protesters" in the movement.

Introduction

Much recent research and discussion on the effects of media on social movements has focused on digital and social media. However, television remains a prominent medium in most contemporary societies. In Hong Kong, television has been crucial in the formation of local identity (Ma, 1998). Historically, the intensive live coverage of many important incidents has shaped people's emotional reactions to events and their collective memories (Chan & Lee, 2010; Ma, 2010). This article contends that in the Umbrella Movement, television played a crucial role in mobilizing the participants and contributing to the scale of the occupation.

A brief account of the beginning of the movement highlights the plausibility of television's effects on mobilization. On the night of 27 September 2014, and after a week of class boycott, student groups protested outside the Central Government Office (CGO). Scholarism, one of the major student groups that had organized the protests, suddenly mobilized the participants to rush into the "Civic Square", an area in front of the East Wing of the CGO, which used to be an open space but had been fenced to prevent public access since early September 2014. Physical conflict between the students and the police occurred. The television news showed screenshots of the police removing the protesting students from the Civic Square with seemingly excessive force. Enraged by the police's violent actions, more people went to the CGO on September 27 and joined the protest.

The unexpected development of this situation compelled the proponents of Occupy Central to declare the beginning of the occupation, which was originally scheduled to begin on 1 October, in the early morning hours of 28 September. In the early afternoon of that day, tens of thousands of citizens hoped to join or support the protest near the CGO (*Apply Daily*, 2014). However, the police blocked the major routes to the CGO area. As more and more citizens arrived, the sidewalks became increasingly overcrowded. Some protesters finally breached the police's blockade line and rushed into Harcourt Road, a main road in the Central Business District (CBD) of Hong Kong. The traffic on Harcourt Road was thus blocked, and the inadvertent occupation of the main roads began.

Around 6 pm, the police shot tear gas to disperse the crowd. The use of tear gas arguably shocked the whole society. The use of tear gas is a rare event in Hong Kong, and the firing of tear gas in the urban landscape of the city's CBD created spectacular images. These images were immediately transmitted to citizens' private homes via television. Throughout the day, 24-hour news channels had been transmitting live broadcasts of the protests.

Nevertheless, the use of tear gas failed to end the protest. Instead, it motivated even more people to participate. In addition to the Admiralty business district, the traffic nodes of two other urban districts – Causeway Bay and Mongkok – were also occupied that night. In news reports, some protesters claimed that they had not intended to join the protest until the police fired tear gas (*Apple Daily*, 2014, September 30). In other words, the police's actions provoked them to participate in the protest. However, their actions probably would not have had a "mobilizing impact" without the presence of television. Hence, it is also appropriate to say that the television images motivated more people to join the protest.

However, how representative were the anecdotal cases shown in the news media? That is, did the television images of tear gas motivate a significant proportion of protesters to join the Umbrella Movement? Moreover, if a substantial proportion of protesters were indeed motivated by the television images of tear gas, did they have the same set of political beliefs as the other protesters? In addition, while the role of digital and social media is in contemporary large-scale protests has been widely acknowledged (Valenzuela, Arriagada, & Scherman, 2012; Tufekci & Wilson, 2012), what roles did these media play in motivating users to join the protest?

This article tackles these questions through analyzing the data collected from a survey of protesters at the occupied area. The answers to these questions should help us better understand not only the onset of the Umbrella Movement, but also the potential of televised images for the mobilization of large-scale social protests. The next section will examine the mobilizing power of television by discussing the concepts of the public screen and mediated instant grievances.

Public screen and mediated instant grievances

The influence of television on social change is often seen as negative. In addition to the argument by technological determinists that the medium of television discourages people from the rational and in-depth discussion of political affairs (Postman, 1985), other early television studies doubted the extent to which television content represents social reality. In their early studies, Gerbner and colleagues argued that television discourages audiences from seeking social change. The medium serves to maintain the status quo by cultivating distorted worldviews (Gerbner & Gross, 1976; Gerbner, Gross, Jackson-Beeck, Jeffries-Fox, & Signorielli, 1978). From a political economic perspective, the institutional collaboration between broadcasters and commercial corporations is a basic concern. Given the high operational costs and the oligopolistic market structure, the TV industry tends to cater to the interests of corporations (Herman & Chomsky, 1988). Where the coverage of social movements and collective actions is concerned, the result is the phenomenon of the "protest paradigm" (Chan & Lee, 1984); that is, the tendency of television news to portray protests and protesters as deviant, violent, and dangerous. Empirical research has indeed shown that audiences exposed to news about protests that was framed according to the protest paradigm were more critical of the protesters (McLeod, 1995; McLeod & Detenber, 1999).

In contrast to the negative effects of television, DeLuca and Peeples (2002) conceptualized the power of television as promoting public criticism and resistance by delivering images based on the concept of the "he d on the c". Focusing on the case of the anti-WTO protests in Seattle in 1999, they argued that the uncivil disobedience of the anarchists led to violent conflict with the police, the visual images of which were widely circulated in the media. The images consequently dominated the news agenda, thus allowing the protest and the violent conflict to define the entire WTO Conference. The images also became discursive materials for aligning various anti-WTO parties with the anti-globalization protests from that point.

Although DeLuca and Peeples (2002) included many kinds of pictorial images – television, computer, and the front pages and photos in newspapers – in their concept of the public screen, television was given a prominent place in their discussion. Theoretically, they argued that the widespread circulation of "screens" entails a new kind of relationship between news information and politics, which the conventional idea of the public sphere does not capture:

> we cannot simply adopt the term "public sphere" and all it entails, a term indebted to orality and print, for the current screen age. The new term takes seriously the work of media theorists suggesting that new technologies introduce new forms of social organization and new modes of perception. (DeLuca and Peeples, 2002, p. 131)

The authors argued that the he authors argued that thepromoted the shift from a that theterm "public sphere" and all ". Different from the dissemination of information by texts, television images are composed of a great variety of signs and meanings that the editors cannot fully control (Fiske, 1987; Hartley, 2003). TV news images thus have a degree of relative autonomy in the sense that the images themselves can potentially speak about the issue.

The relative autonomy of images is even more obvious during live reporting, when editorial staffs in the newsrooms cannot edit the images. They can at most select which camera images to show, and they can interpret the images in voice over narration. However, the images constrain the range of plausible interpretations. Furthermore, when spectacular images are captured, their power can contravene editorial agenda-setting within the newsroom. It is difficult for news editors to ignore the news value of amazing images or move the story down on the news agenda (Bourdieu, 2001). It is usually argued that journalists' obsession with dramatic scenes when reporting social protests tends to produce a negative portrayal of protesters as violent and irrational rioters. Thus, the television medium is sometimes regarded as having a structural bias against social movements (McLeod & Detenber, 1999). However, DeLuca and Peeples (2002) contended that journalists' interest in dramatic images can also work against the interests of established institutions rather than those of the protesters, which is arguably what happened in the Umbrella Movement.

The tear-gassing of the Admiralty business district was a highly spectacular event that was rarely witnessed in Hong Kong. Putting aside the question of whether the police used an appropriate degree of violence, the scene caused the instant shock of what DeLuca and

Peeples (2002) described as "the familiar made strange" (p. 144); that is, something unusual taking place against a background in which every element is familiar to the audience.

In typical news images of protester–police conflicts, the audience cannot easily judge from the images themselves whether the actions of the police are appropriate or not. In contrast, the use of tear gas in this case created war-like scenes that were so surreal that people were likely to question seriously the necessity for the police's action. Based on the war-like images, audience members were also likely to perceive that the use of tear gas involved a high degree of police violence. Because the incident took place on a Sunday evening, many people were at home watching the televised live reports. The timing of the incident thus further enhanced the power and penetration of the television images. Then, later that night, there were rumors that the police might shoot the protesters with rubber bullets if the tear gas did not succeed in dispersing the crowd. The incident became increasingly dramatic and suspenseful, possibly tempting the audience to keep watching their television sets to keep updated about the situation.

Images of the use of tear gas were provocative in the sense that they could have stimulated grievances among the audience. Grievances are regarded as one of the important factors in protest mobilization, in addition to political opportunities and resource mobilization (Simmons, 2014). Moreover, when the grievances are imposed suddenly, the level of mobilization can be further enhanced beyond the original capacity of the movement's organization (Walsh, 1981, 1988). According to Walsh (1981, p. 18), "Suddenly imposed major grievances such as chemical spills, court-ordered busing, or a nuclear accident are more or less likely to spur collectivities to protest mobilization, depending on their structural situation." Kern, Marien, and Hooghe (2015) adopted the notion of grievance to explain the rise in the level of protest mobilization during economic crises despite declines in the resources of movement organizations.

In fact, because Hong Kong society did not expect the use of tear gas, Walsh's (1981, 1988) ideas are pertinent to the present case because some participants became angry that the unexpected use of tear gas was "suddenly imposed". This article proposes the concept of mediated instant grievances to account for the mobilization effect of the visual images disseminated via television on 28 September.

The concept has three core elements. First, the grievances were "instant" in the sense that they were "suddenly imposed" and had an instant effect; that is, the scale of public support for the protest was expanded in a single night. Second, because the grievances were directly due to the action of the police, grievances against the police also became the major purpose for participation by the protesters mobilized by the images. Third, the instant grievances were "mediated" because they could not have existed on a broad scale without the dissemination of images through the medium of television. The word "mediated" covers two meanings. It emphasizes the importance of the visual images disseminated through television. Without the war-like images of the Admiralty business district, the use of tear gas would have been merely an abstract concept and not capable of provoking huge grievances. Moreover, personal television sets served as the key medium delivering the images of the incident. Certainly, the Internet and social media have been playing important roles in circulating the images and updating the information. However, the penetration of television into the living rooms of modern households remains unique, and traditional broadcasters were still credible news organizations with sufficient resources to produce the images of the incident for dissemination in the first place.

Certainly, the above argument needs to be substantiated by empirical evidence. However, it should be noted that the above argument about the influence of television images and the generation of mediated instant grievances is not meant to be about the effects of media on individual citizens. The argument does not imply that everyone exposed to the image would have the same level of anger. In fact, at the individual level, it is plausible that people's reactions to the television images of the use of tear gas would be colored by their pre-existing beliefs about the legitimacy of the protest. It is also possible that some individuals would refrain from going to the protest site because of their perceptions of the danger shown in the television images. In this article, the argument is that mediated instant grievances were generated among a substantial proportion of the watching public, thus contributing to the scale of the Umbrella Movement.

Empirical analysis of mediated instant grievances

An empirical analysis was conducted to demonstrate the power of television images and mediated instant grievances. Specifically, the analysis centered on the variable of the decision to participate. To the extent that the television images of tear gas and mediated instant grievances were crucial to the movement's mobilization, we expected that a substantial proportion of the participants would indicate that they decided to participate in the Umbrella Movement on 28 September. The first research question is therefore as follows:

> Q1: What proportion of the participants in the movement decided to participate on 28 September?

In addition, to further understand the role of the TV screen in mobilization and the kind of participants that were more likely to be affected by the mediated instant grievances, hypotheses related to political attitudes, media beliefs, reasons of participation, and view of self-mobilized actions were proposed.

Political attitude

The argument for "mediated instant grievances" implies that some participants were mobilized mainly by the instant and strong grievances generated by the actions of the police. These participants did not join the movement before they witnessed the police'h actions, which implies that their basic political beliefs and attitudes toward the issue addressed by the movement were not strong enough to prompt them to participate. Hence, it is hypothesized that the people mobilized by mediated instant grievances held a set of distinct political beliefs and views compared to other protesters.

Specifically, it is expected that the two groups of participants varied in terms of their degree of partisanship, support for democracy, and sense of belonging to Hong Kong and China. Partisanship is closely related to interests in politics. However, in the context of Hong Kong, people who are interested in politics do not necessarily become members of political parties (Ma, 2012). However, they would be more likely to be able to name the parties they support. The people who were mobilized by mediated instant grievances were expected to exhibit lower levels of partisanship.

People who were mobilized by mediated instant grievances were also expected to show a relatively lower level of support for democracy. However, the survey did not contain an item that directly measured support for democracy in abstract terms. Instead, support for the commemoration of the June 4 Incident (i.e., the tragic ending through military suppression of the student pro-democracy movement in China in 1989) is used as a surrogate here because attitudes toward the June 4 Incident can reflect people's views of China and democratization (Lee, 2012). In other words, participants mobilized by mediated instant grievances would support the commemoration of 4 June to a lesser degree.

Hong Kong studies have shown that sense of belonging to Hong Kong and China are relevant nt dies have shown that sene city because they reflect people's views of the PRC government and its intervention in the affairs of Hong Kong (C. K. Chan, 2014; Lee & Chan, 2005). In Hong Kong, the issue of democratization is often regarded as involving a conflict between the city and China. People with different senses of belonging to the city and the nation may exhibit different degrees of support for democratization. It is hypothesized that people who joined the movement because of mediated instant grievances would show a weaker sense of belonging to Hong Kong and a stronger sense of belonging to China.

The hypotheses can be summarized as follows:

H1: Participants mobilized by mediated instant grievances were less likely to be supporters of specific political parties or groups compared to other protesters.

H2: Participants mobilized by mediated instant grievances had weaker support for the commemoration of the June 4 Incident compared to other protesters.

H3: Participants mobilized by mediated instant grievances exhibited a weaker sense of belonging to Hong Kong compared to other protesters.

H4: Participants mobilized by mediated instant grievances exhibited a stronger sense of belonging to China compared to other protesters.

Media beliefs

The occupation of urban space as a form of collective action is unprecedented in Hong Kong, and it has been regarded as radical by most commentators. Social media is often seen as the breeding ground of radical ideas and a platform for political mobilization (Chan & Lee, 2012; Leung & Lee, 2014; Luk, 2014). However, because the original plan of Occupy Central had been widely discussed in the society since early 2013, the participants exposed to relevant discussions through social media should have been familiar with the issue and therefore decided to join the protest at the early stage. In contrast, television is probably not the most appropriate medium for explicating and discussing abstract concepts such as civic disobedience. It is therefore hypothesized that the participants mobilized by mediated instant grievances, while relying on television for movement-related information, would also rely less on social media for movement-related information.

In addition, it is hypothesized that the participants mobilized by mediated instant grievances would perceive The Television Broadcast Limited (TVB) – the dominant free-to-air broadcaster in the city – as a credible news source to a larger extent than other protesters who might be more inclined to hold a critical attitude toward TVB as a monopolistic and politically conservative broadcaster (Lee, 2015). In contrast to TVB, *Apple Daily* is a strongly pro-democracy newspaper (Lee & Chan, 2008) and it advocated Occupy Central at a very early stage. The strongest supporters of the movement who decided to participate early were likely to treat *Apple Daily* as a credible news source compared to people who were mobilized by mediated instant grievances.

Hence, another set of four hypotheses is proposed:

H5: Compared to other protesters, the participants mobilized by mediated instant grievances relied less on social media for information related to the movement.

H6: Compared to other protesters, the participants mobilized by mediated instant grievances relied more on television for information related to the movement.

H7: The participants mobilized by mediated instant grievances were more likely than other protesters to perceive TVB as a credible news source.

H8: The participants mobilized by mediated instant grievances were less likely than other protesters to perceive *Apple Daily* as a credible news source.

Reasons for participation

As argued, the participants who were motivated by mediated instant grievances were likely to be less active in politics and hold political beliefs relevant to the movement. Following the rationale expressed in H1 to H4, it is also hypothesized that the participants mobilized by mediated instant grievances were less likely than other protesters to view supporting democracy as the main reason for their participation. It is also expected that those who participated because of mediated instant grievances had weaker social and/or psychological connections with the movement groups organizing the protests. It is therefore hypothesized that they were less likely to regard their own actions as responses to the calls of the movement organizers. Moreover, because the use of tear gas could easily be perceived as the use of violence against youngsters and students, who were seen as the main body of the participants, it is also hypothesized that the people mobilized by mediated instant grievances were more likely to believe that protecting the students was their reason for participation. Lastly and straightforwardly, the people mobilized by mediated instant grievances would be more likely to acknowledge that protesting the use of tear gas was their reason for participation.

The four hypotheses are as follows:

H9: The participants mobilized by mediated instant grievances were less likely than other protesters to regard supporting democracy as their main reason for participation.

H10: The participants mobilized by mediated instant grievances were less likely than other protesters to regard the calls of the movement'r organization as their main reason for participation.

H11: The participants mobilized by mediated instant grievances were more likely than other protesters to regard protecting students as their main reason for participation.

H12: The participants mobilized by mediated instant grievances were more likely than other protesters to regard protesting the use of tear gas as their main reason for participation.

View on self-mobilized action

Self-mobilized protest action is a key feature of social movement in Hong Kong. Despite the fact that efforts by movement organizers are often necessary for the action to take place, many participants claim that they join the action "spontaneously" and not because of the influence of any particular parties (Lee & Chan, 2011; Lee, 2014). In the Umbrella Movement, the idea of self-mobilization and the popular belief in its moral superiority had mutated into controversies regarding whether there should be a "central organizer" or a "central stage" in the Movement (Tsang, 2014; Wong, 2014). As argued above, the participants mobilized by mediated instant grievances were less active in politics and less closely related to movement organizations. They were therefore expected to find the discourse of self-mobilized actions convincing and appealing. Hence, two hypotheses can be stated:

H13: The participants mobilized by mediated instant grievances believed in the positive aspects of self-mobilized actions to a larger extent compared with other protesters.

H14: The participants mobilized by mediated instant grievances were less concerned about the importance of leadership in the movement compared with other protesters.

Method and measurements

The data were derived from an on-site survey that was conducted from 3 pm to 7 pm on 4 and 5 October (Saturday and Sunday) in the occupied area in the Admiralty business district. The interviewers were instructed to walk along a given route and distribute the questionnaire to every 10th person they passed. During the two days, 969 completed questionnaires were collected. The response rate was 95%.

Of the respondents, 56.9% were female. The mean age was 27.7 (SD = 9.19); 47.8% of the respondents were aged 25 or below, and 35.7% were aged 26 to 35. The respondents were asked to indicate the social class to which they belonged: 48.8% of the respondents claimed to belong to the lower class, while 47.6% claimed to belong to the middle class. Moreover, 79.3% of the respondents had tertiary or higher levels of education. However, only 19.1% were current undergraduates when the survey was conducted. The following are the key variables used in the analysis.

Time of participation decision

This is the core variable used to illustrate the effect of the mediated instant grievances. The respondents were asked when they decided to join the movement by choosing one of six options: (i) "before the National People's Congress' decision in late August" (3.6%); (ii) "after the National People's Congress' decision in late August" (5.2%); (iii) "during the week of class boycott" (11.4%); (iv) "September 27 when the conflict at the Civic Square happened" (19.6%); (v) "September 28, after the use of tear gas" (55.8%); and (vi) "yesterday or today" (4.5%). The variable was treated as an ordinal-scaled variable in the multiple regression analysis (M = 4.32, SD = 1.13).

Political attitudes

Regarding partisanship, the respondents were given a list of political parties and asked to indicate which ones they supported; "I don't support any political parties" was an optional category. The variable was recoded into a simple dichotomous item for testing H1 (1 = Not supporting any party; 0 = supporting at least one party, M = 0.54, SD = 0.50). The respondents were also asked whether they agreed with the statement, "I continually support the commemoration of the June 4 Incident." The responses were registered on a five-point Likert scale with 1 = strongly disagree and 5 = strongly agree ($M = 4.16$, $SD = 0.90$). Finally, the respondents were asked to indicate on a 0–10 scale (0 = the weakest and 10 = the strongest) their sense of belonging to Hong Kong ($M = 7.36$, $SD = 1.99$) and to China ($M = 2.38$, $SD = 2.37$) respectively.

Media beliefs

The respondents were given a list of media platforms and asked about the importance of each platform to acquire movement-related information. The responses were registered on a five-point Likert scale ranging from 1 = very unimportant to 5 = very important. The items o 5 e TV coverage" ($M = 4.02$, $SD = 1.10$) and "TV news report" ($M = 3.87$, $SD = 1.16$) were averaged for an index of the perceived importance of TV news ($M = 3.95$, $SD = 1.07$, $r = 0.80$). The items "Whatsapp"h($M = 4.15$, $SD = 1.03$) and "Facebook" ($M = 4.63$, $SD = 0.79$) were averaged on an index on the perceived importance of social media ($M = 4.39$, $SD = 0.77$, $r = 0.42$). The respondents were also asked to indicate on a five-point Likert scale (1 = very not credible and 5 = very credible) their perceptions of the credibility of TVB news ($M = 1.77$, $SD = 0.94$) and *Apple Daily* ($M = 3.78$, $SD = 0.77$).

Reasons for participation

The respondents were given a list of possible reasons for their participation. They were asked to indicate the importance of each reason for their own participation on a five-point Likert scale (1 = very unimportant and 5 = very important). The items "to fight for universal suffrage without filtering", "to fight for civil nomination", and "to protect the freedom of Hong Kong" were averaged for an index on "participate due to support for democratic values" ($M = 4.78$, $SD = .53$, $\alpha = 0.81$). The items "to support the Hong Kong Federation of Students", uto support Scholarism", cto support the organizers of Occupy Central", and "to support other organizations engaged in the movement" were averaged for an index on "participate to support movement organizations"a($M = 2.72$, $SD = 1.04$, $\alpha = 0.88$). "To support and protect the students/classmates" ($M = 4.62$, $SD = 0.74$) and "the use of tear gas" ($M = 4.41$, $SD = 0.99$) were used in the analysis as two single-item variables.

Views of self-mobilized action

The respondents were asked to indicate on a five-point Likert scale (1 = strongly disagree, 5 = strongly agree) whether they agreed with "Self-mobilized action is important for making a purer movement" ($M = 4.03$, $SD = 0.93$), "Self-mobilized action is important to prevent a movement from being kidnapped" ($M = 3.83$, $SD = 1.00$), "The weakness of self-mobilized action is that it leads to a lack of focus" ($M = 3.03$, $SD = 1.17$), or "The weakness of self-mobilized action is that it leads to a lack of leadership" ($M = 3.41$, $SD = 1.16$).

Analysis and findings

Time of participation decision of different groups of protesters

Q1 asks about the number of participants in the Umbrella Movement that decided to join the action on 28 September, which could be a sign of the power of mediated instant grievances. The percentage distribution noted in the method section has already provided the answer.

Table 1. Demographics and timing of participation decision.

	(1)	(2)	(3)	(4)	(5)	(6)	Overall
Gender							
Male	41.9%	54.5%	45.3%	32.9%	44.3%	54.1%	43.1%
Female	58.1%	45.5%	54.7%	67.1%	55.7%	45.9%	56.9%
Age							
25 or below	9.7%	44.4%	69.7%	53.5%	46.6%	48.7%	47.8%
26 to 35	48.4%	31.1%	18.2%	34.7%	39.5%	35.9%	35.7%
36 to 45	3.2%	8.9%	7.1%	7.6%	8.9%	10.3%	8.7%
46 or above	38.7%	15.6%	5.1%	4.1%	5.0%	5.1%	7.7%
SES							
Lower class	26.9%	29.3%	47.8%	52.6%	52.0%	51.4%	48.8%
Middle class	73.1%	65.9%	48.9%	43.5%	44.6%	45.7%	47.6%
Upper class	0.0%	4.9%	3.3%	3.9%	3.4%	2.9%	3.6%
Education level							
Primary school or below	6.5%	2.2%	0.0%	0.6%	0.6%	0.0%	1.0%
Secondary level	9.7%	24.4%	14.3%	16.8%	19.5%	28.9%	19.6%
Tertiary education or above	83.9%	73.3%	85.7%	82.6%	79.8%	71.1%	79.3%

Notes: (1) Before the NPC's decision in late August; (2) After the NPC's decision in late August; (3) During the week of class boycott; (4) September 27; (5) September 28; (6) Yesterday or today.

Excluding the respondents who gave no valid answer to the question, more than 55% of the respondents acknowledged that they decided to join the movement on 28 September.

It should be noted that, except the first and last options, each of the other response categories to the question represents a benchmark or critical moment that could have mobilized substantial number of people to join the movement. For instance, the announcement of the decision of the National People resents a benchmark 31August, which set up a highly restrictive framework for the chief executive election in 2017, led many people to conclude that negotiation with the government would be useless and thus encouraged some to decide to participate in the movement (K. M. Chan, 2014). The one-week long class boycott held between 22 and 26 September, which was initiated by university student unions, was the largest class boycott in Hong Kong after the handover. The class boycott might have mobilized young people to participate in the eventual occupation (*Apply Daily*, 2014, September 27). Although each remarkable moment is significant, the frequencies showed that the use of tear gas was the critical action that provoked people to join the protest. The findings thus support the argument for the power of mediated instant grievances.

Table 1 summarizes the demographics of the protesters who decided to join the movement at different time points. There was a particularly large proportion of females among the people who decided to join the protest on 27 September. This finding might be related to television images showing police violence against female students in uniform during the fight between the police and the student protesters at the Civic Square. In terms of age distribution, the findings showed that the class boycott was particularly important in encouraging young people to join the movement. Almost 70% of the respondents aged 25 or below decided to participate during the week of the class boycott.

Concerning socioeconomic status, the percentage of the lower class that decided to join the movement increased over time, possibly because members of the lower class were less well versed about and attentive to political issues. Hence, it took a longer period for relevant information and messages to diffuse to these protesters. This finding might also indicate that members of the lower class began to be mobilized substantially when the actual actions began (i.e., the beginning of the class boycott). Although the class boycott is not the focus of this article, the findings shown in Table 1 indicate the role played by the class boycott in precipitating the actions and in mobilizing more people to join what would eventually evolve into the Umbrella Movement.

Characteristics of protesters mobilized through mediated instant grievances

To test the hypotheses about the differences between people who were mobilized by mediated instant grievances and other people, the respondents who decided to join the movement on 28 September were treated as one group and compared to all other protesters in the independent samples t-test. Although the answer "yesterday or today" indicated after the use of tear gas, it was grouped together with the answers that indicated before 28 September in order to highlight specifically those who were mobilized by mediated *instant* grievances.

Table 2 summarizes the relevant findings. First, concerning the political attitudes of the participants, H1 to H3 were supported. The participants who decided to participate on 28 September were less likely to support any political parties, showed weaker support for the commemoration of 4 June, and exhibited a weaker sense of belonging to Hong Kong (mean differences = 0.13, –0.24, and –0.46 respectively, $p < 0.001$ for all). These findings are consistent with the argument that mediated instant grievances mobilized people who were relatively less active in politics to join the movement.

Second, the importance of television, which was the key medium in generating mediated instant grievances, was also supported. The findings supported H6 and H7. The participants who decided to join the movement on 28 September relied on television for movement-related information, and they also thought that TVB was more credible compared to other protesters (mean differences = 0.28, and 0.19; $p < 0.001$ and 0.01 respectively).

Nevertheless, it should be acknowledged that among the participants who decided to join the movement on 28 September, the mean score for the importance of social media (4.38) was still higher than that of the importance of television (4.07). Therefore, the findings showed that social media also played a role in communicating movement-related information to the participants mobilized by mediated instant grievances. The findings suggest that the relative reliance on television was a factor in the mobilization of those who participated on 28 September.

Regarding the reasons for participation, only H12 was supported: those who decided to participate on 28 September were more likely to acknowledge the "use of tear gas" as a reason for their participation (mean differences = 0.38; $p < 0.001$). The participants who decided to join the movement on 28 September were also nominally more likely to see "protecting the students" as the reason for their participation, although the difference between the two groups was not statistically significant. Thus, H11 was not supported. Lastly, the participants who decided to participate on 28 September were more likely to see self-mobilized actions as having the function of preventing a movement from being kidnapped (mean differences = 0.21; $p < 0.05$). The finding partly supported H13.

Table 2. t-test comparison of participants having made the decision to join the movement on September 28 and all other protesters.

	Decided on 28 Sept.(n = 484)	Not decided on 28 Sept. (n = 384)	Mean difference
Political attitudes			
Support none of the political parties (t = 3.85***)	0.59	0.46	0.13
Support the commemoration of June 4 (t = 3.90***)	4.04	4.28	−0.24
Sense of belonging to HK (t = 3.35***)	7.14	7.60	−0.46
Sense of belonging to China (t = 0.58)	2.36	2.46	−0.10
Use of media			
Importance of social media (t = 0.75)	4.38	4.42	−0.04
Importance of TV news (t = 3.91***)	4.07	3.79	0.28
Perceived credibility of TVB news (t = 2.89**)	1.83	1.64	0.19
Perceived credibility of *Apple Daily* (t = 0.22)	3.76	3.75	0.01
Reasons of participation			
Support movement organizations (t = 0.52)	2.68	2.71	−0.03
Support core democratic values (t = 0.13)	4.78	4.78	0.00
To protect and support students (t = 1.77)	4.66	4.57	0.09
The use of tear gas (t = 6.21***)	4.58	4.20	0.38
View of self-mobilization			
It enables a purer movement (t = 0.47)	4.05	4.02	0.03
It prevents kidnapping (t = 2.95*)	3.90	3.69	0.21
The movement loses focus (t = 0.20)	3.00	3.02	−0.02
The movement loses leadership (t = 0.46)	3.38	3.41	−0.03

Note: ***$p < 0.001$; **$p < 0.01$; *$p < 0.05$.

Table 3. Predictors of time of participation decision (1 = earliest; 6 = latest).

Variables	β
Demographics	
Age	–0.14***
Gender (M = 0)	–0.00
SES	–0.08*
Education level	–0.03
R^2 change	3.1%***
Political attitudes	
Support none of the political parties	0.22***
Support commemoration of June 4	–0.14***
Sense of belonging to HK	–0.10**
Sense of belonging to CN	0.01
R^2 change	9.4% ***
Use of media	
Importance of social media	–0.10**
Importance of TV news	0.11***
Perceived credibility of TVB news	0.10**
Perceived credibility of *Apple Daily*	0.02
R^2 change	4.0%***
Reasons for participation	
Support movement organizations	–0.01
Support core democratic values	–0.08*
Protect and support the students	0.05
The use of tear gas	0.16***
R^2 change	3.2%***
View of self-mobilization	
It enables a purer movement	0.05
It prevents kidnapping	0.10**
The movement loses focus	0.01
The movement loses leadership	0.04
R^2 change	1.4%**
Total R^2	18.8%***

Notes: N = 820. Except the dependent variable, and variables of the demographics, the missing values of all other variables were replaced by mean.
***$p < 0.001$; **$p < 0.01$; *$p < 0.05$.

Multivariate analysis on timing of participation decision

The findings shown in Table 2 were used to test the hypotheses by distinguishing the participants who were subjected to the effect of mediated instant grievances and those who were not. Although not all hypotheses were supported, all significant differences were in the expected directions. A multiple regression analysis was conducted to examine the predictors of the timing of participation decision, which were treated as an ordinal-scaled variable. That is, instead of presenting mediated instant grievances as a fixed moment, the analysis examined the timing of the participation decision as a linear variable ranging from the earliest to the latest moment. With reference to the evolution of the movement, it was expected that the participants who made earlier decisions tended to be influenced by the original plan of Occupy Central, while those who made later decisions were more affected by mediated instant grievances.

As shown in Table 3, these findings are similar to the results of the bivariate t-tests. In terms of demographics, the participants who made their participation decisions in later stages were younger and had lower socioeconomic status ($\beta = -0.14$ and -0.08; $p < 0.001$ and 0.05 respectively). As discussed earlier, it is likely that it took more time for information to diffuse to junior students (given that the protesters were young overall) and the lower class. Non-support for political parties, support for commemorating 4 June, and sense of belonging to Hong Kong were significantly related to the dependent variable, which was consistent with the findings shown in Table 2 ($\beta = 0.22$, -0.14 and -0.10; $p < 0.001$, 0.001, and 0.01 respectively). The political attitude variables explained 9.4% ($p < 0.001$) of the variance in the dependent variable. The findings strengthened the argument that the mediated instant grievances mobilized people who were relatively less active in politics.

Interestingly, although the results of the t-test were insignificant, the reliance on social media for movement information was negatively and significantly related to time of participation decision ($\beta = -0.10$; $p < 0.01$). That is, people who made an earlier decision were more reliant on social media, suggesting that social media played a mobilizing role among the most interested and efficacious protesters. In contrast, the reliance on television and perceived credibility of TVB were both positively related to time of the participation decision ($\beta = 0.11$ and 0.10; $p < 0.001$ and 0.01 respectively).

Lastly, the acknowledgment of supporting core democratic values as a reason for participation and agreement with the positive value of self-mobilization in preventing a movement from being kidnapped were related to the dependent variable, which was consistent with the argument that the protesters who joined the movement at later stages were relatively more distant from the movement's values and organizations ($\beta = -0.08$ and 0.10; $p < 0.05$ and 0.01 respectively). These findings were also consistent with the findings presented in Table 2.

Discussion

Before 28 September 2014, no one foresaw that Occupy Central, which was supposed to be a disciplined form of civil disobedience, would become a massive and prolonged occupation movement in Hong Kong. Over the previous decade, the city had become used to large-scale but peaceful protest marches as a major form of protest (Lee & Chan, 2011). Hence, the occupation of urban space had been viewed as too radical for the movement culture of the city. Thus, the intriguing question of how protesters could be mobilized to participate in this novel form of protest was raised.

Based on anecdotes and observations of the effects of television images of the police form of lized to, this article draws upon the notions of the "public screen" (DeLuca & Peeples, 2002) and 2) and evision images of the police form of lized to develop the concept of mediated instant grievances to explain how the protest reached the scale of an occupation during the course of a single night. In contrast to the current trend of political communication scholarship, which overwhelmingly emphasizes the importance of digital and social media in protest mobilization, the findings of the present study showed that the medium of television is still pervasive in Hong Kong society, and it mobilized people with relatively lower degrees of digital literacy and political involvement and efficacy to join the Umbrella Movement.

The power of mediated instant grievances is based on the visual nature of the television medium and the technology of live broadcasting. The power does not depend on the political predilection of the television broadcasters. In the case of the Umbrella Movement, it is noteworthy that the protesters mobilized by the use of tear gas tended to rate the credibility of TVB more highly, despite the fact that TVB was widely criticized as a politically conservative and self-censoring broadcaster.

Several qualifications and clarifications of the argument ventured in this article are needed at this point. First, this article does not attempt to argue that television is so powerful that it can replace social media in political mobilization. Within the movement at large, social media and television may work complementarily and form a holistic and integrated media environment for the communication of movement-related information and messages. Nevertheless, this study aimed to highlight the unique significance of live broadcast television.

Second, as already noted in the theoretical section, this study did not test the psychological reactions to television images at the individual level. The cross-sectional survey of participants in the Movement did not include those who did not join the Movement. Millions of citizens stayed at home even after the police's use of tear gas. It is logically possible that the images caused effects in addition to instant grievances. For instance, the war-like images may have discouraged some people from joining the Movement because they feared the danger involved. However, the point of this article is that a substantial number of people were mobilized by the television images to join the protests. How other people reacted to the television images of tear gas flying over the Admiralty business district would not negate the power of the mediated instant grievances. Third, the articulation of the concept of mediated instant grievances does not imply that grievances were the only factor in the mobilization of the Umbrella Movement. Walsh (1981, 1988) acknowledged that the power of "suddenly imposed grievances" was dependent on other situational factors. The comparative research of Koopmans and Duyvendak (1995) on the anti-nuclear movements in Western Europe also revealed that political opportunities and frame alignment had to be considered in examining the power of "suddenly imposed grievances". In the present case, several factors might have primed the public to react to the television images of tear gas in specific ways, including the harsh and ultra-conservative decision by the NPC during the week of class boycott by the students, the conflicts between the student-protesters and the police on 27 September, and so forth.

Fourth, while the concept of mediated instant grievances points to the phenomenon that many protesters were not mobilized by the main movement groups and organizers, the role of the movement organizers should not be underemphasized when the movement as a whole is considered. On one hand, public discourses during the Umbrella Movement often praised the apparently self-mobilizing and spontaneous character of the citizens' action, whereas the organizers of Occupy Central were criticized as being too moderate and falling behind the pace of the evolution of the movement (HKFS, 2014). On the other hand, the original planning and discursive efforts spent on explicating the concept of civil disobedience by the proponents of Occupy Central, as well as the volunteers and resources offered by the group, did contribute to the formation and sustainability of the Umbrella Movement *Ming Pao*, 2014, November 2). As Lee (2014) pointed out, movement organizations and "citizen self-mobilization" are often complementary in the dynamics of collective action campaigns.

To conclude, while this article demonstrated that a significant number of people were mobilized through mediated instant grievances to participate in the Umbrella Movement, it should be kept in mind that the long-term effects of such grievances remain an open question. Some people mobilized through mediated instant grievances might have already been "on the brink" of participation. Some might actually have had a relatively "distant relationship" with politics and were driven to act by the relatively non-political motivations of "protecting the students" and "protesting against the use of tear gas". As many participants highlighted, "enlightenment" was one of the chief missions they hoped to accomplish through joining the movement. When this article was written, all the occupants had retreated from the occupied sites, and the Umbrella Movement was finished. However, the following questions remain: To what extent were these participants mobilized through mediated instant grievances and "enlightened" to become regular activists? To what extent was civil society empowered after the Umbrella Movement, similar to the empowerment after the rally on 1 July 2003 (Ku, 2009; Lee & Chan, 2011)? These questions can only be addressed through the continual observation and monitoring of the situation in Hong Kong.

Disclosure statement

No potential conflict of interest was reported by the author.

References

Apple Daily. (2014, September 27). They made the footprints for democracy. *Apply Daily*, A04. (In Chinese)
Apple Daily. (2014, September 28). Occupy Central begins. *Apply Daily*, A01. (In Chinese)
Apple Daily. (2014, September 30). The silent majority is called to come out. *Apple Daily*, A04. (In Chinese)
Bourdieu, P. (2001). Television. *European Review, 9*, 245–256.
Chan, C. K. (2014). China as "Other": Resistance to and ambivalence toward national identity in Hong Kong. *China Perspectives, 97*, 25–34.
Chan, K. M. (2014, September 8). The beginning of the era of resistance. *Ming Pao*, A28. (In Chinese)
Chan, M., & Lee, C. C. (1984). The journalistic paradigm on civil protests: A case study of Hong Kong. In A. Arno & W. Dissanayake (Eds.), *The news media in national and international conflict* (pp. 183–202). Boulder, CO: Westview.
Chan, M., & Lee, F. L. F. (2010). The puzzle of why Hong Kong does not forget June 4: Media, social organization, nation-state and collective memory. *Mass Communication Research, 103*, 215–260. (In Chinese)

Chan, M., & Lee, F. L. F. (2012). Activating support for social movements: The effect of the Internet on public opinion toward social movements in Hong Kong. *Taiwan Journal of Democracy, 8*, 145–167.

DeLuca, K. M., & Peeples, J. (2002). From public sphere to public screen: Democracy, activism, and the "violence" of Seattle. *Critical Studies in Media Communication, 19*, 125–151.

Fiske, J. (1987). *Television culture*. New York, NY: Routledge.

Gerbner, G., & Gross, L. (1976). Living with television: The violence profile. *Journal of Communication, 26*, 173–199.

Gerbner, G., Gross, L., Jackson-Beeck, M., Jeffries-Fox, S., & Signorielli, N. (1978). Cultural indicators: Violence profile no. 9. *Journal of Communication, 28*, 176–206.

Hartley, J. (2003). *Tele-ology: Studies in television*. London: Routledge.

Herman, E. S., & Chomsky, N. (1988). *Manufacturing consent: The political economy of the mass media*. New York: Pantheon Books.

HKFS. (2014, November 25). To confess is not the reason of withdrawal. *Ming Pao*, A05. (In Chinese)

Kern, A., Marien, S., & Hooghe, M. (2015). Economic crisis and levels of political participation in Europe (2002–2010): The role of resources and grievances. *West European Politics, 38*, 465–490.

Koopmans, R., & Duyvendak, J. W. (1995). The political construction of the nuclear energy issue and its impact on the mobilization of anti-nuclear movements in Western Europe. *Social Problems, 42*, 235–251.

Ku, A. (2009). Civil society's dual impetus: Mobilizations, representations and contestations over the July 1 March in 2003. In M. Sing (Ed.), *Politics and government in Hong Kong: Crisis under Chinese sovereignty* (pp. 38–57). London: Routledge.

Lee, F. L. F. (2012). Generational differences in the impact of historical events: The Tiananmen Square incident in contemporary Hong Kong public opinion. *International Journal of Public Opinion Research, 24*, 141–162.

Lee, F. L. F. (2014). Internet, citizen self-mobilization, and social movement organisations in environmental collective action campaigns: Two Hong Kong cases. *Environmental Politics,*. doi:10.1080/09644016.2014.919749

Lee, F. L. F. (2015). Press freedom and political change in Hong Kong. In G. Rawnsley & M. Y. Rawnsley (Eds.), *The Routledge handbook of Chinese media* (pp. 131–144). London: Routledge.

Lee, F. L. F. & Chan, M. (2005). Political attitudes, political participation, and Hong Kong identities after 1997. *Issues & Studies, 41*, 1–35.

Lee, F. L. F. & Chan, M. (2008). Professionalism, political orientation, and perceived self-censorship: A survey study of Hong Kong journalists. *Issues & Studies, 44*, 205–238.

Lee, F. L. F., & Chan, M. (2011). *Media, social mobilization and mass protests in post-colonial Hong Kong*. London: Routledge.

Leung, D. K. K. & Lee, F. L. F. (2014). Cultivating an active online counter-public: Examining usage political impact of Internet alternative media. *International Journal of Press/Politics, 19*, 340–359.

Luk, Y. C. (2014, October 7). The role of portable Internet devices in Occupy Central. *Apple Daily*, A15. (In Chinese)

Ma, E. K. W. (1998). Re-inventing Hong Kong: Memory, identity, and television. *International Journal of Cultural Studies, 1*, 329–349.

Ma, E. K. W. (2010, August 26). Live reporting: Wounds and anger. *Ming Pao*, B15. (In Chinese)

Ma, N. (2012). Political parties and elections. In W. M. Lam, P. L. T. Lui, W. Wong (Eds.), *Contemporary Hong Kong government and politics* (pp. 159–177). HonHong Kong: Hong Kong University Press.

McLeod, D. M. (1995). Communicating deviance: The effects of television news coverage of social protest. *Journal of Broadcasting and Electronic Media, 39*, 4–19.

McLeod, D. M. & Detenber, B. H. (1999). Framing effects of television news coverage of social protest. *Journal of Communication, 49*, 3–23.

Ming Pao. (2014, November 2). Materials are sufficient for Admiralty, A03. (In Chinese)

Postman, N. (1985). *Amusing ourselves to death: Public discourse in the age of show business*. New York, NY: Viking.

Simmons, E. (2014). Grievances do matter in mobilization. *Theory and Society, 43*, 512–546.

Tsang, H. W. (2014, October 3). Why do we so care about if there are leaders? *Ming Pao*, A36. (In Chinese)

Tufekci, Z., & Wilson, C. (2012). Social media and the decision to participate in political protest: Observations from Tahrir Square. *Journal of Communication, 62*, 363–379.

Valenzuela, S., Arriagada, A., & Scherman, A. (2012). The social media basis of youth protest behavior: The case of Chile. *Journal of Communication, 62*, 299–314.

Walsh, E. J. (1981). Resource mobilization and citizen protest in communities around Three Mile Island. *Social Problems, 29*, 1–21.

Walsh, E. J. (1988). *Democracy in the shadows: Citizen mobilization in the wake of the accident at Three Mile Island*: New York, NY: Greenwood Press.

Wong, M. L. (2014, October 13). The so-called organizers. *Ming Pao*, D05. (In Chinese)

Social media and Umbrella Movement: insurgent public sphere in formation

Paul S. N. Lee, Clement Y. K. So and Louis Leung

The Chinese University of Hong Kong, Hong Kong

> The study examines the role of social media during the Umbrella Movement in Hong Kong that lasted from September to December 2014. By interviewing a random sample of 1011 respondents over the telephone before the end of the Umbrella Movement, it was found that social media had become an insurgent public sphere (IPS) in the protest movement. Data showed that acquisition of political news through social media was related positively to support for the Umbrella Movement and adversely with satisfaction and trust of established political authorities, including the Hong Kong Special Administrative Region government, the Hong Kong police, and the Chinese central government. The insurgent public sphere role of social media, its implications, and likely development vis-à-vis the state and the market are discussed.

On the evening of 28 September 2014, the police fired tear gas to disperse the crowds gathered around Admiralty of Hong Kong Island. This action, however, provoked even more people to come out in support of the students' protest against the Chinese central government's decision to place hurdles to block democrats from being elected as the Hong Kong chief executive in the scheduled 2017 universal suffrage. This unexpected outcome, to everyone's surprise, developed into a 79-day Occupy Movement that became known as the Umbrella Movement worldwide. It was called the Umbrella Movement by foreign media because the protesters used only umbrellas and wet towels to protect themselves from the police's pepper spray and tear gas. In the following, we will use the term "Umbrella Movement" and "Occupy Movement" interchangeably.

New form of mobilization

The Umbrella Movement shared many characteristics of social movements that have sprung up in recent years in the United States (Bennett, 2012; Castells, 2012; Juris, 2012), Egypt (Arditi, 2012; Castells, 2012; Tufekci & Wilson, 2012), Spain, Turkey, Mexico (Rovira Sancho, 2014), Guatemala (Harlow, 2012), and Chile (Valenzuela, Arriagada, & Scherman, 2012). These movements differed from the norms and rituals of conventional social movements and operated with a new "self-help" and "self-actualization" ethos. The participants in the movements conceived of themselves as autonomous individuals submitting themselves to collective actions only through consensus. Collectivity enjoyed no privileged status over individuality in the movements. This ethos resulted in a "leaderless" movement: every participant was equal; no hierarchy or common ideology was adhered to. Bennett (2012) called this phenomenon "do-it-yourself" politics. He observed that while drawing on repertoires of action from the past, the new form of collective action "displayed openness to individual-level innovation aided by clear avoidance of formal organization, leaders, collective identification, divisive ideology, or hierarchy" (p. 30).

Another feature of the new form of mobilization is the active participation of youth and the utilization of highly personalized digital networks to coordinate and maintain the movement's momentum. Young people today are very different from previous generations (Livingstone, 2002; Tapscott, 2009). The young generation today grew up in a digital environment where distinctions between online and offline activities are blurred. This generation does not distinguish between online and offline identities (Palfrey & Gasser, 2008; Wilson, 2006). They are "digital natives" as distinguished from "digital immigrants", who pick up digital skills like learning a new language later in life and speak the new language with an accent; for example, printing out a document written on the computer in order to edit it or telephoning an email recipient to make sure the email has been received. Digital natives, in contrast, like to multi-task, prefer graphics to text, function best when networked, and thrive on instant gratification and frequent awards (Prensky, 2001).

There are other terms for this new generation, including the Net generation (born between 1977 and 1997 [Tapscott, 2009]), Generation Y (born between 1978 and 1990 according to Baggott [2009]; Barzilai-Nahon and Mason [2010]; Childs, Gingrich, & Pillar [2009]; Simons [2010]; Tapscott [2009]; Tulgan and Martin [2001]), the Facebook generation (born between 1976 and 1994 [Clare, 2009]), Generation Z (born since 1995 according to Dorizas [2009]; born around 1990 according to Hogan and Lynch [2011]), or Millennials (born during or after 1982 according to Oblinger [2003] and;Tapscott [2009]). Although various age brackets and labels are used to delineate the new generation, the central characteristic of this generation is that they bathe in bits (Tapscott, 2009) and live with digital media. They have common experiences with digital technology, particularly the Internet, mobile phones, and social media.

According to Bennett (2012), the dominance of neoliberal economics in recent decades has privatized public sectors or subjected them to hybrid market models. The market deregulation philosophy has made relationships between individuals and civic organizations more entrepreneurial and less centrally manageable (Bimber, Flanagin, & Stohl, 2012). There has been a decline in group loyalty and social fragmentation, as well as an increase in personal stress and a sense of responsibility for choices and consequences (Beck, 2006; Bennett, 1998).

The rise of more personalized politics, especially among young people, has become a notable trend. The young generation is more interested in personally meaningful, lifestyle-related political issues than party politics, giving rise to "consumer politics" (Bennett, 2008). Personal action frames displace collective action frames in many protest causes and individuals. Collective actions are mobilized around personal lifestyle values, including causes such as economic justice, environmental protection, and workers and human rights. These causes are more difficult to address by politicians and mainstream media that belong to the previous era. Accompanying personalized politics is a strong mistrust of politicians and mass media because they seem to be irrelevant to young people (Bennett, 2008, 2012). Consequently, alternative personalized media, particularly mobile phones, Internet websites, and social media, constitutes a new platform for alternative views and collective actions.

Networked media and Net Geners

Today, young people incorporate networked media in their lives at a faster rate than any other generation. Researchers found that Net Geners (18- to 29-year-olds) in the United States were most likely to seek news from the Internet and least likely to seek news from the traditional channels of network TV and daily newspapers (Raine, Cornfield, & Horrigan, 2005). Another study showed that 37% of those aged 18–24 obtained campaign information from social networking sites (SNSs), and only 4% aged 30–39 did so. For older-age cohorts, these numbers decreased further (Kohut, 2008). In 2008, Facebook was the most commonly used online social network among American adults; 73% have a profile on Facebook compared with 48% on MySpace and 14% on LinkedIn (Lenhart, Purcell, Smith, & Zickuhr, 2010). Other studies also showed that 96% of Net Geners belong to social networks (Childs et al.,2009), and among all SNSs, Facebook was usually the most popular.

A new media tracking study (Centre for Communication and Public Opinion Survey, 2014) indicated that the situation is similar in Hong Kong. Of youth aged 18 to 29, 44% frequently obtained news from various websites via their mobile phones, whereas only 20% of those aged 60 or older did the same. For people aged 60 or older, 30% never obtained news from their mobile phones, and only 8% of those aged 18–29 did not get news from mobile phones. For the use of social media, the generational divide is even greater. Everyone in the 18–29 age group has used social media such as Facebook, YouTube, or Instagram, whereas more than half (52%) of people aged 60 or older have never used social media of any kind. Although 87% of 18- to 29-year-olds use social media frequently, only 11% of people aged 60 or older did the same. The chasm between Net Geners and previous generations in the use of new media, particularly social media, is serious.

Facebook is the dominant social media site used by Hong Kong youth, particularly during the Umbrella Movement (Ma, Lau, & Hui, 2014). Many youngsters switched their profile pictures on Facebook to yellow ribbons or umbrellas to show their support for the movement. Facebook and WhatsApp were among the major platforms for information distribution and opinion sharing among different groups of people regarding the various incidents related to the movement between September and December 2014 (Li, Tam, Yeung, Yip, & So, 2015; Wu, 2014). One notable example is the teen icon Joshua Wong, who founded the activist group Scholarism and was elected in a *Time* magazine poll as one of the 2014 Persons of the Year. He was described as "updating his Facebook page and WhatsApping madly", and his friends in Scholarism were "absorbed in their own online lives" (Beech & Rauhala, 2014, p. 21).

SNS and political participation

To many people, social media is likely to enable resource-poor political actors to connect, accumulate social capital, and gain a foothold in the public realm through SNSs (Bennett, 2012; Castells, 2009; Loader & Mercea, 2011; Stiegler, 2008). Networked media offer new possibilities of coordinating separated and atomized individuals into a collective entity for certain causes and actions. Bennett (2012) observed, "When conventional political institutions seem on the verge of acting against the interests of diverse and seemingly isolated populations, the social networked communication of digitally networked activism (DNA) can produce surprising results" (p. 29).

Since SNSs are characterized by users' choices and the co-production of content, the hierarchical central control of media production by state and commercial institutions is challenged. Social media is conceived as having a democratic capacity in fostering alternative discourses and empowering marginalized groups including youth (Benkler, 2006; Jenkins, 2006; Leadbeater, 2008). Social and political networks could replace hierarchical institutions and alter existing power relationships (Castells, 1996). Networks allow all citizens to change their relationship to the public sphere. Net citizens are no longer passive consumers and spectators; they have become creators and primary subjects, and in this sense, the Internet democratizes (Benkler, 2006).

However, many studies have shown that social media's role in political participation is mixed and may be overstated. Baumgartner and Morris (2009) found that SNS users are no more inclined to participate in politics than are users of other media, despite the promise of SNS holding for increasing political interest and participation among youth. The general use of SNSs is not related to social capital, civic participation, or online and offline political participation, although the *informational use* and *online network size* are positively related to political participation, online and offline (Gil de Zjuiga, Jung, & Valenzuela, 2012). Kushin and Yamamoto (2010) found that even information seeking in social media is not related to situational political involvement or self-efficacy; only online expression is significantly related to situational political involvement. Another study found that reliance on SNSs such as Facebook and MySpace is positively related to civic participation but not to political participation or confidence in government (Zhang, Johnson, Seltzer, & Bichard, 2010). Similarly, Theocharis, and Quintelier (2014) discovered that Facebook use is positively related to civic participation but not to online or offline political participation.

Nevertheless, there are positive findings about the role of SNSs in political participation. A study by the Pew Research Center found that among those who connected to SNSs, 40% had used the networks to engage in some political activity, from getting information or signing up as a friend of a political candidate to discovering a friend's political interests or affiliations during the 2008 primary season in the United States (Smith & Rainie, 2008). Consuming online news is found related positively to political participation among Net Geners (Quintelier & Vissers, 2008; Tang & Lee, 2013). Bakker and de Vreese (2011) found that "being connected" online itself is positively related to online and offline political participation. Using US national data, Gil de Zuniga et al. (2012) found that seeking information via social media is a positive and significant predictor of people's social capital and political participatory behaviors, online and offline. Tang and Lee (2013) also found that political participation is explained prominently by exposure to shared political information in Facebook, and network structural heterogeneity predicts offline, though not online, participation.

The variations in findings about SNSs' role in political participation can be explained by variations in different studies' measures of SNS uses (for news, information, or entertainment), use duration (frequency or time per day), choices of independent or dependent variables (network size, network heterogeneity, political or civic participation or engagement), definition and operationalization of various concepts (forwarding political messages by email or other behaviors seeking to influence government action), time when the study was conducted (normal period or period with public attention on controversial issues), cultural context of the country (democratic or authoritarian system), etc.

The insurgent nature of SNS

The findings of studies on SNSs' roles in recent social movements all point to the crucial role of SNSs in mobilizing people to participate in collective actions against political authorities and established institutions. In all these movements, SNSs exhibited an "outrage", "radical", "anti-establishment", or "insurgent" role (Arditi, 2012; Bennett, 2012; Castells, 2012; Downing, 2001; Juris, 2012; Rovira Sancho, 2014; Tufekci & Wilson, 2012).

In the present study, we argue that during normal periods when there is no political issue or government election, social media may serve mainly a *social* role, connecting people for social interactions, building and maintaining relationships, exchanging information, and sharing common interests and hobbies in private life. However, when public issues come up, depending on how controversial they are, the *political* role of SNSs will rise in proportion to the intensity of the tension generated in the debates on social, economic, or political issues. The higher the tension, the more likely the SNS will contribute to people's political participation through increased frequency and intensity of discussion on these issues among the networked communities. When confronted with controversial public issues, an SNS will become an insurgent public sphere (IPS) for issue advocates to galvanize into collective action, making demands and putting pressure on the political authorities.

The public sphere conceived by Habermas (1987, 1989, 1992) is a unitary sphere where all members can join with universal access. He believed the rationality of the bourgeois public sphere was capable of extending itself to include other classes and groups. However, many critics have pointed out that the Habermasian public sphere in reality privileged a particular style of "rationality" that largely favored white, wealthy men to the exclusion of other identities including women, proletariats, and racial minorities (Fraser, 1990; McKee, 2005; Negt & Kluge, 1993; Pateman, 1989; Van Zoonen, 2005). The critics argued that there were multiple public spheres in which "subaltern" public spheres existed side-by-side with the dominant public sphere (Fraser, 1990; Squires, 2002). The Umbrella Movement demonstrated clearly the existence of a counterpublic sphere (Squires, 2002) operating side-by-side with the dominant public sphere represented by the dominant mass media. The mass media public sphere, according to Habermas (1989), had changed the culture-debating public into the culture-consuming public, and the essence of critical-rational political discussions in the public sphere was lost. The counterpublics were denied access to the dominant public sphere.

It is observed that during the Umbrella Movement social media became an IPS. We define IPS as a public space for counterpublics to interconnect, discuss issues, construct collective identity, articulate common goals, and engage in collective actions, online or offline, in direct opposition to and confrontation against the dominant public, the state or the market. The IPS emerges when great public controversies appear in society where the dominant public, state, or market stifles free expression, discussion, and debates in traditional mass media that are controlled by the state and/or the market.

Social media can assume an IPS role mainly because it has an *individuated networked structure*. It provides a platform where individuals can express their private dissenting views, yet with the potential of reaching huge and diverse audiences through numerous private and public networks. Previously, dissenting or anti-establishment views needed to reach the wider public through the mass media in order to apply pressure to the state or the market for changes. With the emergence of social media, dissidents and marginalized groups do not need the mass media to publicize their views any more. Through social networking sites, dissidents can reach big audiences in not only their own country but also others. Moreover, the dissidents' views are distributed faster than traditional mass media.

The individuated nature of SNSs, unlike organized institutions such as the press, school, or church, makes state or market control more difficult and costly. However, the cost for SNS users to set up a site or to become a node in a network is much lower. In the conventional form of social mobilization that stresses leadership and discipline, loose groups are usually not included in massive social actions because the cost of coordinating them and putting them within bounds is high. Social media, however, can reduce the costs of coordinating undisciplined groups and facilitate diverse marginalized groups to join hands for a common cause. More importantly, social media helps to create "shared awareness", i.e., understand the situation at hand and understand that everyone else does, which is a crucial form of coordination for collective action (Shirky, 2011). This shared awareness can be increased within a short time because messages are sent out by SNS users horizontally without going through various hierarchies.

Many examples testify to the insurgent role of SNSs. In May 2009, SNSs were used to mobilize an online movement that moved offline in Guatemala in protest against Guatemalan President Alvaro Colom. He was accused of murdering lawyer Rodrigo Rosenberg in a video produced by Rosenberg himself before his death (Harlow, 2012). Online networking sites helped to sustain massive protests for about three months, both online and offline, demanding justice and Colom's ouster. In the uprising in Egypt in early 2011, social media, particularly Facebook and Twitter, played a central role in mobilizing people to protest in Tahrir Square, leading to the downfall of President Mubarak (Tufekci & Wilson, 2012).

An ethnographic study (Juris, 2012) on the Occupy movements in the United States demonstrated that social media had contributed to an emerging logic of aggregation, assembling masses of individuals from diverse backgrounds within physical spaces to confront the establishment. In August 2010 in Chile, a protest broke out against the Barrancones power plant that would have closed a reserve that houses 80% of the world's Humboldt penguins. Within two days after the government had approved the project, 118 groups against Barrancones were created on Facebook (Valenzuela et al., 2012). The protesters stopped the company from building the plant in the reserve area. Facebook use was found to be associated significantly with protest activities in Chile (Valenzuela et al., 2012). After examining various social movements in the last two decades, Rovira Sancho (2014) concluded that with the emergence of Web 2.0, insurgencies are a networked fight for democracy that uses global visibility and freedom on the Net as a condition for its existence.

Hypotheses

In this study, we examine whether social media, in contrast to mass media, played an anti-establishment role in creating an insurgent public sphere for the protestors in the Umbrella Movement. Based on the literature, we put forth the following hypotheses for testing.

H1a: Acquisition of political news on social media is related positively to support among Net Geners for the Umbrella Movement.

H1b: Acquisition of political news on social media is related positively to support across all generations for the Umbrella Movement.

H2a: Acquisition of political news on social media is inversely related to satisfaction with the Hong Kong Special Administrative Region (SAR) government's handling of the Umbrella Movement.

H2b: Acquisition of political news on social media is inversely related to satisfaction with the Hong Kong police's handling of the Umbrella Movement.

H2c: Acquisition of political news on social media is inversely related to satisfaction with the Chinese Central Government's implementation of "one country, two systems" in Hong Kong.

H3a: Acquisition of political news on social media is inversely related to trust in the Hong Kong SAR government.

H3b: Acquisition of political news on social media is inversely related to trust in the Hong Kong police force.

H3c: Acquisition of political news on social media is inversely related to trust in the Chinese central government.

Previous studies showed that consumption of information/news in social media, rather than entertainment, is positively related to political participation (Gil de Zuniga et al., 2012; Quintelier & Vissers, 2008; Tang & Lee, 2013). In this study, we focus on the acquisition of political news on social media as the independent variable. For a study on the impact of social media on social movements, it is essential to examine the use of social media for political news. Since social media is conceived of as "insurgent" during controversial times, we expect to see a significant link between the use of social media for political news and anti-establishment attitudes during the Umbrella Movement.

This study looked at three levels of attitude as the dependent variables: support for; satisfaction with; and trust in the establishment. We chose the following indicators: the level of support for the Umbrella Movement; satisfaction with the Hong Kong Special Administrative Region (HKSAR) government and the Hong Kong police's handling of the Umbrella Movement; satisfaction with the Chinese central government's implementation of the "one country, two systems" model in Hong Kong; and trust in the HKSAR government, Hong Kong police, and Chinese central government. The rationale for these hypotheses is given in order.

First, if social media becomes an insurgent public sphere for marginalized groups to assemble and consolidate into joining offline collective actions during controversial periods, Net Geners, as a marginalized group, are more likely than other age groups to use social media to get related news and tend to be more supportive of collective actions arising from the issues. Hypothesis 1a is intended to see if there are generational differences in the use of social media for political news and in support for the 79-day Occupy Movement. If the marginalized Net Geners tend to use social media for anti-establishment activities or alternative discourses, hypothesis 1a that "acquisition of political news on social media positively is related to support for the Umbrella Movement among Net Geners" should be supported.

Furthermore, if social media really serves as an IPS when controversial issues come up, then no matter how old an individual is, he or she is more likely to support the Occupy Movement if he or she chooses to obtain political news from social media. In that space, people are more likely to get involved in sharing and deliberating anti-establishment or alternative discourses. Hypothesis 1b that "acquisition of political news on social media is positively related to support for the Umbrella Movement across all generations" should also be supported.

We reckon that those who use social media for news more frequently are more likely to feel dissatisfied with the government's and police's methods of handling the Occupy Movement because the IPS is filled with alternative anti-establishment messages and discourses. The government and the police are two major established institutions targeted by protestors during the Umbrella Movement. Similarly, the Chinese central government is the chief culprit responsible for the massive protests; thus, social media news users should also be dissatisfied with the central government's implementation of the "one country, two systems" model in Hong Kong. The IPS role of social media will be established further if H2a to H2c are supported. These hypotheses predict a low level of social media users' satisfaction with the Hong Kong SAR government, the police, and the Chinese central government during the movement.

Hypotheses 3a to 3c are intended to test further the IPS role of social media by examining people's trust in the Hong Kong SAR government, the police, and the Chinese central government. If the IPS role of social media is established, we would see low trust in these three institutions among social media users.

Method

Sample and procedures

The Umbrella Movement started on 28 September 2014, and ended with the eviction of the last protester by the police in the last occupied area of Causeway Bay on 15 December 2014. When the Umbrella Movement was drawing to a close with the government's announcement of the eviction date and the packing up of materials by protesters in the occupied areas, we conducted a survey in 8–12 December 2014.

To derive the sample, phone numbers were first generated by systematic sampling using the most recent residential phone directories. The last two digits of each number were deleted and replaced with the full range of two-digit figures from 00 to 99 to include non-listed numbers. This procedure generated a database from which phone numbers were chosen randomly by computer. The most recent birthday method was used to select the target respondent from a household. We successfully interviewed 1011 Hong Kong residents aged 15 or older on the phone (with a sampling error of 3.1% at the 95% confidence level). The response rate was 44%. All data were weighted by the proportion of gender, age, and education according to the most recent statistics of people aged 15 or older issued by the Census and Statistics Department of the Hong Kong SAR government.

Measures

Generations

Net Geners were operationalized to include those aged between 15 and 29; they were teenagers and young adults. We figured that people born after 1985 should have enough experience with the Internet and digital technologies including social media. In 2000, the oldest Net Geners in this study were 15 years old, and by then, personal computers had about 50% penetration in Hong Kong, and 36% had Internet connections (Go-Globe, 2014). We conceived that those born before 1985 in Hong Kong were likely to be "digital immigrants" rather than "digital natives" bathed in bits since birth. The next generation cohort aged 30–49 is sometimes called Gen Xers. The older generations include those aged 50 or older. They were born in the two decades after the war and are frequently called Baby Boomers.

Social media

By the time when the study was conducted, the most popular social networking sites in Hong Kong were Facebook, Hong Kong Golden Forum, and Discuss.com.hk. Although 19% of respondents mentioned Facebook as the source from which they most frequently obtained political news, less than 1% named the other two. Facebook was therefore taken as the only indicator of social media in this study.

Acquisition of political news
Respondents were asked if they obtained political news from Facebook, which was the most important social media platform during the Umbrella Movement; 19% of respondents named Facebook as the major source from which they most frequently got political news. Facebook ranked third after the mainstream media Television Broadcasts Ltd. (TVB) and Apple Daily, which, respectively, 67% and 33% of respondents named as the source for political news. Similarly, respondents were also asked if they acquired political news from traditional media such as television (TVB, CableTV, and NowTV), newspapers (Apple Daily, Oriental Daily News), and radio (Radio Television Hong Kong, Commercial Radio). Respondents were asked to indicate a "yes" or "no" answer to the use of Facebook as well as other traditional media.

Support for Umbrella Movement
The measure for this variable was a five-point scale ranging from 1 = "strongly not support" to 5 = "strongly support," with 3 = "so-so".

Satisfaction with the Hong Kong SAR government, the police, and the Chinese central government
The respondents were asked if they were satisfied with the way the Hong Kong SAR government and the police had handled the Occupy Movement, as well as the Chinese central government's implementation of the "one country, two systems" model in Hong Kong. A five-point scale ranging from 1 = "strongly dissatisfied" to 5 = "strongly satisfied", with 3 = "so-so", was provided for answers. For the question related to the central government's implementation of "one country, two systems" model in Hong Kong, a scale ranging from 0 = "totally dissatisfied" to 10 = "totally satisfied", with 5 = "so-so", was given.

Trust in the Hong Kong SAR government, the police, and the Chinese central government
Respondents were asked how much they trusted the Hong Kong SAR government, the police, and the Chinese central government in three questions on a scale ranging from 0 = "no trust at all" to 10 = "total trust", with 5 = "so-so".

Results and analysis

The sample was about 48% male and 52% female. We re-grouped the age groups into three broad categories: Net Geners (aged 15–29); Gen Xers (aged 30–49); and Baby Boomers+ (aged 50 or older). About 22% were Net Geners, 34% were Gen Xers, and 44% were Baby Boomers+. About 36% of the sample had received tertiary non-degree education or college degrees, 46% had secondary school education ranging from Form 1 to Form 7, and 18% had primary school education or lower. The sample profile matched the demographics of the Hong Kong population compiled by the Census and Statistics Department of the Hong Kong government with some minor weighting adjustment.

Table 1. Use of Facebook for political news: across generations, support of and on ground participation in Umbrella Movement.

Use of Facebook for political news	Across generations		
	Net Geners (15–29)	Gen Xers (30–49)	Baby Boomers (50 or above)
No	52.1%	80.2%	95.1%
Yes	47.9%	19.8%	4.9%
	(N = 217)	(N = 348)	(N = 446)
	Total N = 1,011; Chi square = 173.43, df = 2, Cramer's V = 0.41***		
Support for Umbrella Movement	Non-Facebook users for news		Facebook users for news
Support	28.0%		62.1%
Not support	72.0%		37.9%
	(N = 793)		(N = 195)
	Total N = 988; Chi square = 80.1, df = 1, Cramer's V = 0.29*		
On ground participation	28.3%		52.4%
Not on ground participation	71.7%		47.6%
	(N = 410)		(N = 168)
	Total N = 578; Chi square = 30.28, df = 1, Cramer's V = 0.23***		

Note: *$p < 0.05$; ***$p < 0.001$.

This study is related to the Umbrella Movement that demanded genuine universal suffrage without pre-screening of candidates by a selection committee controlled by the Chinese central government. The movement by nature is a political one fighting for democracy under Chinese rule. The respondents' political orientation therefore was an important variable to consider in the analysis, and we asked the respondents to indicate their political leaning. Results showed that 29% of respondents claimed they were "neutral-middle," 27% said they had "no political orientation", 33% said they were "pro-democrats", and 10% considered themselves "pro-establishment".

Table 1 shows that great differences exist in the use of social media between the different generations. Although 48% of the Net Geners had used Facebook for political news in the Umbrella Movement, only 20% and 5% of Gen Xers and Baby-boomers respectively did. Table 1 also shows that Facebook users for political news were more likely than non-users to support the Occupy Movement and participated on the ground protesting in person in the occupied areas. Among the Facebook users, 62% expressed their support for the Occupy Movement, whereas only 28% of non-users indicated their support for the Movement (see Table 1). Similarly, among Facebook users, more than half (52%) actually participated *in person* in the occupied areas, whereas only 28% of Facebook non-users did. All differences were statistically significant. These results show that the use of social media for political news made a difference in people's support for and participation on the ground in the occupied areas in the Umbrella Movement.

We then tested our hypotheses, and the results are summarized in Table 2. Acquisition of political news from social media had a significant impact not only on support

Table 2. Means and standard deviations of the influence of acquisition of political news from Facebook and support for Umbrella Movement, satisfaction with and trust in established institutions across generations.

Dependent variables	News acquisition from Facebook	Generations		
		NetGeners (n = 217)	Gen Xers (n = 348)	Baby Boomers + (n = 446)
Support for Umbrella Movement[a]	Yes	3.76 (1.04)	3.68 (1.33)	3.94 (1.60)
	No	3.31 (1.19)	2.52 (1.41)	2.29 (1.52)
		t = −2.95***	t = −6.19***	t = −5.01***
Satisfaction				
with Hong Kong SAR government's handling of the Umbrella Movement[b]	Yes	1.59 (.80)	1.71 (1.00)	1.45 (.90)
	No	2.24 (1.07)	2.52 (1.20)	2.84 (1.44)
		t = 5.02***	t = 5.15***	t = 4.53***
with police's handling of the Umbrella Movement[b]	Yes	1.94 (1.00)	2.22 (1.21)	1.79 (1.27)
	No	2.52 (1.19)	3.10 (1.32)	3.27 (1.42)
		t = 3.89***	t = 5.02***	t = 4.77***
with Chinese central government's practice of "one country, two systems" in Hong Kong[c]	Yes	3.49 (2.45)	3.30 (2.91)	1.57 (.91)
	No	4.61 (2.63)	5.05 (2.88)	2.35 (.88)
		t = 3.23***	t = 4.50***	t = 4.11***
Trust[d]				
in Hong Kong SAR government	Yes	2.88 (2.23)	3.19 (2.72)	2.18 (2.77)
	No	4.14 (2.41)	5.09 (2.73)	5.58 (3.09)
		t = 4.01***	t = 5.14***	t = 5.12***
in Hong Kong police force	Yes	3.88 (2.58)	4.00 (2.82)	3.15 (3.51)
	No	4.62 (2.80)	6.24 (2.64)	6.36 (3.02)
		t = 2.02*	t = 6.21***	t = 4.71***
in Chinese central government	Yes	2.47 (2.35)	2.93 (2.79)	2.00 (2.76)
	No	3.93 (2.81)	5.00 (2.77)	5.61 (3.29)
		t = 4.14***	t = −5.46***	t = 5.02***

Notes: [a]Scales: 1 = strongly not support; 3 = so-so; 5 = strongly support.
[b]Scales: 1 = very dissatisfied; 3 = so-so; 5 = very satisfied.
[c]Scales: 0 = totally dissatisfied; 5 = so-so; 10 = totally satisfied.
[d]Scales: 0 = no trust at all; 5 = so-so; 10 = total trust.
*$p < 0.05$; ***$p < 0.001$.

Table 3. Hierarchical regression of influences on support for Umbrella Movement, satisfaction with, and trust in Hong Kong SAR government.

Predictors	Support for Umbrella Movement[a] β	Satisfaction with HK SAR government[b] β	Trust in HK SAR government[c] β
Block 1: demographics			
Gender (Male = 1)	0.02	−0.02	−0.03
Age	−0.08**	0.05	0.06*
Education	0.03	−0.06*	−0.02
R^2	0.09***	0.07***	0.07***
Block 2: political orientation			
Pan-democrat	0.33***	−0.22***	−0.21***
Middle-neutral	−0.01	0.01	0.03
Pro-establishment	−0.14***	0.18***	0.20***
No orientation	0.01	−0.01	−0.03
R^2	0.23***	0.16***	0.17***
Block 3: political news Acquisition via traditional news media			
TVB	−0.12***	0.06*	0.10***
Cable TV	0.01	0.01	−0.01
Now TV	0.07**	−0.06*	−0.08**
RTHK	0.04	−0.03	−0.06
Oriental Daily News	−0.11***	0.12***	0.12***
Apple Daily	0.18***	−0.15***	−0.20***
R^2	0.06***	0.05***	0.07***
Block 4: political news Acquisition via social media			
Facebook (Yes = 1)	0.16***	−0.17***	−0.16***
R^2	0.02***	0.02***	0.03***
R^2	0.40	0.30	0.34
Total adjusted R^2	0.39	0.29	0.33
F	74.94***	47.39***	55.96***

Notes: Figures are standardized beta weights from final regression equation with all blocks of variables in the model. Missing values were replaced by means in regression analyses.
[a]Scale: 1 = strongly not support, 3 = so-so, 5 = strongly support.
[b]Scale: 1 = very dissatisfied, 3 = so-so, 5 = very satisfied.
[c]Scale: 0 = no trust at all, 5 = so-so, 10 = total trust.
*p < 0.05; **p < 0.01; ***p < 0.001; N = 1,011.

for the Umbrella Movement but also on satisfaction with and trust in established institutions, including the Hong Kong SAR government, the police, and the Chinese central government. A detailed examination of Table 2 shows a systematic pattern of the impact of

Facebook on all the test variables. Within each generation, namely Net Geners, Gen Xers, and Baby Boomers+, the use of Facebook for political news was consistently accompanied by more support for the Umbrella Movement and lower satisfaction with and lower trust in the HKSAR government, the Hong Kong police, and the Chinese central government.

For example, the use of Facebook for political news was linked to increased support for the Umbrella Movement among the Net Geners (3.76 compared with 3.31 of Facebook non-users). This was also true for the Gen Xers (3.68 vs 2.52), as well as the Baby Boomers+ (3.94 vs 2.29). In contrast, the use of Facebook for political news resulted in less trust in the Chinese central government compared with non-use, especially among the Baby Boomers+, who had the lowest mean score of 2.00 (compared with the mean score of 5.61 of Facebook non-users). Therefore, all hypotheses were supported.

The exceptionally low score of Facebook users for trust of the Chinese central government among the Baby Boomers+ (aged 50 or older) can partly be explained by the fact that many of them or their parents had fled communist rule in China during the second half of the twentieth century. If they chose to obtain news from Facebook, they would get much more information unfavorable to the Chinese central government, which has rarely been reported in mainstream media since Hong Kong's reversion to China in 1997. The claim that social media has an insurgent role during periods of controversy can be further corroborated by the fact that non-Facebook users among the Baby Boomers+ had the highest trust level in the Chinese central government across all generations, but once they used social media as their major source for political news, they then had the lowest level of trust in the Chinese central government among *all* generations. The political backdrop of the Baby Boomers+ may also explain why the Facebook users of this group, contrary to our original expectations, supported the Umbrella Movement more than Facebook users among the Net Geners and experienced the lowest satisfaction with and trust in the Hong Kong SAR government, the Hong Kong police, and the Chinese central government.

It is evident from this study that if a person got his or her political news from sources other than social media, he or she was more likely to have more trust in and satisfaction with the established authorities, including the government and the police, irrespective of which generation he or she belonged to. This reflects in a certain way that traditional mass media tended to be more pro-establishment, while social media tended to be insurgent or anti-establishment.

These results also indicate that Gen Xers and Baby Boomers+, though in smaller numbers than Net Geners, also used social media for news, and mobilized in the insurgent public sphere for collective actions. Protests and anti-establishment activities therefore cannot be explained alone by generational difference. The use of social media, however, is demonstrated to have a consistent impact on people's support for the protest movement and anti-establishment sentiment.

To delineate further the insurgent role of social media, we ran a hierarchical regression to examine the relationship between social media and the Umbrella Movement, and satisfaction with and trust in established authorities, including the Hong Kong SAR government, the Hong Kong police, and the Chinese central government. In the hierarchical regression, we controlled three major sets of independent variables: demographics; political orientation; and acquisition of political news in traditional mass media. These three sets of independent variables are normally assumed to be influential in determining one's support for a social protest. Since we want to examine the unique impact of social media in insurgencies, these variables must be controlled.

The findings showed a systematic and consistent pattern of relationships in all test variables: social media was a positive predictor for support of the Umbrella Movement and a negative predictor for the levels of satisfaction with and trust in the Hong Kong SAR government, the Hong Kong police, and the Chinese central government. Without burdening readers with too much detail, we use only regression results of social media on people's satisfaction with and trust in the Hong Kong SAR government to illustrate the pattern of relationships. The results are shown in Table 3.

As expected, using Facebook for political news was a significant positive predictor of support for the occupy movement ($\beta = 0.16, p < 0.001$), and a significant negative predictor of satisfaction ($\beta = -0.17, p < 0.001$) with and trust ($\beta = -0.16, p < 0.001$) in the Hong Kong SAR government. Acquisition of political news from Facebook accounted for 2% of the variance for support of the Umbrella Movement and satisfaction with the HKSAR government. For trust in the HKSAR government, the use of Facebook for political news accounted for 3% of the variance. This incremental variance was explained beyond that accounted for by all the control variables (Table 3).

An examination of the control variables for the regression of social media on support for Umbrella Movement showed that pan-democratic orientation ($\beta = 0.33, p < 0.001$), Now TV ($\beta = 0.07, p < 0.01$), and *Apple Daily* ($\beta = 0.18, p < 0.001$) had a positive impact on support for the movement whereas age ($\beta = -0.08, p < 0.01$), pro-establishment orientation ($\beta = -0.14, p < 0.001$), TVB ($\beta = -0.12, p < .001$), and *Oriental Daily News* ($\beta = -0.11, p < 0.001$) had a negative impact (Table 3). TVB was the source most frequently used for political news during the Umbrella Movement (67%). It was the most popular television service in Hong Kong and known to be pro-establishment. The political stance of the *Oriental Daily News* fluctuated but was basically pro-China in recent years. However, the *Apple Daily*, which ranked second (33%) as the major source from which respondents frequently got political news, was known to be "anti-government" and "anti-China", while Now TV was seen to lean slightly toward the protestors during the Umbrella Movement. The traditional mass media selected in the regression analysis all had 9% or more respondents naming it as a major source of political news.

In the regression of social media on satisfaction with the way the Hong Kong SAR government handled the occupy movement, a reverse pattern was found in the impact of the control variables. Pan-democratic orientation ($\beta = -0.22, p < 0.001$), Now TV ($\beta = -0.06, p < 0.05$), *Apple Daily* ($\beta = -0.15, p < 0.001$), and education ($\beta = -0.06, p < 0.05$) became negative in its impact on satisfaction with the HKSAR government, whereas pro-establishment orientation ($\beta = 0.18, p < 0.001$), TVB ($\beta = 0.06, p < 0.05$), and *Oriental Daily News* ($\beta = 0.12, p < 0.001$) became positive (Table 3).

Similarly, the regression of social media on trust in the Hong Kong SAR government resulted in a pattern similar to that of satisfaction with the HKSAR government. Pan-democratic orientation ($\beta = -0.21, p < 0.001$), Now TV ($\beta = -0.08, p < 0.01$), and *Apple Daily* ($\beta = -0.20, p < 0.001$) had negative impact, whereas age ($\beta = 0.06, p < 0.05$), pro-establishment orientation ($\beta = 0.20, p < 0.001$), TVB ($\beta = 0.10, p < 0.001$), and *Oriental Daily News* ($\beta = 0.12, p < 0.001$) had positive impact (Table 3).

All the blocks, demographics ($\Delta R^2 = 0.09; \Delta R^2 = 0.07; \Delta R^2 = 0.07$), political orientation ($\Delta R^2 = 0.23; \Delta R^2 = 0.16; \Delta R^2 = 0.17$), use of traditional mass media for political news ($\Delta R^2 = 0.06; \Delta R^2 = 0.05; \Delta R^2 = 0.07$), and use of social media for political news ($\Delta R^2 = 0.02; \Delta R^2 = 0.02; \Delta R^2 = 0.03$), contributed significantly ($p < 0.001$) to predicting support for the Umbrella Movement and satisfaction with and trust in the HKSAR government respectively. Altogether they explained 40%, 30%, and 34% of the variance in support for the movement and satisfaction with and trust in the HKSAR government respectively. Political orientation, understandably, had the strongest explanatory power among the four blocks of variables.

The findings indicate that the use of social media had a positive and significant, albeit small, contribution to people's support for the social movement. Most people today still use mass media as their major source of news and information, and people's political orientation is influential in determining their support for a social movement. However, when the young generation ages, more and more people will use a form of social media, which will displace mass media as the major source of information. The impact of social media will then become more powerful and significant. We ran a general ordinary least squares (OLS) regression model that included all variables at one time instead of a hierarchical model for all test variables, but we found that the explanatory power of social media did not change much. For example, the standardized betas for Facebook predicting support for the Umbrella Movement, satisfaction with the HKSAR government, and trust in the HKSAR government were 0.16, –0.17, and –0.17 respectively. When we ran them in hierarchical fashion, they were in the following order: 0.16, –0.17, and –0.16 (see Table 3); there was almost no change. The present finding of a small yet significant role of social media in the Umbrella Movement echoes Curran's (2012) observation regarding the Arab Spring. He pointed out that digital media might not cause the uprisings, which had deep-seated economic, political, and religious causes, but it helped to strengthen them (p. 54).

Discussion and conclusion

Our study shows that during the Umbrella Movement, the use of social media for political news increased support for the Occupy Movement and reduced satisfaction with the HKSAR government's method of handling the Movement and trust in the HKSAR government, as well as satisfaction with and trust in the Hong Kong police and the Chinese central government. Social media served as an IPS for counterpublics to mobilize and act against the dominant public and state.

Some explanations can be offered for the anti-establishment and insurgent role of social media at a time of great controversy. First, social media enables the autonomous construction of social networks controlled and guided by their users (Castells, 2012). Marginalized groups, including the Net Geners who are excluded from mainstream politics and mass media (Bennett, 2012; Castells, 2012; Loader & Mercea, 2011), have easy access to SNSs and make their views known to large networked communities instantly. Once dissenting views are known in the public sphere, those who are excluded from or are subordinate to the mainstream society due to unequal power relationships (Asen, 2000; Warner, 2002) can connect through the SNS, seeking solidarity and forming large counterpublics with collective actions (Leung & Lee, 2014; Palczewski, 2001; Warner, 2002).

Second, interpersonal discussion on public issues enhances political participation (McLeod, Scheufele, & Moy, 1999). Since SNSs facilitate and encourage interpersonal discussion on various topics, including controversial public issues, the IPS becomes a powerful platform for political mobilization. By allowing multiple channels for interpersonal feedback, peer acceptance, and reinforcement of group norms, SNSs promote the construction of personal and group identities that are key antecedents of protest behavior (Dalton, Sickle, & Weldon, 2009; Valenzuela et al., 2012). Seeking and being exposed to information in SNSs also enhance individuals' social capital (Ellison, Gray, Lampe, & Fiore, 2014; Putnam, 2000) and mutual support (Gil de Zuniga et al., 2012; Tang & Lee, 2013; Valenzuela et al., 2012), thus preparing the counterpublic to get together for collective actions.

Third, social media not only help to activate latent ties that may be crucial to the mobilization of networked publics, but also enables expression and information sharing that liberates the individual and the collective imagination (Papacharissi, 2014). The audience base of anti-establishment networking sites can be expanded quickly through many-to-many and mass self-communication (Castells, 2009), solving the long-existing problem of using alternative media but failing to reach a large audience (Owens & Palmer, 2003).

Another factor contributing to the IPS nature of social media is the "filtering" effect of the individual network (Pariser, 2011). Since social media users are engaged in "private" communication and have control over the content to which they are exposed, they are likely to confine their contacts to like-minded people and to avoid those whom they would like to ignore. This echo chamber effect (Garrett, 2009) will reinforce existing and inclining views embraced by the counterpublics. Without exposure to opposing or alternative views, the IPS may end up becoming overly critical and extreme in its discourses and actions.

Finally, despite that surveillance in the form of big data on users are still being dominated by big corporations, the users' autonomy in the choice of materials, co-production of content, multilayered channels, multifarious messages, and instant transmission of speech make social media basically difficult to be fully monitored by the central government. The discourses in SNSs are not dominated by the state or business (Earl & Kimport, 2011; Loader & Mercea, 2011). Alternative views, including anti-establishment discourses, appear much more frequently in the IPS.

Undoubtedly, with the increasing influence of social media in politics and economy, the state and the market will try to control and manipulate social media similar to mass media. These institutions will try to dominate the public spheres that threaten their power and interests. Meanwhile, when the older generations are gone, with more and more people using social media, which will gradually displace the information and entertainment role of traditional mass media, prominent SNSs controlled by the state or the market will emerge. However, it is doubtful whether these state- or market-controlled SNS will become the dominant public sphere and thus nullify the IPS role of social media. As discussed earlier, the individual and low-cost nature of SNS allow people to easily set up alternative and insurgent sites. Unless the state imposes a total ban on social media, IPSs are not likely to be rooted out. A total ban on social media and networked communication will harm the economy and alienate otherwise pro-state citizens. The state at best resorts to censorship and restricts access to anti-establishment information on the Internet at a high cost. Social media mainly provides a platform for socializing during normal periods, such as exchanging information and sharing common interests among friends, and can become an IPS suddenly when controversial issues appear. It is difficult for the state to distinguish insurgencies from socializing activities. Surveillance of social media incurs heavy economic and political costs.

Since the Umbrella Movement had an avowed goal of "genuine universal suffrage" under the "one nation, two systems" designed by the Chinese government, the movement was essentially a political democratic movement. Judging from the successful organization of the occupy movement for 79 days, and reliance on Facebook for political news by most supporters (62%) of the movement, social media, as an IPS, has a democratizing role in society. This role is realized through its help in building up dissent, cultivating a common consciousness and identity for a cause, and disseminating dissenting views and insurgent activities across the city and to the wider world. The IPS, once formed and expanded, will be likely put under the spotlight of the world stage. Once put on the world stage, the local dominant public and the state will be subject to the surveillance of a global audience, which will curtail much of the freedom of action by the state or the dominant public in its response to the counterpublics, especially actions that violate human rights and international norms. No matter whether the insurgents' goal is finally obtained, the IPS presents an opportunity for counterpublics to advance dissenting views, have an open debate of issues ignored by the dominant public, and enhance free speech as well as diversity of ideas.

In the foreseeable future, social media will continue to play an IPS role, especially during controversial times and under autocratic rule (Willnat & Aw, 2014). With the increasing use of social media for information, entertainment, and public discourses, the state and the market will certainly encroach upon this new media to exert additional control and influence that they already have. However, the control of this individuated networked media by the state and market will not be easy as resistance to their control can be mobilized much faster and with broader support. Moreover, as Dean (2010) notes, the affective flow and affective links in social media remain and resonate with networked publics even after the specific links to the content have been shut down. Affective attachments to media cannot produce communities but may produce "feelings" of community. When the time comes, the IPS will form again quickly based on such imagined community.

Future studies may examine the encroachment of the state and the market on social media, and how they engulf this insurgent public sphere and attempt to turn it into a dominant public sphere that disseminates mainstream discourses supporting the state and the market. In the present study, we did not examine the discourses in the IPS in the Umbrella Movement. Future studies should analyze the discourses in the social media and traditional mass media. The IPS role of social media would become even more distinct with such analysis.

Disclosure statement

No potential conflict of interest was reported by the authors.

References

Arditi, B. (2012). Insurgencies don't have a plan, they are the plan: Political performatives and vanishing mediators in 2011. *Journalism, Media and Cultural Studies, 1*(1), 1–16.
Asen, R. (2000). Seeking the "counter" in counterpublics. *Communication Theory, 10*(4), 424–446.
Baggott, C. (2009). If we build it, the will come. *National Civic Review, 98*(3), 30–33.
Bakker, T. P. & de Vreese, C. H. (2011). Good news for young people, Internet use, and political participation. *Communication Research, 38*, 451–470.
Barzilai-Nahon, K. & Mason, R. (2010). How executives perceive the Net generation. *Information, Communication & Society, 13*(3), 396–418.

Baumgartner, J. C. & Morris, J. S. (2009). MyFaceTube politics: Social networking web sites and political engagement of young adults. *Social Science Computer Review, 28*, 24–44.

Beck, U. (2006). *Power in the global age: A new global political economy.* Cambridge: Polity Press.

Beech, H. & Rauhala, E. (2014 October 20). Voice of a generation. *Time, 184*(15), 16–21.

Benkler, Y. (2006). *The wealth of networks: How social production transforms markets and freedom.* New Haven, CT: Yale University Press.

Bennett, W. L. (1998). The uncivic culture: Communication, identity, and the rise of lifestyle politics. *PS: Political Science & Politics, 31*(4), 740–761.

Bennett, W. L. (2008). Civic learning in changing democracies: Challenges for citizenship and civic education. In P. Dahlgren (Ed.), *Young citizens and new media: Learning and democratic engagement* (pp. 59–78). New York: Routledge.

Bennett, W. L. (2012). The personalization of politics: Political identity, social media and changing patterns of participation. *The Annals of the American Academy of Political and Social Science, 644*, 20–39.

Bimber, B., Flanagin, A., & Stohl, C. (2012). *Collective action in organizations: Interaction and engagement in an era of technological change.* New York: Cambridge University Press.

Castells, M. (1996). *The information age: The rise of the network society.* Vol. 1. Malden, MA: Blackwell.

Castells, M. (2009). *Communication power.* Oxford: Oxford University Press.

Castells, M. (2012). *Networks of outrage and hope: Social movements in the Internet age.* Malden, MA: Polity Press.

Centre for Communication and Public Opinion Survey, Chinese University of Hong Kong. (2014). *New media tracking study.* Retrieved from http://www.com.cuhk.edu.hk/ccpos/en/research/New%20Media_Survey%20Results_2012_ENG.pdf

Childs, R., Gingrich, G., & Pillar, M. (2009). The future workforce: Gen Y has arrived. *The Public Manager, 38*(4), 21–23.

Clare, C. (2009). Generational differences: Turning challenges into opportunities. *Journal of Property Management, 74*(5), 41–43.

Curran, J. (2012). Rethinking internet history. In J. Curran, N. Fenton, & D. Freedman (Eds.), *Misunderstanding the Internet* (pp. 34–65). London: Routledge.

Dalton, R., Sickle, A., & Weldon, S. (2009). The individual–institutional nexus of protest behavior. *British Journal of Political Science, 40*, 51–73.

Dean, J. (2010). Affective networks. *Media Tropes eJournal, 2*(2), 19–44.

Dorizas, A. (2009). Generation next. *Government News, 29*(5), 18–19.

Downing, J. (2001). *Radical media: Rebellious communication and social movements.* Thousand Oaks, CA: Sage.

Earl, J. & Kimport, K. (2011). *Digitally enabled social change: Activism in the Internet age.* Cambridge, MA: MIT Press.

Ellison, N., Gray, R., Lampe, C., & Fiore, A. (2014). Social capital and resource requests on Facebook. *New Media and Society, 16*(7), 1104–1121.

Fraser, N. (1990). Rethinking the public sphere: A contribution to the critique of actually existing democracy. *Social Text, 25*(26), 56–80.

Garrett, R. (2009). Echo chambers online? Politically motivated selective exposure among Internet news users. *Journal of Computer-Mediated Communication, 14*(2), 265–285.

Gil de Zuniga, H., Jung, N., & Valenzuela, S. (2012). Social media use for news and individuals' social capital, civic engagement and political participation. *Journal of Computer-Mediated Communication, 17*, 319–336.

Go-Globe. (2014, August 6). Internet usage in Hong Kong: Statistics and trends. Retrieved from http://www.go-globe.hk/blog/internet-usage-hong-kong/

Habermas, J. (1987). *The theory of communicative action: Lifeworld and system: A critique of functionalist reason.* Boston, MA: Beacon.

Habermas, J. (1989). *The structural transformation of the public sphere: An inquiry into a category of bourgeois society.* Cambridge, MA: MIT Press.

Habermas, J. (1992). Further reflections on the public sphere. In C. Calhoun (Ed.), *Habermas and the public sphere* (pp. 421–461). Cambridge, MA: MIT Press.

Harlow, S. (2012). Social media and social movements: Facebook and an online Guatemalan justice movement that moved offline. *New Media & Society, 14*(2), 225–243.

Hogan, J., & Lynch, K. (2011, September). *How Irish political parties are using SNS to reach generation Z: An insight into a new online social network in a small democracy.* Paper presented at the annual meeting of the American Political Science Association. Retrieved from http://ssm.com/abstract=1901792

Jenkins, H. (2006). *Convergence culture: Where old and new media collide*. New York: New York University Press.

Juris, J. (2012). Reflections on Occupy Everywhere: Social media, public space, and emerging logics of aggregation. *American Ethnologist, 39*(2), 259–279.

Kohut, A. (2008). *Social networking and online videos take off: Internet's broader role in campaign 2008*. The Pew Research Center for the People and the Press. Retrieved from http://www.Pweinternet.org/pdfs/Pew_MediaSources_jan08.pdf

Kushin, M. & Yamamoto, M. (2010). Did social media really matter? College students' use of online media and political decision making in the 2008 election. *Mass Communication & Society, 13*, 609–630.

Leadbeater, C. (2008). *We-think*. London: Profile Books.

Lenhart, A., Purcell, K., Smith, A., & Zickuhr, K. (2010). *Social media and young adults: Social media and mobile Internet use among teens and young adults*. Washington, DC: Pew Internet & American Life Project. Retrieved from http://www.pewinternet.org/Reports/2010/Social-Media-and-Young-Adults.aspx

Leung, D. K. K. & Lee, F. L. F. (2014). Cultivating an active online counterpublic: Examining usage and political impact of Internet alternative media. *The International Journal of Press/Politics, 19*(3), 340–359.

Li, X. X., Tam, H. W., Yeung, K. L., Yip, T. W., & So, C. Y. K. (2015, January 21). The role of social news media in the Occupy Movement. *Media Digest*. Retrieved from http://app3.rthk.hk/mediadigest/content.php?aid=1990 [In Chinese].

Livingstone, S. (2002). *Young people and new media: Childhood and the changing media environment*. London: Sage.

Loader, B. & Mercea, D. (2011). Networking democracy? *Information, Communication & Society, 14*(6), 757–769.

Ma, W. K., Lau, H. C., & Hui, Y. H. (2014, September 12). 2014 news and social media use survey. *Media Digest*. Retrieved from http://app3.rthk.hk/mediadigest/content.php?aid=1960 [In Chinese].

McKee, A. (2005). *The public sphere: An introduction*. Cambridge: Cambridge University Press.

McLeod, J., Scheufele, D., & Moy, P. (1999). Community integration, local media use and democratic processes. *Communication Research, 23*, 179–209.

Negt, O. & Kluge, A. (1993). *Public sphere and experience: Toward an analysis of the bourgeois and proletarian public sphere*. Minneapolis, MN: University of Minnesota Press.

Oblinger, D. (2003). Boomers, gen-Xers and millennials: Understanding the new students. *Educause Review, July/August*, 37–47.

Owens, L. & Palmer, K. (2003). Making the news: Anarchist counter-public relations on the World Wide Web. *Critical Studies in Media Communication, 20*(4), 335–361.

Palczewski, C. (2001). Cyber-movements: New social movements, and counterpublics. In R. Asen & D. C. Brouwer (Eds.), *Counterpublics and the state* (pp. 161–186). Albany, NY: State University of New York Press.

Palfrey, J. & Gasser, U. (2008). *Born digital: Understanding the first generation of digital natives*. New York: Basic Books.

Papacharissi, Z. (2014). On networked publics and private spheres in social media. In J. Hunsinger & T. Senft (Eds.), *The social media handbook* (pp. 144–158). New York: Routledge.

Pariser, E. (2011). *The filter bubble: What the Internet is hiding from you*. New York: Penguin.

Pateman, C. (1989). *The disorder of women: Democracy, feminism and political theory*. Cambridge: Polity Press.

Prensky, M. (2001). Digital natives, digital immigrants. *On the Horizon, 9*(5), 1–6.

Putnam, R. (2000). *Bowling alone: The collapse and revival of American community*. New York: Simon & Schuster.

Quintelier, E. & Vissers, S. (2008). The effect of Internet use on political participation: An analysis of survey results for 16-year-olds in Belgium. *Social Science Computer Review, 26*(4), 411–427.

Raine, L., Cornfield, M., & Horrigan, J. (2005). *The Internet and campaign 2004*. Washington, DC: Pew Internet and American Life Project. Retrieved from http://www.pewinternet.org/pdfs/PIP2004Campaign.pdf

Rovira Sancho, G. (2014). Networks, insurgencies, and prefigurative politics: A cycle of global indignation. *Convergence: The International Journal of Research into New Media Technologies, 20*(4), 387–401.

Shirky, C. (2011). The political power of social media: Technology, the public sphere, and political change. *Foreign Affairs, January/February*, 28–41.

Simons, N. (2010). Leveraging generational work styles to meet business objectives. *Information Management, 44*(1), 28–33.

Smith, A., & Rainie, L. (2008). *The Internet and the 2008 election*. Retrieved from http://www.pewinternet.org/pdfs/PIP_2008_election.pdf

Squires, C. (2002). Rethinking the black public sphere: An alternative vocabulary for multiple public spheres. *Communication Theory, 12*(4), 446–468.

Stiegler, B. (2008). *Acting out*. Stanford, CA: Stanford University Press.

Tang, G. & Lee, F. L. F. (2013). Facebook use and political participation: The impact of exposure to shared political information, connections with public political actors, and network structural heterogeneity. *Social Science Computer Review, 31*(6), 763–773.

Tapscott, D. (2009). *Grown up digital: How the Net generation is changing your world*. New York: McGraw-Hill.

Theocharis, Y. & Quintelier, E. (2014). Stimulating citizenship or expanding entertainment? The effect of Facebook on adolescent participation. *New Media & Society, 1–20*, doi:10.1177/1461444814549006

Tulgan, B. & Martin, C. (2001). *Managing Generation Y: Global citizens born in the late seventies and early eighties*. Amherst, MA: HRD Press.

Tufekci, Z. & Wilson, C. (2012). Social media and the decision to participate in political protest: Observations from Tahrir Square. *Journal of Communication, 62*, 363–379.

Valenzuela, S., Arriagada, A., & Scherman, A. (2012). The social media basis of youth protest behavior: The case of Chile. *Journal of Communication, 62*, 299–314.

Van Zoonen, L. (2005). *Entertaining the citizen: When politics and popular culture converge*. Lanham, MD: Rowman & Littlefield.

Warner, M. (2002). *Publics and counterpublics*. Cambridge, MA: MIT Press.

Willnat, L. & Aw, A. (2014). Conclusion. In L. Willnat & A. Aw (Eds.), *Social media, culture and politics in Asia* (pp. 276–299). New York: Peter Lang.

Wilson, B. (2006). Ethnography, the Internet and youth culture: Strategies for examining social resistance and 'online–offline' relationships. *Canadian Journal of Education, 29*(1), 307–328.

Wu, A. (2014). Hong Kong's "alternative" revolution: Facebook. *House News, and Passion Times*. Retrieved from http://www.huffingtonpost.com/amy-wu/hong-kongs-alternative-re_b_6028004.html

Zhang, W., Johnson, T. J., Seltzer, T., & Bichard, S. L. (2010). The revolution will be networked: The influence of social networking sites on political attitudes and behaviour. *Social Science Computer Review, 28*(1), 75–92.

Media and information praxis of young activists in the Umbrella Movement

Alice Y. L. Lee and Ka Wan Ting

Hong Kong Baptist University, Hong Kong

> Young people were key participants in the Umbrella Movement in Hong Kong and the media also played an important role in this protest. This study examines how Hong Kong's young activists developed communication strategies and media practices to mobilize this social movement. A framework termed "media and information praxis of social movements" is proposed for the analysis. The findings showed that in their praxis, the young activists used their media and information literacy skills to initiate, organize, and mobilize collective actions. They not only used social media and mobile networks but also traditional mass media and street booths in a holistic and integrated approach to receive and disseminate information. Hence, these young activists served as agents of mediatization. The results also indicated that the young activists moved away from the traditional movement mode which just tried to motivate a large number of people to protest in the streets. They actively engaged in the new movement mode, which emphasizes the media and information power game. Their praxis in the Umbrella Movement reflects the trend toward the mediatization of social movements in Hong Kong.

In Hong Kong, young people took the lead in the 2014 Umbrella Movement. It has been observed that these "digital natives" made heavy use of different kinds of media. In recent years, mediatization has emerged as an influential concept in communication studies and political science. Adopting the mediatization thesis, this study explores the central role of media practices in the Umbrella Movement.

With the advancements in digital technology, the amount of research on the mediatization of politics has increased significantly. Many social movement scholars have studied the role of media in various social movements around the world (Cammaerts, 2012; Mattoni & Trere, 2014; Van de Donk, Loader, Nihon, & Rucht, 2004). However, mediatization studies have been criticized as overly media-centric, because they "posit the media as agents of change and holders of power – rather than particular individuals or social groups" (Deacon & Stanyer, 2014, p. 1034). Moreover, many studies have over-emphasized the importance of digital media, overlooking the contribution of other communication channels to social movements.

This study, therefore, shifts the research focus to the actors. The staff of social movement organizations, public relations people, and the spin doctors of political parties can be regarded as agents of mediatization. However, in recent years many young people around the world have enthusiastically participated in collective action, and their role has become more prominent. Therefore, in this study techno-savvy young activists are regarded as agents of mediatization. This study examines how they used their media and information literacy skills to develop communication strategies and media practices to initiate and organize the Umbrella Movement. The theoretical framework, "media and information praxis of social movements", is proposed to explore the mediatization phenomenon. Young activists in Scholarism, a post-1990s student group and one of the major social movement organizations in the Umbrella Movement, were chosen as the subjects of this research. These young people are typical "Net Geners".

This study aims to answer two research questions: (i) How did the young people serve as agents of mediatization and apply their media and information skills in the Umbrella Movement? (ii) Did the young activists rely only on digital and mobile media to launch the Movement? If not, how did they use the traditional media at the same time?

Digital youth and social movements

The Umbrella Movement in Hong Kong happened during the 79 days between 28 September and 15 December 2014. Local surveys indicated that young people were the key participants in the Movement. While the average age of the demonstrators at the occupation sites was 27.7 years, 48.8% of the demonstrators were under 25 years (Chan & Lee, 2014).

It is well known that young people tend to participate enthusiastically in social movements. Another trend worth noting is that young people like to apply their media knowledge to political actions. Many recent studies on the involvement of youth in social movements have emphasized their use of the media. A research report on the Kinder & Braver World Project pointed out that many young people today are active and creative in movement strategies and in the production and use of media (Costanza-Chock, 2012). Peer-to-peer learning is an integral part of social movement activity, and digital media literacy is one of the most common topics discussed among youth. Youth organizers have built networks for sharing their organizational and media-making skills. A study on European social movements found that youth movements were characterized by "a high use of information and communication technologies" (Fominaya, 2012, p. 2). Moreover, Friedman (2014) described young activists as "square people", as they connect to one another by massing in physical squares or virtual squares. Friedman remarked that these young people use the Internet and social media as tools to observe the world, and they have the new media tools to voice their opinions and take political action.

Many communication studies have pointed out that a natural bond exists between young people and the media. Westlund and Bjur (2014) argued for the naturalization effect of the media in young people's lives. As everything in everyday life becomes mediatized, the media become "invisible". Young people use the media without thinking: they live "in" rather than "with" the media. They do not simply use the media, but live a media life (Weslund & Bjur, 2014, p. 24).

Hong Kong's young activists are digital natives; that is, they live a media life. According to Tapscott (2009), they have grown up digitally as the Net Generation. A local survey indicated that college students spent 13 hours on average each day using various media platforms (So, 2011). Hong Kong is a technologically advanced city. The results of a public opinion survey showed that nearly 90% of teenagers owned a registered social network account, and 98% of young people used Facebook frequently (Public Opinion Programme, 2010). Hence, young activists in Hong Kong are nurtured in a highly technological environment.

Although the Umbrella Movement has no formal leader, two student groups played a particular role in bringing the Movement forward: the Hong Kong Federation of Students and Scholarism. Many media commentators recognized the importance of how these young people used Facebook, WhatsApp, alternative media, and other media forms in the Movement. Hence, this study chose young activists as the main research target and investigated their role in the mediatization of social movements.

Mediatization of social movements

In recent years, social movement theorists have recognized the importance of the media. Scholars have agreed that communication is a significant tool of resource mobilization (Van de Donk et al., 2004). Studies have indicated that the media in Hong Kong are central to the development of a social movement. They not only have served as facilitators of large-scale demonstrations but also have helped to frame the reality of protest (Chan & Lee, 2007). In the context of the rapid development of communication technologies, many scholars have pointed out that in the new participatory media environment, social actors will choose to "bypass the mass media and use their own channels for direct communication" (Schulz, 2004, p. 95). Lovink (2005) put forward the idea of tactical media and the cheap "do-it-yourself" media. Previous research on environmental protests has documented how activists applied the online tactical media strategy to attract and bypass the mass media (Lester & Hutchins, 2009). Bennett and Segerberg (2012) even argued that digital media have changed the rules of the game for social movements. The logic of connective action has replaced the logic of collective action. Castells (2012) even termed this new form of protest as the networked social movement.

As the media play an increasingly essential role in social movements, there is a need to theorize how media and communication both enable and constrain activists of collective action in the new technological environment (Cammaerts, 2012). Hence, mediatization has become an influential concept in addressing the issue. This study adopts the institutionalist view of mediatization, which regards mediatization as "a process in which non-media social actors have to adapt to media rules, aims, production logics and constraints" (Deacon & Stanyer, 2014; Mazzoleni & Schulz, 1999, p. 249). The mediatization of social movements is then defined as "the employment of media logic by social activists in the launch of collective action" (Mazzoleni & Schulz, 1999, p. 249).

The concept of mediatization is intertwined with the concept of media logic (Klinger & Svensson, 2014). Media logic refers to the form of communication through which the media present and transmit information. It is the way that information is selected, organized, and presented in different medium platforms. Altheide and Snow (1979) argued that many social institutions have become part of media culture because of the changes that have resulted from the presentation and interpretation activities that use media logic. According to them, the mass media are a major social influence because their logic and format have become incorporated within the logic of social institutions. Hence, the way in which mass media present information has become accepted as current practice in all kinds of institutional contexts, including the political context of social movements.

In the field of political science, the mediatization of politics usually refers to two institutional changes: (i) political actors change their individual strategies; and (ii) they rearrange resources of political organizations. Hence, if we look at the mediatization of social movements, we have to examine how social activists modify their strategies and re-allocate their organizational resources when they adopt media logic. With the advancement of information and communication technologies (ICTs) in the twenty-first century, many activists have used digital media and Internet platforms to support their protests. Therefore, mediatization is no longer limited to the adaptation of traditional mass media logic; it also applies new media logic. The logic of new media format is characterized by immediate, horizontal, interactive, and highly personalized communication (Klinger & Svensson, 2014; Van Dijck & Poell, 2013).

Current research on mediatization has been criticized for narrowly conceptualized (Deacon & Stanyer, 2014). First, the media was regarded as the sole agent of mediatization, and it is assumed to be innately powerful, ignoring the roles of other social actors (e.g., movement activists). Second, there is no clear idea about the changing communicative practice. Some scholars regarded the social media as essential to the mobilization of social movements, but others were less enthusiastic and saw "slacktivism". They thought that social media activism could not motivate people to make real sacrifices and take high risks. Instead, traditional media are still effective (Gladwell, 2010; Morozov, 2010). It is therefore necessary to examine the mediated functions of different types of media and the roles of social activists.

To understand how mediatization occurred and analyze the role of the media in the Umbrella Movement, a theoretical framework was developed to guide the empirical research.

Media and information praxis of social movements

Many studies have shown that young activists are techno-savvy. However, such studies on youth social movements tend to be descriptive and lack conceptual rigor. Most of these studies merely describe how youth use social media and the Internet. Although they may mention media-related competencies, general terms such as media sophistication are used without being more specific.

In this study, we use UNESCO's concept of media and information literacy (MIL) to precisely define the communication competencies of young activists. A theoretical framework, the media and information praxis of social movements, is developed to analyze the use of media by young activists in the Umbrella Movement.

UNESCO suggests that media and information literacy is an essential life skill in the current digital age, particularly for young people, and it is a holistic concept that integrates media literacy, information literacy, and ICT skills. It is defined as:

> a set of competencies that empowers citizens to access, retrieve, understand, evaluate and use, to create as well as share information and media content in all formats, using various tools, in a critical, ethical and effective way, in order to participate and engage in personal, professional and societal activities. (UNESCO, 2013, p. 29)

Media and information literacy comprises the following components: (i) access to and retrieval of media and information from all channels (online and offline); (ii) evaluation and understanding of media and information; and (iii) communication, use, and creation of media and information. Access is related to obtaining, finding, and choosing media to inform or entertain by using appropriate technologies. Evaluation involves understanding, assessing, critically analyzing, evaluating, and organizing media content or information as knowledge. Communication and creation refer to the ability to master the production know-how of information and how to use, monitor and communicate effectively with other people (Lee, 2013; UNESCO, 2013).

As organizers and participants, the activists in a social movement need to be informed, keep connected, deliver movement ideology, and mobilize collective action. Based on their media and information literacy competencies, this study proposes that young activists followed the media and information praxis to engage in the Umbrella Movement.

Table 1. Media and information praxis of social movements.

Components	Communicative strategies and media practices	Key characteristics
Information aggregation (gathering and verifying information on social movements)	• Use of ICT skills (digital technologies and social media) • News and information searching • Transmedia navigation • Cognitive load management: discriminating and filtering information for importance • Evaluation of relevancy, currency, reliability, completeness, accuracy and quality of movement information • Verification and triangulation (particular for rumors)	• Immediacy • Reliability
Connective communication (connectivity among movement participants)	• SMO's recruitment of members and followers • Effective networked communication and information sharing among SMO members and movement participants • Crowdsourcing • Virtual partnership building • Network smart: understanding the network structure and boundaries • Privacy and security practices	• Personalization • Networked customization
Discourse dissemination (promotion of the movement)	• Delivery of movement discourse • Ideological positioning • Displaying the SMO's stand • Influencing media representation • Creative media production for publicity	• Produsage • Spreadability
Communicative mobilization (motivation for collective action)	• Public mobilization • Call for action	• Participation • Liveness

Praxis is established practices. It comprises informed and committed actions that depend on the exercise of skills, usually involving creativity (Smith, 2011). Praxis requires a person to make "a wise and prudent practical judgment about how to act" in a certain situation (Carr & Kemmis, 1986, p. 190).

Thus, the media and information praxis of social movements refers to the communicative strategies that the activists use in the movement to seek, evaluate, produce, and disseminate information, as well as to mobilize participation in collective action. The communicative strategies involve the wise use of information from various communication platforms. The strategies integrate both mass media logic and new media logic in the operation of the social movement.

This framework of media and information praxis has four components (see Table 1). The first is information aggregation, which refers to the collection and verification of information about the social movement. Young people, whether organizers or participants in the social movement, need to obtain up-to-date and accurate information from various media platforms so that they can make correct judgments about their subsequent actions. The second component is connective communication. Young activists need to build communication networks in order to conduct efficient communication among the activists and connect the participants in the movement. These networks are personalized and customized. The third component is discourse dissemination. The delivery of the movement's goals and values through various media channels is essential. The advocates of the movement need to articulate their ideological position and try to influence media representation through creative media production or media publicity. The fourth component is communicative mobilization. The activists' most important task is to use the media to mobilize collective actions. This study uses the four components of this framework to investigate how the members of Scholarism participated and promoted the Umbrella Movement in Hong Kong.

Scholarism and the Umbrella Movement

In this study, the case of Scholarism was selected to examine how young Hong Kong activists strategically used the media during this prolonged social movement. Scholarism is a Hong Kong student activist organization that was founded by a group of post-1990s secondary students on 29 May 2011 to protest against the Moral and National Curriculum. The group strongly believes that students have the right and power to influence government policies (Scholarism, 2014). Members of Scholarism, together with other social groups, initiated the Anti-Moral and National Education Movement,[1] which in 2012 successfully forced the Hong Kong government to set aside the curriculum guide for Moral and National Education. The organization subsequently turned its attention to political reform.

On 31 August 2014, the National People's Congress Standing Committee passed the election framework for the 2017 Hong Kong Chief Executive Election. Members of Scholarism then accused the framework of failing to meet the international standards for a truly democratic and open election. On 22 September 2014, the Hong Kong Federation of Students announced a five-day class boycott across tertiary institutions in support of a truly democratic election. On 26 September, secondary school students motivated by Scholarism joined the boycott. On the same night, students outside the Government Headquarters, led by Scholarism's convener, Joshua Wong, stormed into Civic Square and triggered the start of the Occupy Central Movement, which brought the city to a standstill for almost three months. The last occupied site in Causeway Bay was finally cleared on 15 December, marking the end of the Umbrella Movement.

Although Scholarism was not the only leading student group in the Umbrella Movement, its leaders and members did play an important role in the protest. For example, Joshua Wong was a central figure. Its members initiated the boycott of classes, joined the occupation of Civic Square, and conducted the hunger strike.

Research methods

This study was conducted in 2014. Several data collection methods were used, including a small-scale questionnaire survey, focus group sessions, interviews, content analysis of Scholarism's Facebook pages, and document analysis. First, questionnaires were sent to all core members of Scholarism (around 50 members), and 27 valid questionnaires were collected. The survey aimed to understand the media usage by individual members. Second, the core members of Scholarism were invited to participate in two focus groups, each of which comprised five core members. The focus groups were designed to explore the participants' rationale for their media choices and to collect their views on social and political issues. Third, in-depth interviews were conducted with three key members of

Scholarism (interviewees A, B, and C) to examine the strategic use of the media from an organizer's perspective. Other interviewees included young activists associated with Scholarism (interviewees D and E), university lecturers who cooperated closely with Scholarism (interviewees F and G), and the producer of a documentary on Joshua Wong (interviewee H). The identities of all participants in the survey, the focus group studies, and the interviews were kept anonymous.

Fourth, a content analysis of three Facebook pages was carried out to understand how the young activists used social media: the Facebook pages of Scholarism and *Dash* (Scholarism's in-house publication), and the public Facebook page of Joshua Wong. The content analysis covered the period from 31 August to 15 December 2014. As there was a huge number of postings, only postings related to five incidents were selected for analysis. A total of 232 postings were coded. The five incidents were as follows: the class boycott and occupation of Civic Square; the tear gas crackdown; the Mongkok clearance; the siege of the government's headquarters; and the hunger strike. These incidents were chosen because the members of Scholarism were heavily involved in these events. Joshua Wong took the lead to storm into Civic Square. He initiated the hunger strike, and he was arrested during the Mongkok clearance. Fifth, news reports published during the Movement were collected for analysis. We retrieved 69 articles related to Scholarism's communications from the Wisenews database. In addition, books written by Joshua Wong and other Umbrella Movement participants were analyzed to help understand the media practices of the young activists.

Information aggregation and verification

In the Umbrella Movement, the members of Scholarism were well aware of the importance of gathering news and information, and they were effective users of such information. Many previous studies on young activists, such as those on the Arab Spring, focused only on their use of social media (e.g., Facebook, Twitter, and YouTube). This study took a broader perspective and found that Hong Kong's young activists were very knowledgeable about the characteristics of many media platforms, and they had sophisticated search skills. In the Umbrella Movement, they strategically gathered information through three types of sources: (i) new media (social media, online forums, blogs, online alternative media); (ii) traditional media and their online sites/apps; and (iii) mobile personal networks.

Our mini-survey of 27 members of Scholarism showed that the most common media used to obtain daily social, political, and news information were Facebook (70%), WhatsApp (67%), YouTube (26%), Instagram (26%), and Hong Kong Inmedia (15%). During the Umbrella Movement, the activists also turned to alternative online media, such as *SocREC*, *hkdash*, *memhk*, and *VJMedia*. In particular, they accessed the specific Facebook pages of Scholarsim, *Dash*, Joshua Wong's public Facebook, the Hong Kong Federation of Students, and the student publications of local universities.

The activists treated social media and new media as their basic information sources. Our survey findings showed that the factors that influenced their choice of media sources were ease and convenience (81%), fast updating of information (63%), and whether they could be obtained freely (56%). When the focus group participants were asked why they preferred to use new media to receive daily information, member C in the second focus group firmly replied "Quick! Speed!" During the Movement, the members of Scholarism needed to know immediately what was happening around them. Moreover, the new media have a sharing function, which made it more convenient to exchange information. Member A pointed out that using the Internet and Facebook had become part of their daily lives.

Joshua Wong, the convener of Scholarism, revealed that he obtained information mainly through online media and mobile apps. On Scholarism's Facebook page, he described his daily routines as follows: "Got up at 9:00 am to read news in order to know the latest development, then wrote articles and updated my Facebook page" (Scholarism Facebook Page, 2 November 2014). It was revealed that Joshua had been addicted to the Internet from Grade 6 onwards, and he was called a "geek" or "otaku" (Yim, 2014, p. 42). He used social media and the Internet to learn about the social structure of Hong Kong society. Although previous social movements in Hong Kong had made little use of the Internet, the Anti-Express Rail Link (Anti-XRL) Movement[2] in 2009 successfully used it to discuss, investigate, organize, promote, and mobilize. Joshua said that in that year he obtained much information about the Anti-XRL Movement through Facebook, Twitter, and YouTube, and he became familiar with many young activists. From then on, it became a "ritual" for him to "spend at least half an hour every day to read online news and Facebook postings" (Wong, 2014a, p. 28). He began to discuss and debate social issues with his online friends.

According to Wong, Facebook is his "base", the main channel for obtaining news. Because he had hundreds of Facebook friends in different parties and groups, he had immediate access to the hottest news of the day whenever he searched his Facebook page (Wong, 2014a, p. 36). Subsequently, he used Facebook to recruit members and co-found Scholarism. He and his comrades effectively used communication strategies and successfully launched the Anti-Moral and National Education Movement in 2012. From the media experience gained through previous social movements, he learned to use social media and the Internet to access, retrieve, and evaluate information during the Umbrella Movement. Wong's case reflects that young people learned media logic through their daily media practice and their participation in the Movement.

Meanwhile, the young members of Scholarism recognized the equal importance of the traditional media. The interview findings indicated that *Apple Daily*, *Ming Pao Daily*, *iCable News*, *Now TV News*, and *RTHK*[3] were also common news sources for the activists. They tended to choose media that they believed to be neutral and credible. Moreover, the young activists in the Movement knew the difference between the roles of the new and the old media. In an in-depth interview, a key member of Scholarism (interviewee B) explained:

> the target audiences of many online alternative media were the pan-democratic groups, but the audiences of traditional media were all the citizens in Hong Kong. Therefore, the traditional media can be regarded as the thermometer of public opinion. If you want to know the public sentiment of the Movement, you have to turn to the traditional media instead of the new media.

Another key member of Scholarism (interviewee A) also asserted that the traditional media had greater credibility than social and online media. He also found out that some of the alternative online media had secret sponsors with special political agendas.

In addition to selecting information from both new and old media, the activists developed their own mobile personal networks in order to obtain up-to-date and trustworthy information. They set up many WhatsApp and Telegram groups. In particular, when they wanted the latest information about the demonstrations, conflicts, and police crackdowns, they asked their friends who were at the frontline to provide live reports. These young people not only were eager to obtain comprehensive and timely information but also emphasized the verification of information. A key member of Scholarism (interviewee A) commented that "as movement organizers, we not only need to select and filter information, but also need to know how to analyze every piece of information", indicating that verification and cautious interpretation were important to him. During the Umbrella Movement, they developed a sophisticated information-checking mechanism. When they were in doubt, they sought professional help. They also went directly to the related organizations or parties to gets answers to their questions. The major design of their verifying mechanism was to set up an investigative surveillance team to get first-hand information. Every morning, around five or six members of Scholarism were sent out to the frontlines and the occupied sites to obtain and verify new information. During the evening, more than 10 students were involved in this kind of investigation and surveillance. The Scholarism activists tended to believe eyewitness accounts and investigative reports by their own members, who were nicknamed the "pigeons" (i.e., the messengers).

During the Movement, many rumors and stories circulated at the occupied sites. For example, there was news that rubber bullets were ready for use by the police. The young activists understood that they must correctly judge the political situation by fully understanding, evaluating, and analyzing all information. A key member (interviewee A) commented that "If you judge the political situation in a wrong way and mobilize some kind of collective action, it will be very risky. It may cost lives!" In fact, during the Movement, unfounded rumors spread widely. A group of journalism students from the University of Hong Kong set up a Facebook page called "Live: Verified updates", which aimed to help verify user-generated texts about the protests (Beam, 2014). The young activists were critical information users who were highly literate in media and information skills. They formed a full picture of a situation by integrating information collected from online new media, mass media, and personal mobile networks.

Connectivity among young activists and Movement participants

To launch a social movement, it is necessary to recruit activists, attract participants, and keep them together. The young activists were very capable of building communication networks.

When it was first established in 2011, Scholarism effectively used Facebook to recruit secondary and tertiary students. During the Umbrella Movement, it continued to use Facebook to recruit volunteers and "Friends of Scholarism" (i.e., citizen supporters), although the activists also developed more personalized networks to connect the Movement's participants. According to a key member of Scholarism (interviewee A), Facebook and WhatsApp were the two most common communication methods used to connect core members. Nonetheless, for important matters, they still chose to meet face-to-face to exchange views. Scholarism has several hundred members. The organization includes various WhatsApp groups, Facebook groups, and email chatrooms for its members to keep in touch. Before the Umbrella Movement, WhatsApp was used to liaise with members regarding less serious issues and everyday conversation. However, during the Movement, WhatsApp became an important channel for networking. According to interviewee B, the Anti-Moral and National Education Movement depended almost entirely on Facebook for communication. During the Umbrella Movement, however, the communication channels became much more diversified and personalized because the technology had advanced and more members had smartphones. WhatsApp was used more frequently. The members also used Telegram and Instagram to keep in touch and exchange information. The communication networks were also useful for crowdsourcing and collecting necessary equipment for the Movement, such as water, masks, medicine, and so forth.

The young activists used WhatsApp, Telegram, and SMS for different purposes. Telegram is similar to WhatsApp, but it can accommodate up to 200 people in a group, and it can send attached documents (Telegram, 2014). The huge number of postings on WhatsApp and Telegram meant that important messages could easily be "drowned". The young activists used SMS to deliver important notices to ensure that the target members received essential messages. In other words, the activists customized their mobile personal networks to connect with fellow members and the active participants in the Movement. Hence, smartphones played a very important role in their communication network.

The activists involved in the social movement needed to communicate with essential partners. Interviewee F, a partner of Scholarism, commented that the three most important means of communication were WhatsApp, followed by face-to-face discussion and telephone conversation. It is noteworthy that this group of youngsters never used email for communication and discussion. A media professional (interviewee H), who filmed Joshua Wong in a documentary, revealed that he communicated with Joshua mainly through text messages that were usually very short – "one word talk". This finding suggests that the activists preferred customized and efficient communication.

Discourse dissemination

During the Umbrella Movement, the activists developed "we media" to deliver the Movement's political discourse and mission even as they mastered media logic and practiced spinning to shape the representation of the Movement in the media. Although Scholarism worked closely with the mass media, it did not depend on the mainstream media to interact with the public. Instead, it established an official website and a Facebook page to express its views and deliver its message. After the Anti-Moral and National Education Movement, it developed a new publication, *Dash*, as well as its Facebook page. Joshua Wong also set up a public Facebook page in addition to his private page, to facilitate communication with the general public. According to a local study on the popularity of Facebook in the Umbrella Movement, the Scholarism Facebook page ranked third with 320,000 likes, and the *Dash* Facebook page ranked 12th with 100,000 likes (Chan & Fu, 2014). Both Facebook pages gained widespread attention from young people in Hong Kong.

The activists regarded the construction of their own media channels as important because they could attract and consolidate supporters. The *Dash* platform was used to report on civil society from the youngsters' point of view (Wong, 2014a). *Dash* is basically run by the members of Scholarism. Many young people, particularly secondary school students, were encouraged to voice their opinions there. For example, it published an article written by a secondary student, which explained that he joined the Movement because he loved Hong Kong and wanted to be a responsible citizen. He expressed that social justice was extremely important and civil disobedience should not be deemed a criminal activity.

Dash played a key role in the Umbrella Movement, and it was regarded as useful in circulating Movement information. Referring to *Dash*, interviewee D commented that it was easier for young people to learn how to build a new media platform than a traditional media channel because it cost less and required few professional skills. In the early stage, a group of online editors was invited to work with Scholarism members for a short period to develop *Dash*. The young activists picked up the skills very quickly and ran it by themselves.

Scholarism's Facebook page and *Dash* were effective in disseminating its political discourse, which included the goals, ideals, and key values of the Umbrella Movement that were expressed through texts and images. Many articles and postings on Scholarism's "we media" conveyed the key messages of "fight for true democracy", "call for universal suffrage", "insist on civil nomination", "civil disobedience is necessary", and "challenge the high wall with eggs (i.e., challenge the authority with bravery)".

As digital natives, these young people creatively managed the production of media and strategically used the new media platforms. Like their European counterparts, they practiced learning by doing (Costanza-Chock, 2012). They made use of their resources and experiences and expressed their messages in creative and interesting ways. Because they understood that young demonstrators in the Movement preferred to read visual images, they used many "lazybones picture packages" on their websites and Facebook pages. A lazybones picture package refers to a picture with a brief explanation, which easily draws the attention of the young audience to a particular issue.

For instance, they used the lazybones picture package to express the students' determination to fight for civil nomination, saying that the National People's Congress Standing Committee's decision on the Chief Executive election was unacceptable. They amended photos to create a "kuso" effect, such as demonizing the Legislative Council Members who belonged to the pro-Beijing bloc. The innovative campaign, "one person one school uniform photo for supporting class boycott", was also initiated by Scholarism through its Facebook pages, and it received wide support from Hong Kong citizens. These can be regarded as what Lovink (2005) referred to as tactical media strategies. By building its own media platforms, Scholarism achieved two goals. First, it bypassed the mass media and directly sent messages and views. Second, it obtained access to the mass media by launching gimmicky activities. Many journalists kept a close eye on the young activists' "we media" platforms. Their political statements and open letters were then published by the traditional media and thus disseminated to the general public.

In the present study, the content analysis of their three Facebook pages showed that of the 232 postings analyzed, 54.3% used lazybones picture packages and only 26.3% contained no visual element. Moreover, emphasizing the spreadability of their messages, they used their Facebook fan pages to cover the Movement's incidents and provide "breaking news".

They also knew that different platforms could be used to achieve different goals. A division of labor existed between the Scholarism site and *Dash*. They used the Scholarism site to promote Scholarism and state its position, whereas they used *Dash* to cover the Movement's incidents. The activists were aware that the discourse distributed through these social media not only reached participants of the Movement and the general public but also influenced the mainstream media because many reporters visited their websites and social media pages to find news.

In addition to using social media, Scholarism used traditional methods to deliver their messages about political reform and the boycott of classes, which included setting up street booths and delivering promotional pamphlets. They also knew how to use the strategy of cross promotion. They printed the *Dash* website address at the back of their pamphlets so that they could lead the audience to their online publications and Facebook page.

Of course, the Scholarism members did not ignore the mass media. On the contrary, they attempted to shape discourse in the mainstream media about the Movement. Interviewee B, another key member of Scholarism, pointed out that it was necessary to "reframe" some of the stories in the mass media and shape the public's mindset. One example is the response to the Education Bureau's announcement in the mainstream media. The education authority made appeals to the parents and teachers by asking them not to let their children and students join the unlawful collective action. To reframe this issue, Scholarism's media platforms posted numerous speeches and stories by professors and celebrities to explain the meaning of civil disobedience and the importance of fighting for true democracy. The spokesperson for Scholarism also conveyed this stand to the organization's media friends.

In order to shape the public's mindset through the mass media, they developed several media strategies. First, they treated press interviews seriously. During the Umbrella Movement, hundreds of local and foreign reporters stayed in the occupied sites to cover the Movement. It was regarded as a great opportunity for the press to express the activists' views. Scholarism assigned several members to serve as spokespersons. They received media training from their seniors and learned to act professionally. Agnes Chow, one of the spokespersons, is fluent in Cantonese, English, and Japanese. She granted daily interviews to numerous foreign reporters and gained the nickname, the "Goddess of Scholarism". Joshua Wong was also a media attraction. When he led the students to rush into the Civic Square, he was only 17. His young age, outspokenness, and leadership skills made him a movement celebrity. He appeared on the cover of *Time* magazine under the title "The Face of Protest". He is a sophisticated media user and he knows how to handle the press, creating international headlines, such as "Taking back Hong Kong's future" (Wong, 2014b). It is worth noting that Scholarism was eager to gain the attention of not only the local press but also the global media.

Second, Joshua and several members of Scholarism wrote articles for the traditional media, in which they expressed their views. They also joined radio and online programs to gain media exposure. Third, they mastered media logic and skillfully delivered information to journalists. Scholarism set up several WhatsApp groups to keep in touch with different types of reporters. They learned how to attract the attention of the press. Joshua Wong said that in the beginning they did not think of calling the press until they worked with the Hong Kong Federation of Students (HKFS). They learned how to write a press release and arrange a press conference (Wong, 2014a). They even knew when to provide exclusive stories to certain newspapers and when to make appeals to all media.

Fourth, they created pseudo-events to attract the media's attention. They chased after a high-ranking Chinese government official visiting Hong Kong and tried to challenge him with questions about political reform. Together with HKFS, they wrote a letter to the President of China, Xi Jinping. They also went on a hunger strike to raise public awareness of the call for "one man, one vote!" According to interviewee C, during the hunger strike, the strikers met the press and visitors many times a day to get media exposure. These strategies and media events were regarded as useful in drawing public attention to the Movement. They fit the scenario that Chan and Lee (1984) described as the "protest paradigm", which focuses on tactics, spectacles, and dramatic actions.

The findings indicated that the young activists understood that both the social media and traditional media were important in delivering their movement discourse. They had already mastered media logic and were capable of handling the press. Their media practices echoed Lester and Hutchins's (2009) findings on environmental protest. The techno-savvy activists knew how to play power games by engaging the news media and using the "we media" to sustain the Movement's momentum and attract the world's attention.

Communicative mobilization

According to the key members of Scholarism, Facebook was the main channel of mobilization. The findings of the content analysis showed that 20.9% of the themes of the Facebook postings were related to mobilization. For example, during the incident "Class Boycott and Occupy the Civic Square", Scholarism's Facebook page asked for the citizens' support. Regarding participation in civil disobedience, Joshua Wong provided the following suggestions on his Facebook page: (i) do not take weapons to avoid arrest; (ii) do not attack the police; and (iii) do not throw anything because it may stimulate violence by the police.

Scholarism's Facebook page also shared the postings of other Facebook pages to give advice about collective action. For example, regarding the collective action of surrounding the government's headquarters, it re-posted HKFS's posting, which explained obtaining legal support in the case of police arrest (Scholarism Facebook Page, 1 December 2014).

During the collective action surrounding government buildings, the young activists' Facebook pages became the news center that provided breaking news and up-to-date information for participants in the Movement. Scholarism's Facebook team was closely linked to their surveillance team (the pigeons) at the frontline. For instance, during a confrontation between the police and the demonstrators, Scholarism sent members to the frontline to monitor the situation. They then used their mobile networks to report the latest developments, such as the number of policemen, the number of people arrested, and whether tear gas or pepper spray was being used. Hence, they managed to do live reporting.

The content analysis found that 56.2% of the themes of Facebook postings were classified as "factual reporting on the Movement", while 8.5% were on "Scholarism's position statement". In fact, these factual reports and Scholarism's position statements enhanced the citizens' participation by promoting the Movement's values. For example, they shared interviews about civil disobedience, talks about democracy, the progress of the hunger strike, and other activities among the "villagers" of the occupied sites. Smartphones were the most often used device by the activists in the Movement. WhatsApp and Telegram played an extremely important role in the demonstrations and confrontations.

Conclusion and discussion

Hong Kong has a long history of protest. In the past two decades, numerous demonstrations have taken place in this city. Local research showed that the mass media have been the great facilitator of those large-scale demonstrations (Chan & Lee, 2007). Studies on the Anti-Express Rail Link Movement and the Anti-Moral and National Education Movement indicated that apart from the traditional media, social media were heavily employed to promote mobilization in these two movements (Ting, 2014; Wang, 2011). The findings of this study further indicate that media practices played a central role in launching the Umbrella Movement. The trend toward the mediatization of social movements is evident in social protests from the 2003 Anti-Basic Law Article 23 Demonstration[4] to the 2014 Umbrella Movement.

The case of Scholarism showed that these young activists were able to develop a "media and information praxis" to organize and promote the Umbrella Movement. The findings of this study showed that they were sophisticated in aggregating and evaluating information, connecting participants, promoting movement discourse, and enhancing movement participation.

Marx defined praxis as a revolutionary, critical-practical activity (Smith, 2011). The media practices of the young activists certainly had a critical dimension. The findings of our study showed that the activists were critical and skeptical media users. In information aggregation, they emphasized immediacy and reliability. Through the use of social media and new mobile technologies, the activists built a personalized and customized communication network to connect the participants in the Umbrella Movement. Most importantly, they were highly conscious of security issues, and they developed ways to protect their information.

Young activists are prosumers. In the Movement, they did not depend solely on the mass media to air their views and cover their stories, but they developed their own media to disseminate their discourse and explain their stand against the government. They were concerned about produsage and spreadability, yet they did not ignore the power of the traditional media. They learned not only social media logic but also mass media logic to handle the press and shape their media representation. Some key members even developed the skills of spin doctors. With their media arsenal, the young activists were able to call for territory-wide participation.

Scholarism was not the only leader of the Umbrella Movement, but it worked together with other young groups to promote and launch the protest. The present study of its involvement revealed that its members acted as mediatization agents. It seems that not one of the actions of the Movement excluded the consideration of the use of media. *Fortune* magazine even listed Joshua Wong among the top 10 of the world's greatest leaders. The magazine endorsed the power of the techno-savvy students in the Movement. It commented that although this young man had just one cellphone, he was able to influence the movement that paralyzed Hong Kong for three months (Lai, 2015). Moreover, the Umbrella Movement itself became a global media spectacle.

Theoretically, this study found that the media are not necessarily the sole agents of mediatization. No matter how powerful the media, they need people who know how to make good use of them. Young activists equipped with sophisticated MIL skills are indeed important agents of mediatization.

As digital natives, the activists were knowledgeable in using digital media in the daily operations of the Movement, and the smartphone was their main media device. However, the findings also showed they did not depend completely on digital media, but strategically used all media platforms, including social media, mass media, personal mobile networks, street booths, and pamphlet distribution. Nonetheless, social media, particularly Facebook, played an essential role in connecting the participants and mobilizing the collective action in this social movement.

Gladwell (2010) and Morozov (2010) raised a debate about how effectively social media could mobilize a social movement. They had serious doubts about the political power of social media as proposed by Shirky (2011). They argued that social media are only effective in increasing the motivation to participate in a non-risky campaign. However, as the findings showed, in the Umbrella Movement, Facebook, WhatsApp, and Telegram played an essential role in mobilizing the participants to join high-risk confrontations with the police. The young activists even prepared to meet a violent police crackdown that included the use of pepper spray, tear gas, and batons. The social media were effective in rousing the "shared awareness", a concept proposed by Shirky (2011), about political reform among young students in Hong Kong. It was proved by the large number of "likes" and "shares" for the young activists' Facebook fan pages, as well as by the huge turnout at the demonstration sites. The slacktivism argument does not work in this case. On the contrary, the media practices of the young activists fit Castell's (2012) description of a "networked social movement". Armed with media and information literacy, the activists formed their own network to counter the network of the authoritarian bloc, which is the Alliance for Peace and Democracy.

With the advancement of communication technologies, the technological form of life has equipped people with the capabilities of learning by doing and producing (Lash, 2001). Social movements are now launched in a very different mode. During the last two decades in Hong Kong, as shown by the study of Chan & Lee (2007), activists have employed the mass media logic (e.g., invite political stars to make appeals for protest through the press) to mobilize large-scale demonstrations. However, in the Umbrella Movement, the young activists were engaged in a something very different.

"Scholarism is not following the path of traditional social movements," asserted interviewee A, a key member of Scholarism. This is, he claimed, the age of media warfare. It is no longer enough just to take to the streets to demonstrate. Social movement activists need to fight a public relations battle. The case of Scholarism showed that the young activists no longer followed the old way of organizing a movement but adapted to media rules, aims, and production logics to launch their campaign. These youngsters had high media and information literacy and they accumulated their media experience from previous social movements, in which they had mastered the knowledge and skills of media logic. They created pseudo-events, used media gimmicks, and handled the news media tactically. They not only dealt with the "media" but also mastered "information". They sought, evaluated, and produced information. Hence, they engaged in the media and information power game.

The 79-day Umbrella Movement was successful in raising the political consciousness of people in Hong Kong, particularly among the younger citizens. However, it did not yield concrete political results. It was not able to push the government to change its plan for universal suffrage. Nonetheless, it seems that the sophisticated media skills of the young activists has aroused the "shared awareness" of "true democracy" among many Hong Kong citizens, and it has already influenced the democratic development in Hong Kong.

Regarding social movements that took place around the world in 2014, including those in Ferguson and Hong Kong, Christian Davenport, an expert on social movements at the University of Michigan, commented:

> activists proved good at getting people into the street, which is often exciting, and not so good at following up – things like lobbying, reading legislative drafts, monitoring a law after its been passed, sitting through a legal proceeding. (cited in Hampson, 2014, p. 3).

After the Umbrella Movement, the young activists seemed to have recognized this. They are now moving to employ their media and information praxis in the traditional political arena, such as in district board elections, to promote the development of democracy. Further research on the agents of mediatization could pay attention to the ongoing role of young activists in the mediatization of politics in Hong Kong.

Disclosure statement
No potential conflict of interest was reported by the authors.

Notes
1. Moral and National Education refers to the school curriculum previously proposed by the education authority in Hong Kong. The subject was controversial in praising the nationalist ideology of the Chinese Government and was accused of "brain-washing" Hong Kong students. Public demonstrations, joint signatures, and hunger strikes were launched. These collective actions finally forced the Hong Kong SAR Government to leave aside its curriculum guide in October 2012.
2. The Anti-Express Rail Link Movement was launched between mid-2009 and early 2010. Some social groups in Hong Kong protested against the proposed costly construction of the Hong Kong section of the Guangzhou–Shenzhen–Hong Kong Express Rail Link.
3. *Apple Daily* is a popular newspaper with a pro-democracy stance, whereas *Ming Pao Daily News* is a quality newspaper that emphasizes objectivity and neutrality. Both *iCable News* and *Now TV*

News are paid TV channels. *Radio Television Hong Kong (RTHK)* is a government department, but it strives to be a public broadcaster.
4. Article 23 of the Hong Kong Basic Law deals with anti-subversion. In September 2002, the Hong Kong SAR Government released a legislative proposal concerning Article 23. The proposal caused a major controversy, and half a million people took to the streets to protest against it. The proposed bill was eventually shelved.

References

Altheide, D. L., & Snow, R. P. (1979). *Media logic*. Beverly Hills, CA: Sage.
Beam, C. (2014). Rumors are spreading like fire through Hong Kong protest. *Newrepublic.com*. Retrieved from http://www.newrepublic.com/article/119707/hong-kont-protest-rumors-how-separate-truth-falsehood
Bennett, W. L., & Segerberg, A. (2012). The logic of connective action. *Information, Communication & Society, 15*(5), 739–768.
Cammaerts, B. (2012). Protest logics and the mediation opportunity structure. *European Journal of Communication, 27*(2), 117–134.
Carr, W., & Kemmis, S. (1986). *Becoming critical: Education, knowledge and action research*. London: The Falmer Press.
Castells, M. (2012). *Networks of outrage and hope: Social movements in the Internet age*. Cambridge: Polity.
Chan, D. K., & Fu, K. W. (2014, December 14). Blocks of Facebook special pages in the occupied era. *Ming Pao Daily News*, p. S07.
Chan, J. M., & Lee, C. C. (1984). The journalistic paradigm on civil protests: A case study of Hong Kong. In A. Arno & W. Dissanayake (Eds.), *The news media in national and international conflict* (pp. 183–202). Boulder, CO: Westview.
Chan, J. M., & Lee, F. L. F. (2007). Media and large-scale demonstrations: The pro-democracy movement in post-handover Hong Kong. *Asian Journal of Communication, 17*(2), 215–228.
Chan, J. M., & Lee, F. L. F. (2014, November 10). Preliminary exploration of the new structure of the Occupy Central Movement. *Ming Pao Daily News*, p. A29.
Costanza-Chock, S. (2012). *Youth and social movements: Key lessons for allies*. Cambridge, MA: Born This Way Foundation & Berkman Center for Internet & Society.
Deacon, D., & Stanyer, J. (2014). Mediatization: Key concept or conceptual bandwagon. *Media, Culture & Society, 36*(7), 1032–1044.
Fominaya, C. F. (2012). *Youth participation in contemporary European social movements*. Brussels: European Centre for International Affairs.
Friedman, T. L. (2014, May 13). The square people, part 1. Retrieved from http://www.nytimes.com/2014/05/14/opinion/friedman-the-square-people-part-1.html?_r=0
Gladwell, M. (2010). Small change. *Newyorker.com*. Retrieved from http://www.newyorker.com/magazine/2010/10/04/small-change-malcolm-gladwell
Hampson, R. (2014). 2014 protests: From Ferguson to Hong Kong, impact unclear. *Usatoday.com*. Retrieved from http://www.usatoday.com/story/news/nation/2014/12/25/ferguson-staten-island-protest-2014/20435471/

Klinger, U., & Svensson, J. (2014). The emergence of network media logic in political communication: A theoretical approach. *New Media & Society*. Retrieved from http://nms.sagepub.com/content/early/2014/02/18/1461444814522952.full.pdf+html

Lai, Y. K. (2015). Who's the real leader? Joshua Wong in Fortune top 10 as CY Leung gets thumbs down. *Scmp.com*. Retrieved from http://www.scmp.com/news/hong-kong/article/1748566/whos-real-leader-joshua-wong-fortune-top-10-cy-leung-gets-thumbs-down

Lash, S. (2001). Technological forms of life. *Theory, Culture & Society, 18*(1), 105–120.

Lee, A. Y. L. (2013). *Media and information literacy in a networked era*. Paper presented at the 18th International Education Technology Conference "Social Media 2013," 1–3 August, 2013, Hong Kong.

Lester, L., & Hutchins, B. (2009). Power games: Environmental protest, news media and the Internet. *Media, Culture & Society, 31*(4), 579–595.

Lovink, G. (2005). Tactical media, the second decade. *Tacticalmediafiles.net*. Retrieved from http://www.tacticalmediafiles.net/articles/3410/Tactical-Media_-the-Second-Decade;jsessionid=02E-CA580BC711D79A05D03D372A5B15E

Mattoni, A., & Trere, E. (2014). Media practices, mediation processes, and mediatization in the study of social movement. *Communication Theory, 24*, 252–271.

Mazzoleni, G., & Schulz, W. (1999). Mediatization of politics: A challenge for democracy? *Political Communication, 16*(3), 247–261.

Morozov, E. (2010). Think again: The Internet. *ForeignPolicy.com*. Retrieved from http://foreignpolicy.com/2010/04/26/think-again-the-internet/

Public Opinion Programme. (2010). Youth survey on usage of Internet and social network websites. *HKU PoP Site*, Retrieved from http://hkupop.hku.hk/english/report/microsoft10/index.html

Scholarism. (2014, April 16). About us. Retrieved from http://scholarism.com/?page_id=13

Schulz, W. (2004). Reconstructing mediatization as an analytical concept. *European Journal of Communication, 19*(1), 87–101.

Shirky, C. (2011). The political power of social media: Technology, the public sphere, and political change. *Foreign Affairs, 90*(1), 28–41.

Smith, M. K. (2011). *What is praxis? Infed.org. Encyclopaedia of informal education*. Retrieved from http://www.infed.org/biblio/b-praxis.htm

So, C. Y. K. (2011). Revelations of media "24-hour famine". *Expanding Thinking, 64*, 18–20.

Tapscott, D. (2009). *Grown up digital: How the net generation is changing your world*. New York, NY: McGraw-Hill.

Telegram (2014). Telegram FAQ. *Telegram*. Retrieved from https://telegram.org/faq

Ting, K. W. (2014). *Media and social engagement of the Hong Kong bomb generation: A case study of the Scholarism*. (Unpublished undergraduate thesis). Hong Kong Baptist University, Hong Kong.

UNESCO (2013). *Global media and information literacy assessment framework: Country readiness and competencies*. Paris: UNESCO.

Van de Donk, W., Loader, B. D., Nihon, P. G., & Ruht, D. (Eds.). (2004). *Cyberprotest: New media, citizens and social movements*. London: Routledge.

Van Dijck, J., & Poell, T. (2013). Understanding social media logic. *Media and Communication, 1*(1), 2–14.

Wang, J. (2011). *An identity formation through collective action in a new social movement in Hong Kong: A case study of the post-80s anti-express rail link youth*. (Unpublished master's thesis). Hong Kong Baptist University, Hong Kong.

Westlund, O., & Bjur, J. (2014). Media life of the young. *Young, 22*(1), 21–41.

Wong, J. C. F. (2014a). *I am not a hero*. Hong Kong: Crystal Window Books.

Wong, J. C. F. (2014b, October 29). Taking back Hong Kong's future. *Nytimes.com*. Retrieved from http://www.nytimes.com/2014/10/30/opinion/joshua-wong-taking-back-hong-kongs-future.html?_r=0

Yim, C. H. (2014). The passionate dreamer. In J. C. F. Wong (Ed.), *I am not a hero* (pp. 12–15). Hong Kong: Crystal Window Books.

Social movement as civic education: communication activities and understanding of civil disobedience in the Umbrella Movement

Francis L. F. Lee

The Chinese University of Hong Kong, Hong Kong

> Occupy Central, which would later evolve into the Umbrella Movement, was conceived as a civil disobedience campaign when it was first proposed in early 2013. Although the history of civil disobedience in Hong Kong arguably spans decades, the concept was seldom discussed in the public arena, and the practice was not well established in the society's repertoire of contentious actions. The years 2013 and 2014 thus constituted a "critical discourse moment" in which the concept of civil disobedience was intensively discussed and debated. This study seeks to determine whether the Occupy Central campaign and the Umbrella Movement had an educational function that led to increased levels of the public's understanding of civil disobedience. The analysis of the responses to two surveys conducted in September 2013 and October 2014 showed that the public's understanding of civil disobedience increased substantially over the year. After the Umbrella Movement started, attitudinal support for and actual participation in the movement, the political use of social media, and discussions with disagreeing others significantly predicted the understanding of civil disobedience. The theoretical and social implications of the findings are discussed.

Introduction

On 16 January 2013, Benny Tai, a law professor at Hong Kong University, published "The most lethal weapon of civil disobedience" in the *Hong Kong Economic Journal*, which criticized the government's lack of commitment to genuine democratic reform. He expressed doubts about the efficacy of the tactics of previous movements in forcing the government to respond. He thus put forward the idea of "Occupy Central," which was to occupy roads in Central, the financial district to "paralyze the political-economic center" of the city (Tai, 2013). The idea aroused serious interest among pro-democracy politicians, activists, and intellectuals. Within three months, Tai was joined by sociologist Chan Kin Man and Reverend Chu Yiu-ming. Together they initiated the "Occupy Central with Love and Peace" campaign. Eighteen months later and after two days of student protests in front of the government's headquarters, Tai announced the beginning of Occupy Central in the early morning of 28 September 2014. The protest then quickly evolved into the Umbrella Movement.[1]

Civil disobedience is not completely new to the city. Commentators have traced the history of civil disobedience in Hong Kong back to 1966, when a citizen went on a hunger strike against rising ferry prices, which consequently led to large-scale riots. Nevertheless, civil disobedience was rare. It was by no means a well-established item in the city's repertoire of contentious actions (Tilly, 1995, 2008). When Tai published his piece in early 2013, the public arguably had limited understanding of the concept of civil disobedience.

Given the historical background, the Occupy Central campaign and the Umbrella Movement[2] thus created a "critical discourse moment" (Gamson & Herzog, 1999; Gamson & Modigliani, 1989) in which the concept of civil disobedience was publicly explicated and intensively debated. Consequently, one probable effect of Occupy Central and the Umbrella Movement is "educational." Through intensive public discourse, the Hong Kong public may have gained a better understanding of the concept of civil disobedience.

This study examines the effect of the movement on civic education in Hong Kong. It asks the following: To what extent did Hong Kong people understand the idea of civil disobedience before and after the collective action of the Umbrella Movement began? What factors explain the knowledge about the concept of civil disobedience? What are the roles of media and communication activities in generating people's understanding of the concept?

This study contributes to social movement studies by examining one hitherto seldom explored phenomenon: social movements as civic education. While studies have focused on the educational effect of social movements on activists (e.g., Ollis, 2011), little research had studied how movements can educate the public at large. The present study enhances the literature on communication and public opinion and our understanding of how citizens acquire and develop political knowledge within a communication environment composed of mass media, digital media, and interpersonal communication. The analysis also furthers recent efforts to develop "oppositional knowledge" as a distinctive type of political knowledge (Lee, 2015). Locally, this article takes seriously the fact that the Umbrella Movement emerged after an extended period of intensive sense-making activities. Hence, it should contribute to the development of a contextualized understanding of the movement. Furthermore, the analysis also informs us about the likelihood of the establishment of civil disobedience in the repertoire of contentious actions in Hong Kong.

The next section provides the conceptual underpinnings for the study. Background about the Umbrella Movement will then be given, and the specific research questions and hypotheses will be stated, followed by the analysis of data collected from two representative surveys.

Repertoire of contentious actions and oppositional political knowledge

Collective contentious actions can take various forms, but people in different societies and at different times may tend to undertake certain forms of action rather than others (e.g., Ekiert & Kubik, 1998; Wada, 2012). Tilly (1995, 2008) used the metaphor of "repertoire" to refer to the range of actions that people in a society at a specific point in time may adopt in making contentious claims. Repertoires of contentious actions evolve over time because protest actions are "learned cultural creations" (Tilly, 1995, p. 42), that is, forms of protest action can be invented, learned from others, or sometimes stumbled upon by the protesters.

Scholars have spent much effort in examining the factors leading to the adoption of new tactics. Some researchers, including Tilly (1995), emphasized the importance of the structure of the political opportunity and the type of regime in shaping the forms of contentious action (e.g., Allam, 2014; De Fazio, 2012). Others focused on the mechanisms of diffusion (e.g., Biggs, 2013) and learning through collaboration (e.g., Wang & Soule, 2012). The advancement of digital media technologies has also facilitated the emergence of new "e-tactics" that have enriched the repertoires of social movements (Earl & Kimport, 2011; Strange, 2011).

Nevertheless, regardless of origin, movements need to engage in discursive work to promote the new tactic and establish its feasibility, legitimacy, and effectiveness (Biggs, 2013). Hayes (2005), for example, discussed the expansion of the repertoires of French environmental protests, especially the rise of civil disobedience in the early 2000s. He argued that the transnational diffusion of protest tactics needs to be understood as well as the national reception and justification of such actions. Local narratives are important for promoting the internalization and legitimization of innovative behavior. In the case of the environmental protests in France, civil disobedience was positioned as Republican. Activists drew upon the national myths of resistance to mobilize people to support civil disobedience campaigns. Hayes (2005) thus concluded that "the adaptation of innovative behavior takes place within a legitimizing and naturalizing set of cultural, social and political discourses" (p. 836).

It is beyond the scope of this article to examine how civil disobedience was discursively articulated and legitimized during the Occupy Central campaign in Hong Kong. Instead, premised on the fact that the activists who organized the campaign had indeed engaged in intensive discursive work surrounding the idea of civil disobedience, this study focuses on whether and how the public acquired understanding of the concept. Another key concept relevant to this present study is "oppositional political knowledge."

Political scientists who are interested in citizens' political knowledge have typically adopted measures focusing on citizens' grasp of basic facts about established political institutions (e.g., Boudreau & Lupia, 2011; Delli Carpini & Keeter, 1996; Fraile, 2013; Ostman, 2012). However, scholars have also noted that the political knowledge of citizens can be domain specific (Iyengar, 1990; Kim, 2009), that is, people may be knowledgeable about certain areas of public affairs but not others. In addition, different types of political knowledge can have different antecedents and consequences (Johann, 2012; Kaufhold, Valenzuela, & Gil de Zuniga, 2010). It follows that political knowledge that focuses on established institutions may not be the best predictor of people's attitudes toward and participation in social movements. Lee (2015) thus developed the notion of oppositional political knowledge, which is defined as knowledge about facts and concepts that are instrumental in the formation of critical attitudes toward dominant power and generate support for or actual participation in oppositional actions. This type of political knowledge is particularly pertinent to movement-related attitudes and behavior.

The concept of oppositional knowledge is based on the idea that people often fail to challenge the existing political system or policies because they are uninformed or misinformed (Lewis, 2001). It also encompasses the idea that certain types of knowledge, such as knowledge about social injustices, oppositional groups, movement tactics, and so on, can be instrumental in the formation of what movement scholars have called "oppositional consciousness" (Mansbridge, 2001) and "generalized action potential" (Jenkins & Wallace, 1996).

It is therefore important to understand the factors contributing to the formation of oppositional knowledge. Lee (2015) further differentiated three types of oppositional knowledge: (1) factual information about oppositional groups and figures; (2) negative considerations about the dominant power; and (3) understanding of concepts that are central to oppositional discourses and/or contentious actions. The understanding of civil disobedience was used in this earlier study to represent the third type of oppositional knowledge. The empirical analysis found that education, age, external efficacy, interpersonal discussion, support for democratization, and the use of online alternative media were among the most important predictors of oppositional knowledge. Moreover, oppositional knowledge mediated the influence of support for democratization, external efficacy, and the use of online alternative media on protest participation and attitudinal support for the planned Occupy Central campaign.

This article extends Lee's (2015) study but provides a sharper focus on the understanding of civil disobedience in particular. While Lee (2015) reported an analysis based on a survey conducted in September 2013 (i.e., six months after the beginning of the Occupy Central campaign and one year before the beginning of the Umbrella Movement), this study draws upon both the September 2013 survey and a survey conducted in October 2014, two weeks after the beginning of the Umbrella Movement. This extended period allows the examination of whether the public understanding of civil disobedience had risen over the year and discern the factors that predicted the public understanding of civil disobedience when the movement materialized.

Research questions and hypotheses

As noted, civil disobedience has not been a prominent form of protest in Hong Kong although its history can be traced to the 1960s. The term did not appear in the index pages in Lui and Chiu's (2000) comprehensive volume on social movements in the city. In addition, when it arose, civil disobedience was arguably not well received by public opinion. Ku (2004, 2007) analyzed the public discourse surrounding a civil disobedience campaign in 2000. The protest challenged the Public Order Ordinance, which stipulated that protests had to gain a "notice of no objection" from the police. At the time, activists organized several unauthorized protests. According to Ku (2007), the media discourses were supportive of the movement at the beginning but "quickly yielded to the rationality of institutional order" (pp. 193–194). She concluded that a hegemonic framework of "order versus chaos" underlies public discourses in the city. The prevalence of the "order imagery" also explains media representations of other "violent" or "radical" protests (e.g., Lee, 2008; Leung, 2009). However, especially since the historic protest of 1 July 2003, "being peaceful and rational" was generally hailed as the ideal character of protest actions in Hong Kong (Lee & Chan, 2011).

The emphasis on "peace and rationality" in the city's public culture explains why Benny Tai titled the campaign "Occupy Central for Love and Peace." Beginning with his first article on January 16, Tai repeatedly emphasized that the movement had to be non-violent. However, Tai's ideas still aroused criticism by both conservative forces and "radical" activists. The former regarded the public call for illegal acts dangerous and threatening; the latter regarded the insistence on non-violence self-limiting.

An intensive social debate about the definition, nature, merits, and demerits of civil disobedience thus ensued. A search on Wise News showed that in 2000, 125 articles in the news sections of eight Hong Kong newspapers[3] mentioned "civil disobedience" (i.e., the year of the Public Order Ordinance controversy). From 2001 to 2012, the number dropped to between 17 and 90. However, it jumped to 774 in 2013 and to 1507 in 2014 (823 by September 28).

Civil disobedience is undoubtedly a complicated concept. Rawls (1973) defined it as "a public, nonviolent, conscientious yet political act contrary to law usually done with the aim of bringing about a change in the law or policies of the government" (p. 364). However, among other issues, philosophers and social theorists have debated the necessity of non-violence, the justifiability of "coercive" civil disobedience, in addition to how unjust a law has to be to render civil disobedience justifiable (Cohen & Arato, 1992; Chaim, 1992; Quill, 1992). We certainly cannot expect all citizens to become well versed with Thoreau, Gandhi, Martin Luther King, John Rawls, and Ronald Dworkin. However, the intensive debate should help citizens to obtain basic ideas about what civil disobedience (CD) refers to and how it differs from sheer law breaking. Hence, the first research question and hypothesis are stated as follows:

RQ1: What are Hong Kong people's levels of understanding of CD?
H1: Citizens' understanding of CD increased between the time of the Occupy Central campaign and after the beginning of the Umbrella Movement.

The analysis will then examine the predictors of public understanding of civil disobedience after the Umbrella Movement began. The extant literature pinpointed motivation, ability, and opportunity as the main factors behind political learning (Delli Carpini & Keeter, 1996; Luskin, 1990). Hence, it should not be surprising that education (an indicator of ability and possibly opportunity) and general political interest (an indicator of motivation) can explain the understanding of civil disobedience. The following analysis is not aimed at testing a general model of political knowledge, however. Instead, it focuses on oppositional conceptual knowledge with the expectation that support for and participation in the Umbrella Movement can explain the understanding of civil disobedience. This is expected partly because those who understood the concept were more likely to support and participate in the Umbrella Movement and partly because attitudinal support can provide the motivation to learn, while actual participation can provide the opportunities to learn.[4] Two hypotheses are therefore asserted:

H2: Support for the movement relates positively to the understanding of CD.
H3: Participation in the movement relates positively to the understanding of CD.

Media use and interpersonal discussion have long been established as predictors of knowledge (Delli Carpini & Keeter, 1996; Norris, 2000). Generally, in the "motivation, ability, and opportunity" model, news consumption and other political communication activities primarily constitute opportunities to learn about politics. At the same time, people's interest in and thus motivation to learn about politics can also be enhanced through communication (Eveland, 2004). In addition, to the extent that prior political knowledge is crucial for the uptake of new information (Price & Zaller, 1993), media use and interpersonal discussions can also enhance people's ability to learn.

However, different communication activities may have varying effects on political learning, especially when oppositional knowledge is concerned. Lee (2015) found that mainstream news consumption did *not* contribute to oppositional knowledge. He argued that the mainstream media exhibited a structural bias toward the establishment and might not contain much oppositional knowledge. Instead, contemporary movements often employ new media platforms for communication (Bennett & Sederberg, 2013; Chan & Lee, 2015). Moreover, the more interactive nature of online political communications may be conducive to the uptake of *conceptual knowledge* (in contrast to the uptake of simple factual information). Hence, this study expects that the political use of social media will have a stronger influence on the understanding of civil disobedience compared to that of mainstream news consumption. To avoid hypothesizing a "non-relationship" (i.e., between mainstream media use and knowledge), H4 and H5 are asserted as follows:

H4: The political use of social media relates positively to the understanding of CD.
H5: The political use of social media relates to the understanding of CD more positively than mainstream news consumption does.

This study expects that discussion alone does not necessarily generate the understanding of civil disobedience. Instead, by debating with disagreeing others, citizens may come to understand civil disobedience better. This is because debate can force people to clarify and elaborate their thoughts and ideas, which can help to develop and articulate the understanding of abstract concepts. This argument is consistent with recent research on the importance of exposure to disagreement in generating political knowledge (Lee, 2009; Mutz, 2006). Hence, H6 is stated as follows:

H6: Discussion with disagreeing others relates positively to the understanding of CD.

Finally, this study explores the possibility that the factors explaining the understanding of civil disobedience may vary across individuals. It is plausible that communication activities enhance the understanding of civil disobedience mainly among those who are positively predisposed to the idea of protest. Theoretically, people are psychologically motivated to protect their existing political worldviews. Hence, they can exhibit selective exposure, selective attention, and motivated information processing, which in turn affects political learning (e.g., Meirick, 2013; Tworzecki & Markowski, 2014; Wicks, Wicks, & Morimoto, 2014). Supporters of movements, compared to their opponents, should be more likely to be exposed to discussions of civil disobedience, to pay closer attention to such discussions, and to process the discussions more seriously. Consequently, the relationship between communication activities and the understanding of civil disobedience is likely to be stronger among movement supporters than among their opponents. For the sake of simplicity, the last hypothesis is stated as the following summary:

H7: Various communication variables have a stronger positive relationship with the understanding of CD among movement supporters.

Data and method
Sampling and sample characteristics
The data analyzed were derived from two telephone surveys conducted by the Center for Communication and Public Opinion Survey at the Chinese University of

Hong Kong in early September 2013 and October 8 to 15, 2014, respectively. In the former survey, the respondents are Cantonese-speaking Hong Kong residents aged between 18 and 70. In the latter survey, the target respondents are aged 15 or above. The sampling procedures used were the same in both surveys. All telephone numbers from the 2005, 2007, and 2009 directories were compiled. The last two digits of the numbers were replaced by the full set of 100 double-digit figures from 00 to 99. Specific numbers were randomly selected by computers during the fieldwork. The most-recent-birthday method was adopted to select a respondent from a household.

The sample sizes were 782 and 802 and the response rates were 40% and 37% (following AAPOR RR3) for the 2013 and 2014 surveys, respectively. Demographically, the 2013 survey oversampled women and people with high family income levels, whereas the 2014 survey oversampled people with high levels of education and income. Both surveys were weighted so that the samples matched the Hong Kong population in age, sex, and education.[5]

Operationalization of key variables

Understanding of civil disobedience. In both surveys, the respondents were asked if they had heard of the term "civil disobedience." If they answered yes, they were asked if they understood the term. The answers included "not at all," "a little," "quite well," and "very well." Those who said they understood at least "a little" were then asked to name a maximum of two differences between "civil disobedience" and "typical law-breaking behavior." The respondents' answers were rated on an index ranging from 0 to 2. Those who had not heard of the term, did not understand the term, or could not name any valid differences between civil disobedience and typical law-breaking behavior scored 0. Others scored 1 or 2 based on whether they named one or two valid differences between civil disobedience and typical law-breaking behavior. Obviously, what constitutes a valid difference is a matter of judgment. The analysis created two indices based on the "activists' definition" and a "broad definition" of civil disobedience. The details of the coding and the descriptive statistics of the indices, as well as how the indices were interpreted, are discussed in the next section.

Support for and participation in the Umbrella Movement. The 2014 survey asked: "An occupy movement has occurred in Hong Kong recently. Do you personally support this movement?" The term "occupy movement" was used because it was a commonly used label in everyday discourse at the time. The answers were registered on a five-point Likert scale ranging from $1 =$ very unsupportive to $5 =$ very supportive ($M = 3.06$, $SD = 1.47$). Those who were very supportive, supportive, or "so-so" toward the movement were then asked if they had gone to the occupied areas to support the movement. The answers include "$1 =$ no," "$2 =$ have gone there one day," "$3 =$ have gone there two to three days," and "$4 =$ have gone there more than three days." The opponents to the movement were presumed not to have gone to the occupied areas to support the movement. They scored 1. 8.5%, 8.4%, and 5.7% of all respondents that had gone to the occupied areas one day, two to three days, and more than three days, respectively ($M = 1.42$, $SD = 0.87$).

Mainstream news consumption. The respondents were asked to report on a six-point scale (1 = none; 6 = more than an hour) how much time they had spent daily (1) reading newspapers and (2) watching TV news in the previous three weeks. The answers were averaged on an index of news exposure ($M = 4.12, SD = 1.37, r = .29$). The respondents were also asked which newspaper they read the most frequently. During at least the early stages of the movement, *Apple Daily* and *Ming Pao* stood out as relatively (or even strongly) supportive of the movement. A dummy variable of reading of pro-movement papers was created and readers of *Apple* and *Ming Pao* were coded as 1 (43.4%).

Social media use. The respondents were asked to indicate on a scale (from 1 = not using at all to 5 = more than 180 minutes per day) how much time they had spent daily on "Facebook, Twitter, or other social networking sites" in the previous three weeks ($M = 2.04, SD = 1.20$). The sheer amount of time spent on social media may not affect political attitudes, however, because people may use social media for various purposes (Baumgartner & Morris, 2010; Gil de Zuniga, Jung, & Valenzuela, 2012). Social media users were asked how frequently they (1) obtained political and public affairs information, (2) expressed views on politics and public affairs, (3) joined groups about public affairs, and (4) paid attention to the actions of parties, movements, and news commentators via social media. They were also asked (5) how many of their social media "friends" were political party members, movement activists, or news commentators. The answers were given on a five-point scale (1 = not at all to 5 = very frequently/very large number) and averaged on an index of political use of social media, with non-users of social media having the score of 1 ($\alpha = 0.70, M = 1.75, SD = 0.84$).

Disagreeable discussion. The respondents were asked to indicate (1 = not at all to 5 = very frequently) if they had discussed the movement with their family or friends. They were also asked if they had disputes with "family or relatives" and "friends" about the movement. Based on the responses to the two latter questions, each respondent had a score of 0, 1, or 2, representing the amount of disputes they had. The index of disagreeable discussion was the product of frequency of discussion and amount of dispute ($M = 1.18, SD = 2.24$).

Control variables. The control variables used in the multivariate analysis included four demographics (sex, age, income, and education), interest in politics, internal efficacy, collective efficacy, external efficacy (each represented by the average of agreement with two statements), and past participation in protests (measured by a number of items about participation in specific protests).

Analysis and findings

Levels of understanding of civil disobedience

As explained, the understanding of civil disobedience was measured by whether the respondents could differentiate between civil disobedience and typical law-breaking behavior. In his published writings, Occupy Central initiator Benny Tai pinpointed three core characteristics of civil disobedience: (1) it aims at achieving social justice instead of personal gain; (2) it takes peaceful and nonviolent forms; and (3) the participants are willing to bear the legal consequences. Many respondents indeed named one or two of these three points. An index labeled "activists' understanding" of civil disobedience was created. The respondents' scores represent whether they named 0, 1, or 2 of the three points highlighted by Tai.

However, as pointed out in the theoretical section, political philosophers and theorists have debated the proper definition of civil disobedience. Tai's characterization of civil disobedience is not the only possible one and not necessarily the best one. For instance, some scholars may argue against the necessity of nonviolence, whereas others may add other requirements for an act of civil disobedience to be justifiable (e.g., some theorists may require that the law to be broken by an act of civil disobedience is the unjust law itself) (Chaim, 1992; McCausland, O'Sullivan, & Brenton, 2013; Quill, 1992).

Therefore, to be precise, the respondents' scores on the "activist understanding" index should be understood as the extent to which the respondents had taken up or shared the discourses of the proponents of Occupy Central. Not naming the points highlighted by Tai does not entail a complete lack of understanding of civil disobedience. Indeed, many respondents provided a range of other valid answers, such as "civil disobedience is a form of collective action," "civil disobedience aims at winning the support of the majority of the public," "civil disobedience is conscientious action," and so on. Inevitably, there was a grey area: the validity of some answers could be debatable. An example is "civil disobedience is consistent with the moral value of the majority in a society." On the one hand, the goal espoused by a civil disobedience campaign may not be that which the majority is already supporting (especially when the campaign is fighting for minority rights). On the other hand, civil disobedience (and social movements in general) typically appeals to the fundamental cultural values of a society in order to gain support (Alexander, 2005). Hence, there is also a sense in which civil disobedience is – or has to be – consistent with certain moral values of the majority in the society.[6]

A second index not based on the Occupy Central proponents' definition is needed to ascertain the degree to which the public understanding of civil disobedience had indeed increased (as opposed to merely appearing in the discourses of the proponents). However, it would be inappropriate for the author of this study to impose a highly specific definition of civil disobedience. Therefore, the second index was termed a "broad understanding" of civil disobedience: a respondent scored 1 or 2 if s/he could name 1 or 2 differences that were at least arguably correct (i.e., answers falling into the "grey area" were also counted as correct).

Table 1 summarizes the respondents' levels of understanding of civil disobedience as found in the two surveys. The results helped answer RQ1 and tackle H1. In September 2013, Hong Kong citizens could name on average 0.21 of the three differences between civil disobedience and law breaking pinpointed by Benny Tai, and they could name on average 0.39 differences that were at least arguably correct. Notably, citizens' understanding of civil disobedience significantly improved in 2014. In focusing only on respondents aged between 18 and 69 (in order to make the findings most comparable since the 2013 survey included respondents only between 18 and 70), the mean scores of the two indices were 0.39 and 0.51 respectively. The increases were statistically significant in both cases. Therefore, H1 is supported.

Table 1. Public understanding of civil disobedience.

	Activists' understanding	Broad understanding
Total		
2013	.21	.39
2014 (only 18–69)	.39	.51
t-value	5.94***	2.91**
2014 (full sample)	.39	.52
By Age		
Young		
2013	.26	.49
2014	.48	.72
t-value	3.28**	2.54*
Middle-age		
2013	.22	.37
2014	.36	.45
t-value	3.07**	1.46
Senior		
2013	.20	.41
2014	.37	.48
t-value	3.92***	1.24
By Education		
Low		
2013	.12	.22
2014	.24	.28
t-value	2.43*	1.03
Medium		
2013	.17	.32
2014	.33	.46
t-value	3.73***	2.43*
High		
2013	.34	.62
2014	.52	.69
t-value	3.64***	1.16

Notes. Entries are mean scores on a 0–2 index. When comparing the 2013 and 2014 surveys, only respondents aged between 18 and 69 in the 2013 survey was included so as to make the two samples as comparable as possible. Young: 18–30 for 2013 and 18–29 for 2014; Middle-aged: 31–50 for 2013 and 30–49 for 2014; Senior 51–70 for 2013 and 50–69 for 2014. *** $p < .001$; ** $p < .01$; * $p < .05$.

The bottom part of Table 1 provides information about the levels of understanding of civil disobedience in different age and educational groups. The levels of the activists' understanding increased significantly between 2013 and 2014 in all groups. The levels of broad understanding also increased nominally in all groups. However, the increase was statistically significant only in the youngest age group and for people with medium levels of education.

Interestingly, the increase in understanding between 2013 and 2014 was the most conspicuous among young people. A different approach to analyzing the data would show that the levels of understanding of civil disobedience in the three age groups did not differ significantly in 2013 regardless of the activists' understanding or broad understanding ($F = 0.23$ and 1.23, respectively in one-way ANOVA, $p > .20$ in both cases). However, in October 2014, significant differences were found among the three age groups ($F = 4.11$ and 10.91 for activists' understanding and broad understanding respectively, $p < .02$ in both cases). The youngest group exhibited the highest level of understanding of civil disobedience.

The relatively larger increase in understanding among the young was probably related to the fact that young people constituted the group that was the most supportive toward and the most likely to have participated in the Umbrella Movement. As hypothesized, attitudinal support for and participation in the movement are likely to generate higher levels of understanding of civil disobedience. The predictors of understanding of civil disobedience are analyzed below.

Predictors of understanding of civil disobedience

The analysis of the predictors of the understanding of civil disobedience focused only on the 2014 survey partly because the sets of relevant predictors existing in the 2013 and 2014 surveys were not exactly the same and partly because the predictors of the understanding of civil disobedience in the 2013 survey were already reported in Lee (2015). A hierarchical multiple regression analysis was conducted to examine H2 to H6, which posited support for the Umbrella Movement and participation in the movement. A series of media and communication variables were used as predictors of understanding of civil disobedience. The independent variables were included as four blocks in the model: (1) four demographics; (2) the basic political attitudes and past protest participation; (3) support for and participation in the Umbrella movement; and (4) the set of media and communication variables. The four blocks of variables were based on their plausible theoretical relationships (e.g., basic political attitudes and past protest participation can be considered primary "causes" of support for the current movement and communication activities). Nevertheless, for the purpose of the present discussion, it sufficed to focus on the results in the full model.[7]

Table 2 summarizes the findings. The regression model predicted about 22% to 25% of the variance in the two dependent variables. Interestingly, different from previous findings in studies on political knowledge, education and political interest did not relate consistently significantly with the two dependent variables. Instead, people who had lower levels of external efficacy, i.e., those who saw the political system as irresponsive to public opinion, were more likely to exhibit some understandings of civil disobedience. Supporting H2 and H3, both attitudinal support and actual participation in the movement significantly predicted the understanding of civil disobedience.

The findings also supported H4 to H6. The political use of social media was strongly positively related to both dependent variables, illustrating that social media have become a channel for citizens to acquire oppositional political knowledge. Notably, the time spent on social media was related significantly and negatively to the understanding of civil disobedience. In line with previous research on the political effect of social media, sheer usage frequency did not necessarily generate knowledge because people use social media for a wide range of purposes. It is the political use of social media that facilitated political learning.

Consistent with H5, unlike the political use of social media, neither news exposure nor reading of pro-movement newspapers was significantly related to the dependent

Table 2. Predictors of understanding of civil disobedience.

	Activists' understanding	Broad understanding
Demographics		
Sex	−.04	−.03
Age	.07	.05
Education	.06	.10*
Family income	.03	.01
ΔR^2	.055***	.076***
Basic political attitude & protest participation		
Political interest	.08*	.07
Internal efficacy	.09*	.11**
Collective efficacy	.05	.06
External efficacy	−.12**	−.13**
Past protest participation	.08*	.04
ΔR^2	.142***	.136***
Movement support & participation		
Movement support	.13**	.13**
Movement participation	.11**	.09*
ΔR^2	.027***	.024***
Media & communication		
News exposure	.02	.03
Reading pro-movement papers	−.04	−.03
Time spent on social media	−.12**	−.10*
Political use of social media	.16**	.20***
Disagreeable discussion	.09**	.09**
ΔR^2	.019**	.025***
Adjusted R^2	.227***	.246***

Notes. Entries are standardized regression coefficients in the final model. Missing values were replaced by means. $N = 802$. *** $p < .001$; ** $p < .01$; * $p < .05$.

variables. The additional statistically analysis showed that the coefficients of the political use of social media significantly differed from the coefficients of news exposure ($t = 2.80$ and 3.44 in the cases of activists' understanding and broad understanding, respectively, $p < .01$ in both cases) and those of reading pro-movement newspapers ($t = 7.83$ and 9.05 in the cases of activists' understanding and broad understanding respectively, $p < .001$ in both cases). Finally, consistent with H6, disagreeable discussion had a significant effect on both activists' understanding and a broad understanding of civil disobedience.

Finally, H7 predicted that the influence of communication activities, most notably the political use of social media and disagreeable discussion, is more pronounced among movement supporters. The split-sample method (instead of creating interaction terms) was employed to tackle this hypothesis because the supporters and opponents can be considered two distinct groups of people. The split-sample approach was used to determine whether the power of other predictors also varied between the two groups. The same hierarchical regression model was conducted separately for the supporters and non-supporters. The non-supporters included opponents, those who replied "so-so," or those who did not give a valid answer to the question.

Table 3. Predictors of understanding of civil disobedience for supporters and non-supporters.

	Activists' understanding		Broad understanding	
	Non-supporters	Supporters	Non-supporters	Supporters
Sex	−.04	−.05	−.03	−.05
Age	.04	.11	.02	.08
Education	.14*	−.03	.15**	.04
Family income	.05	−.02	.04	−.05
Political interest	.05	.12	.07	.09
Internal efficacy	.09	.10	.06	.15*
Collective efficacy	.01	.06	.04	.04
External efficacy	−.12*	−.06	−.11*	−.09
Past protest participation	.13**	.02	.14**$_a$	−.06$_a$
Movement support	.06	−.07	.05	.00
Movement participation	.14**	.13	.11*	.09
News exposure	.04	−.00	.04	.01
Reading pro-movement papers	−.05	−.02	−.09	.04
Time spent on social media	−.06	−.15	−.06	−.16
Political use of social media	.11	.24*	.13*	.29**
Disagreeable discussion	.05	.11	.04	.14*
Adjusted R^2	.165***	.110***	.168***	.139***

Notes. Entries are standardized regression coefficients in the final model. Missing values were replaced by means. $N = 499$ and 303 for "non-supporters" and "supporters" respectively. Pairs of coefficients sharing the same subscript differ from each other significantly at $p < .05$. *** $p < .001$; ** $p < .01$; * $p < .05$.

Table 3 summarizes the results (for the sake of simplicity, the increases in R^2 by block are not shown because they are not the concern here). The predictors of the understanding of civil disobedience did not vary between the two groups. The only independent variable that obtained a pair of significantly different regression coefficients was past protest participation. It was significantly positively related to a broad understanding of civil disobedience only among non-supporters of the movement. Regarding the communication variables, the positive effects of the political use of social media and disagreeable discussion were nominally stronger among movement supporters regardless of whether the activists' understanding or a broad understanding were concerned. The consistency of the findings is suggestive. However, in none of the cases were the corresponding coefficients statistically significantly different from each other. Therefore, H7 is not supported.

Concluding discussion

The above analysis indicated that the Hong Kong public's understanding of civil disobedience increased substantially between September 2013 and October 2014. It is difficult to evaluate whether this level of understanding is high or low in an absolute sense. However, public opinion surveys typically found that citizens do not have a very good grasp of even the basic facts of politics (Delli Carpini & Keeter, 1996). In fact, the September 2013 survey also contained several questions about factual knowledge. For example, only 25.6% of the respondents could correctly name the

Secretary for Transport and Housing of the Hong Kong Government, and only 11.5% could name the official title of another government bureau chief. In other words, even in 2013, citizens' understanding of civil disobedience was apparently no worse than their ability to identify key government officials. Although we do not have pre 2013 data, it is reasonable to assume that people had already started to learn about civil disobedience in the beginning stages of the Occupy Central campaign.

Admittedly, the results of two surveys are not sufficient to trace precisely the development of citizens' understanding of civil disobedience between 2013 and 2014. However, the findings suggests that the beginning of the Umbrella Movement also played a role in generating further learning. The evidence is that both attitudinal support for and participation in the Umbrella Movement explained the understanding of civil disobedience. As discussed earlier, political learning relies on motivation, ability, and opportunity. While support for the movement should have led to a willingness to learn about the rationale behind the movement, actual participation led to opportunities to learn, ranging from the civic lessons offered by pro-movement academics in the occupied areas to constant interaction with fellow participants. It is therefore theoretically significant that both attitudinal support and behavioral participation were related to the understanding of civil disobedience; the two variables probably promoted such understanding through different mechanisms.

Consistent with Lee (2015), the consumption of mainstream news did not lead to understanding of civil disobedience. In Lee (2015), the lack of influence by the mainstream media was explained in terms of the pro-establishment bias of mainstream media and hence the likelihood that they do not contain much oppositional knowledge. However, it was noted earlier that mentions and discussions of civil disobedience were widespread in the mainstream media in both 2013 and 2014. Moreover, the analysis found that even reading pro-movement newspapers did not affect the understanding of civil disobedience. Therefore, the lack of influence in the present case was probably not caused by the lack of discussion of civil disobedience in the mainstream media. Instead, a plausible argument is that the mainstream media typically only "mentioned" civil disobedience in the news without providing much explanation. More detailed explications and debates were available mainly through the op-ed sections, but these sections were probably read only by a very small group of the most educated citizens. The mainstream media thus failed to constitute a major channel through which the majority of the people could gain an understanding of civil disobedience.

In contrast, the political use of (but not sheer amount of time spent on) social media contributed substantially to the understanding of civil disobedience. This finding confirms the previous findings on the role of social media in social movements and protest politics in Hong Kong (Chan & Lee, 2015; Tang & Lee, 2013). In addition to being a platform where pro-movement discourses are widely available, another reason for the effectiveness of social media is that it allows a high degree of interactivity, which can be particularly important in the uptake of conceptual, instead of merely factual, knowledge. This latter argument about the effectiveness of interactive forms of communication also helps explain the effectiveness of interpersonal discussion with disagreeing others in promoting the understanding of civil disobedience. People discussing with disagreeing others often need to elaborate and defend their positions, and in the process they could come to a more articulate understanding of the ideas that support their claims.

The findings did not support the hypotheses regarding the influence of communication activities on supporters vs. non-supporters of the movement. Although increases in the understanding of civil disobedience found between the two surveys were particularly conspicuous among young people, who did constitute the main participants in the movement, the 2014 survey failed to provide robust evidence for the hypothesis that communication leads to the understanding of civil disobedience mainly among movement supporters. One possible reason is that when the Umbrella Movement began, movement supporters already had a relatively high level of understanding of civil disobedience. Knowledge gain thus was not particularly strong compared to that of the non-supporters of the movement.

Theoretically, this study illustrates that social movements can play an educational role in the society at large, especially if they can successfully create what movement scholars have called a "critical discourse moment" (Gamson & Modigliani, 1989). This possible effect of social movements has received only scant attention in the literature. Moreover, the findings of this study also suggest that the introduction of a new movement tactic or form of protest action into a society requires intensive discursive work that could allow pro-movement citizens as well as the population at large to gain an understanding of the rationale and legitimacy of the tactic or form of action. Past research has examined the characteristics of the discursive work surrounding a society's repertoire of contentious actions (e.g., Hayes, 2005). This study contributes to the literature by examining the effects of such discursive work on public opinion.

This study also supports Lee's (2015) broader claim that oppositional knowledge constitutes a distinctive category of knowledge with distinctive antecedents and consequences. The findings showed that education and political interests, for instance, have limited influence on the understanding of civil disobedience in Hong Kong. Instead, the understanding of the concept was seemingly more "attitude-based," and support for the movement as well as external efficacy were among the strongest and most consistent predictors of the two indices.

For Hong Kong in particular, this study can help explain why the Umbrella Movement was successful in remaining largely non-violent. Because it was scripted and understood by the general public as non-violent, the public expected that the action would remain non-violent and the occupiers would be willing to bear the legal consequences of the action. During the movement, however, there were indeed occasional physical conflicts between the police and the protesters. Moreover, in the later stage of the movement, there was pressure from the radical faction of the movement to "escalate." Nevertheless, in the end, no large-scale physical confrontation took place. Benny Tai and other core proponents of Occupy Central surrendered to the police in early December, and when the police cleared the occupied areas in mid-December, the protesters did not resist with physical force. Although Tai had said that Occupy Central had already evolved into the different Umbrella Movement, to a certain extent the ending of the occupation returned to the "script" that was written over the preceding two-year period.

This study also suggests that one "success" of the Occupy Central campaign and the subsequent Umbrella Movement was the spread of the idea of civil disobedience. Although civil disobedience occurred before the movement, Hong Kong society had not considered the concept as seriously and explicitly as they did during 2013 and 2014. The successful promotion of the concept among the general public may have paved the way for actions and campaigns of civil disobedience in the future.

A limitation of this study is that it addresses the understanding of civil disobedience but not the acceptance of the idea. The surveys did not include questions that asked about the general acceptance of civil disobedience partly because given that they were conducted during Umbrella Movement, such acceptance would probably have been heavily conflated with support for the movement itself. However, the close connection between support for and participation in the movement and the understanding of civil disobedience suggests that an understanding of the concept alone may generate acceptance of the idea. Alternatively, it could be argued that understanding is a necessary, if not sufficient, condition of acceptance. Future research conducted in "normal times" could trace the evolution of both the understanding and acceptance of civil disobedience among the Hong Kong public.

Future research could also adopt qualitative methods to conduct a more nuanced examination of the public understanding of civil disobedience. When the proponents of the Occupy Central campaign promoted the concept of civil disobedience, they inevitably had to take into account and respond to certain basic features of the city's public culture, such as its emphasis on "peaceful and rational protests" (Lee & Chan, 2011) and the hegemony of "law and order" (Ku, 2007). How do Hong Kong people understand civil disobedience in relation to these other ideas, values, and discursive categories? Will the idea of civil disobedience be "domesticated" (in the sense of both being localized and being pacified) to fit the local protest culture? Alternatively, will the idea of civil disobedience become the basis for the re-articulation of protest culture in Hong Kong?

Finally, future research could also focus on how the most involved and committed participants and activists in the Umbrella Movement understood civil disobedience and how their understanding evolved over time. For instance, in the later stages of the Umbrella Movement, the government and the conservative forces successfully applied for court injunctions against the occupation. On 28 October 2014, the Hong Kong Bar Association issued a statement expressing concerns about the refusal of the participants in the movement to obey the court order.[8] At this juncture, the earlier articulation of the justifiability of civil disobedience by the Occupy Central proponents became inadequate. The participants also needed to reconsider their stances and arguments regarding the nature and characteristics of civil disobedience. Unfortunately, no data are available on whether and how the core participants' thinking regarding civil disobedience evolved. Hence, another task of future research would be to track the evolution of the activists' perspectives on civil disobedience.

Notes

1. The international media created the label "Umbrella Revolution" based on the image of protesters using umbrellas to protect themselves against tear gas. However, local academics and commentators emphasized that the movement did not aim at overthrowing the Hong Kong and Chinese governments and thus preferred the term Umbrella Movement.
2. For consistency, unless otherwise indicated, the term "Occupy Central" refers to the discursive campaign surrounding the proposal of Occupy Central between January 2013 and late September 2014, whereas the "Umbrella Movement" refers to the actual collective action campaign that started on 28 September 2014.
3. The search was limited to eight newspapers because the number of newspapers in the city varied over time. The limit was needed to make the figures more comparable. The eight

newspapers are *Apple Daily, Oriental Daily, Sing Tao Daily, Ming Pao, Hong Kong Economic Times, Hong Kong Economic Journal, Wen Wei Pao,* and *Ta Kung Pao.*
4. "Learning" was indeed emphasized as part of the movement experience. Specifically, many local academics organized "civic classes" in "mobile classrooms" in the occupied areas.
5. Details of sample characteristics are omitted because of limited space. Suffice it to say that the discrepancies are by no means extreme. Income was not weighted because of the lack of detailed information about the education X income distribution and the propriety of employing the same weighting procedure for the two samples. The sample – population difference in income should not have affected the substantive findings in this study because income was not a significant predictor of knowledge after controlling for education, and further analyses found that the core relationships tested in this study were not significantly moderated by income.
6. A few answers given by some respondents were definitely incorrect. The examples included "civil disobedience is legal" and "the right to civil disobedience is established in the law." In addition, several respondents simply claimed that there was no difference between civil disobedience and typical law breaking. While individual respondents could hold this belief, it did not constitute a valid answer to the question.
7. The model includes a relatively large number of control variables because many of the controls are theoretically plausible predictors of political knowledge. The model thus provides a rigorous test of the possible impact of media and communication activities. Notably, despite the inclusion of many controls, multicollinearity was not a serious issue. The independent variables with the highest variance inflation factor (VIF) are time spent using social media and political use of social media, with VIFs of 2.39 and 2.87, respectively. However, these values are still much lower than the value of 8 to 10, which is regarded as problematic in social science studies (Stevens, 1996).
8. The statement is available at: http://www.hkba.org/whatsnew/misc/20141028 - Statement of Hong Kong Bar Association Relating to Mass Defiance of Court Orders (Eng) - FINAL1.pdf. Last accessed on March 22, 2015.

Disclosure statement

No potential conflict of interest was reported by the author.

References

Alexander, J. (2005). *The civil sphere*. New Haven, CT: Yale University Press.
Allam, N. (2014). Blesses and curses: Virtual dissidence as a contentious performance in the Arab Spring's repertoire of contention. *International Journal of Communication, 8*, 853–870.
Baumgartner, J. C., & Morris, J. S. (2010). My FaceTube politics: Social networking web sites and political engagement of young adults. *Social Science Computer Review, 28*(1), 24–44.
Bennett, W. L., & Segerberg, A. (2013). *The logic of connective action*. New York, NY: Cambridge University Press.
Biggs, M. (2013). How repertoires evolve: The diffusion of suicide protest in the twentieth century. *Mobilization, 18*(4), 407–428.

Boudreau, C., & Lupia, A. (2011). Political knowledge. In J. N. Druckman, D. P. Green, J. H. Kuklinski, & A. Lupia (Eds.), *The Cambridge handbook of experimental political science* (pp. 171–186). New York, NY: Cambridge University Press.

Chaim, G. (1992). *Philosophical anarchism and political disobedience.* Cambridge: Cambridge University Press.

Chan, J. M., & Lee, F. L. F. (2015). Media and social mobilisation in Hong Kong. In G. Rawnsley & M. Y. Rawnsley (Eds.), *The Routledge Handbook of Chinese Media* (pp. 145–160). London: Routledge.

Cohen, J., & Arato, A. (1992). *Civil society and political theory.* Cambridge, MA: MIT Press.

De Fazio, G. (2012). Legal opportunity structure and social movement strategy in Northern Ireland and Southern United States. *International Journal of Comparative Sociology*, *53*(1), 3–22.

Delli Carpini, M. X., & Keeter, S. (1996). *What Americans know about politics and why it matters.* New Haven, CT: Yale University Press.

Earl, J., & Kimport (2011). *Digitally enabled social change.* Harvard, MA: MIT Press.

Ekiert, G., & Kubik, J. (1998). Collective protest in post-communist Poland, 1989-1993: A research report. *Communist and Post-communist Studies*, *31*(2), 91–117.

Eveland, Jr, W. P. (2004). The effect of political discussion in producing informed citizens: The roles of information, motivation, and elaboration. *Political Communication*, *21*, 177–193.

Fraile, M. (2013). Do information-rich contexts reduce knowledge inequalities? The contextual determinants of political knowledge in Europe. *Acta Politica*, *48*(2), 119–143.

Gamson, W. A., & Herzog, H. (1999). Living with contradictions: The taken-for-granted in Israeli political discourse. *Political Psychology*, *20*(2), 247–266.

Gamson, W. A., & Modigliani, A. (1989). Media discourse and public opinion on nuclear power: A constructionist approach. *American Journal of Sociology*, *95*(1), 1–37.

Gil de Zúñiga, H., Jung, N., & Valenzuela, S. (2012). Social media use for news and individuals' social capital, civic engagement and political participation. *Journal of Computer-Mediated Communication*, *17*, 319–336.

Hayes, G. (2005). Vulnerability and disobedience: New repertoires in French environmental protests. *Environmental Politics*, *15*(5), 821–838.

Iyengar, S. (1990). Shortcuts to political knowledge: Selective attention and the accessibility bias. In J. Ferejohn & J. Kuklinski (Eds.), *Information and the democratic process* (pp. 160–185). Champaign: University of Illinois Press.

Jenkins, J. C., & Wallace, M. (1996). The generalized action potential of protest movements: The new class, social trends, and political exclusion explanations. *Sociological Forum*, *11*(2), 183–207.

Johann, D. (2012). Specific political knowledge and citizens' participation: Evidence from Germany. *Acta Politica*, *47*(1), 42–66.

Kaufhold, K., Valenzuela, S., & de Zuniga, H. G. (2010). Citizen journalism and democracy: How user-generated news use relates to political knowledge and participation. *Journalism & Mass Communication Quarterly*, *87*(3–4), 515–529.

Kim, Y. M. (2009). Issue publics in the new information environment: Selectivity, domain specificity, and extremity. *Communication Research*, *36*(2), 254–284.

Ku, A. S. (2004). Negotiating the space of civil autonomy in Hong Kong: Power, discourses and dramaturgical representations. *China Quarterly*, *179*, 647–664.

Ku, A. S. (2007). Constructing and contesting the "order" imagery in media discourse: Implications for civil society in Hong Kong. *Asian Journal of Communication*, *17*(2), 186–200.

Lee, F. L. F. (2008). Local press meets transnational activism: News dynamics in an anti-WTO protest. *Chinese Journal of Communication*, *1*(1), 57–78.

Lee, F. L. F. (2009). The impact of political discussion in a democratizing society: The moderating role of disagreement and support for democracy. *Communication Research*, *36*(3), 379–399.

Lee, F. L. F. (2015). International alternative media use and oppositional knowledge. *International Journal of Public Opinion Research*. Online first: doi: 10.1093/ijpor/edu040.

Lee, F. L. F., & Chan, J. M. (2011). *Media, social mobilization, and mass protests in post-colonial Hong Kong*. London: Routledge.

Leung, L. (2009). Mediated violence as "global news": Co-opted "performance" in the framing of the WTO. *Media, Culture & Society*, *31*(2), 251–270.

Lewis, J. (2001). *Constructing public opinion*. New York, NY: Columbia University Press.

Lui, T. L., & Chiu, S. W. K. (Eds.). (2000). *The dynamics of social movements in Hong Kong*. Hong Kong: Hong Kong University Press.

Luskin, R. (1990). Explaining political sophistication. *Political Behavior*, *12*(4), 331–361.

Mansbridge, J. (2001). The making of oppositional consciousness. In J. Mansbridge & A. Morris (Eds.), *Oppositional consciousness* (pp. 1–19). Chicago, IL: University of Chicago Press.

McCausland, C., O'Sullivan, S., & Brenton, S. (2013). Trespass, animals and democratic engagement. *Res Publica*, *19*, 205–221.

Meirick, P. C. (2013). Motivated misperception? Party, education, partisan news, and belief in "death panels.". *Journalism & Mass Communication Quarterly*, *90*(1), 39–57.

Mutz, D. (2006). *Hearing the other side*. New York, NY: Cambridge University Press.

Norris, P. (2000). *A virtuous circle*. New York, NY: Cambridge University Press.

Ollis, T. (2011). Learning in social action: The informal and social learning dimensions of circumstantial and lifelong activists. *Australian Journal of Adult Learning*, *51*(2), 248–268.

Ostman, J. (2012). Information, expression, participation: How involvement in user-generated content relates to democratic engagement among young people. *New Media & Society*, *14*(6), 1004–1021.

Price, V., & Zaller, J. (1993). Who gets the news? Alternative measures of news reception and their implications for research. *Public Opinion Quarterly*, *57*(2), 133–164.

Quill, L. (2009). *Civil disobedience*. New York, NY: Palgrave McMillan.

Stevens, J. (1996). *Applied multivariate analysis for the social sciences*. Mahwah, NJ: LEA.

Strange, M. (2011). "Act now and sign our joint statement!" What role do online global group petitions play in transnational movement networks? *Media, Culture & Society*, *33*(8), 1236–1253.

Tai, B. Y. T. (2013, January 16). The most lethal weapon of civil disobedience. *Hong Kong Economic Journal*, A16.

Tang, G. K. Y., & Lee, F. L. F. (2013). Facebook use and political participation: The impact of exposure to shared political information, connections with public political actors, and network structural heterogeneity. *Social Science Computer Review*, *31*(6), 763–773.

Tilly, C. (1995). *Popular contention in Great Britain, 1758-1834*. Cambridge, MA: Harvard University Press.

Tilly, C. (2008). *Contentious performances*. Cambridge: Cambridge University Press.

Tworzecki, H., & Markowski, R. (2014). Knowledge and partisan bias: An uneasy relationship. *East European Politics and Societies*, *28*(4), 836–862.

Wada, T. (2012). Modularity and transferability of repertoires of contention. *Social Problems*, *59*(4), 544–571.

Wang, D. J., & Soule, S. A. (2012). Social movement organizational collaboration: Networks of learning and the diffusion of protest tactics, 1960-1995. *American Journal of Sociology*, *117*(6), 1674–1722.

Wicks, R. H., Wicks, J. L., & Morimoto, S. A. (2014). Partisan media selective exposure during the 2012 presidential election. *American Behavioral Scientist*, *58*(9), 1131–1143.

A legal realist view on citizen actions in Hong Kong's umbrella movement

John Nguyet Erni

Department of Humanities & Creative Writing, Hong Kong Baptist University, Hong Kong

> This article considers the legal validity of citizens' actions in civil disobedience as it pertains to the umbrella movement in Hong Kong. It introduces the critical approach of "legal realism" in order to reconsider normative law, such as police enforcement and court interventions, in relation to political struggle. It has been argued that the legal precepts of rights, responsibility, and the rule of law are capable of contingent and contextually appropriate interpretations by different legal actors, including citizens who participate in civil disobedience. In politics, justice, and most importantly law, civil disobedience offers an alternative legal normativity to consider the citizen's right, and even duty, to express dissent. Furthermore, this right or duty is legally persuasive and conducive to guarding democratic principles.

As soon as the defiant protesters of Hong Kong commenced the Occupy movement, the governments of both the HKSAR and Beijing declared it illegal. However, in many ways, the mass protests represented the strongest challenge yet to the supposed legality of Beijing's decision (handed down on 31 August 2014) to reject open nominations of candidates for the territory's leadership, although the constitutional structure purportedly allows semi-autonomous democracy. Moreover, according to the government, the use of force in the crackdown of the movement was not only mild and tolerant but also unambiguously legal. By December 2014, weakened by political fatigue, the movement was dispersed largely through a series of court orders.

The foregoing is a rough outline of some crucial elements in the legal terrain of the umbrella movement, where normative laws, such as police enforcement and court interventions, were exercised. However, the same ground exposed considerable legal ambiguities. Chief among them are questions about the constitutional guarantees of the Basic Law (to determine the conduct of the territory's own elections) and about the legal understanding of civil disobedience as the exercise of citizens' rights. Much has been written about the constitutional conundrums raised by the Basic Law in what seems to be an endless struggle for clarification. This article focuses on a more urgent issue, namely how to inject new meanings into our understanding of the practice of civil disobedience, especially its fundamental obligation to challenge a system that is perceived as unjust. This obligation, it will be argued, is legally persuasive and conducive to guarding democratic principles.

In *R v Jones (Margaret) & Others* (2006, p. 39), the often-cited Lord Hoffman famously said:

> My Lords, civil disobedience on conscientious grounds has a long and honourable history in this country. People who break the law to affirm their belief in the injustice of a law or government action are sometimes vindicated by history. The suffragettes are an example that comes immediately to mind. It is the mark of a civilized community that it can accommodate protests and demonstrations of this kind.

To understand the "honourable history" of civil disobedience and how it demands the formation of a "civilized community", thus implying the tolerance of conscientious protests, it is important to return to the normative framework regarding the inter-articulation among three major notions: *rights*, *duties*, and *laws*. This entails a return to basic legal philosophy and theory. One lesson of the umbrella movement is the need for a productive debate in Hong Kong regarding the basic precept of normativity in legal positivism and the production of natural rights. Instead of blanket pronouncements about the alleged illegality of the movement, proper deliberation is necessary. This commentary provides a legal realist view of the questions of rights, duties, and laws in the effort to reconcile the political divide arising from the perceived opposition between citizen civil disobedience and the rule of law.

Another normativity is possible: situating civil disobedience in the umbrella movement

From the outset, it must be said that the legal precepts of rights, responsibility, and the rule of law are subject to contingent and contextually appropriate interpretations by different legal actors. In the critical legal realist position, which challenges the view that orthodox legal institutions and doctrines provide an autonomous and self-executing system of legal discourse untainted by politics, it is necessary to recognize the overdetermined nature of legal reasoning and the legal process itself (see Coombe, 2001; Erni, 2011, 2012; Sarat & Simon, 2003). This necessitates rethinking three problematics.

First, we need to recognize that the question of the site of legal knowledge – that is, the assumption that the legislature, courts, and law societies as the singular formation or site of legal knowledge – needs to replaced by the recognizing that there is a multiplicity of legal consciousness and uses by citizens that form the social origin of law. A famous aphorism by Oliver Wendell Holmes Jr. (1963, p. 5), an early proponent of American legal realism, is "The life of the law has not been logic; it has been experience". It is here that the notions of rights, duties, and laws connect strongly with the politics and lived experience of "the popular". During the umbrella movement, it was little wonder that a societal tug-of-war existed regarding who could speak about the law, interpret it, and even challenge it.

Second, the problem of doctrinalism – that is, the assumption that legal principles are the essence of law or its only source of value – needs to be replaced by the understanding of the radically contingent nature of legal interpretations in empirical situations, especially in "crisis governance" (Lazar, 2009). This connects to the tradition within critical legal studies of liberal constitutionalism in which activist liberal law professors and public-interest lawyers argue that legal interpretivism is *already* built into law itself, especially in the provisions guaranteeing various rights kinds (see Kennedy, 2002).

Friedrich von Hayek (1960) and other conservative legal positivists would argue that the correct role of government is best confined to establishing clear, fixed rules of law that amount to a stable set of minimum rules that are applied in a uniformed, non-discretionary manner. In contrast to legal positivism, Benny Tai, one of the key architects of the Occupy Central movement and a specialist in constitutional law, exemplifies the aspirations of legal interpretivism by explaining his view on the various "levels" of governance by law. According to Tai, the "low levels" consist of a basic recognition of the law and an absolute obedience to the law (Tai, 2014). These two strata are built upon minimal elements, such as the clarity and transparency of the law and the proper institutionalization of legal practice. Tai considers these "low" levels because they are generally incapable of restraining power:

> Beginning-stage governance by law lacks an effective means to restrict power. The determination of how the law would be exercised properly relies solely on the government or the legislator's subjective view. Because this kind of governance by law makes little or no demand on the substance of the law, the legal infrastructure ends up being utilized to maintain power, at the expense of protecting basic citizen rights. To leap toward a higher level of governance, the law would have to be transformed from functionalities (as the tool of the powerful) to a system of checks and balances (affording a restriction to power), which can then lead to the actualization of legal purpose (the chief purpose of the law is to practise justice). (Tai, 2014, A37, author's translation)

Tai's legal interpretivism is set in normative terms. Without straying from basic legal theory, he nonetheless rejects blind adherence to predetermined law. In philosophical terms, legal interpretivism adheres to the Kantian assumption of the moral imperative of "means without ends". More accurately, in the context of civil disobedience as citizen action, it is politics without ends. Perhaps one of the most influential thinkers who takes to heart the conviction of "politics without ends" in her writing on human rights is Hannah Arendt. I shall return to Arendt towards the end of this brief article.

Third, the question of legal essentialism – the assumption that there is stable and universal distinction between legal and non-legal practices and relations – needs to be replaced by the recognition that legal relations are always partly discursive or relationally produced. Here, "non-legal" means at least two things. It means all aspects of life that neither express themselves through law nor embody law. However, it also means that which is fundamentally important to human life and therefore will be incorporated into law and policy. Both meanings of the term render any fixed or absolute distinction between law and non-law untenable, thereby returning us to the anti-reductionist ethos of legal realism. According to this view, the plethora of human creativity expressed individually or collectively during the umbrella movement from artwork, songs, and slogans to the ad hoc mobilization of medical and other services provided in make-shift tents evidences a discursive sphere that must be recognized as constituting (non-legalistic) patterns of order and civility, restraint from violence, peaceful collective formation, and self-respect. Legal realist thinking incorporates all empirical social behaviour that spawns a respectable social order as part of the totality of social law, grounded in an anti-reductive understanding of the social functions of law.

In short, the legal determination of the social totality is not simpler nor more monolithic than any other levels of determination, whether economic, political, or cultural. The modernist roots of law do not and cannot negate the fact that law is radically contextual and situationally contingent. The power exercised by law, it must therefore be insisted, is a matter of contextual struggle whereby the constitutive power of law enters into an intricate negotiation with the sites in which it is supposed to constitute its own power.

I understand that not everyone is necessarily convinced of the preference given to the critical legal realist view over either the conventional or the postmodern views of law. No matter how vigorously we work to depict law without denying or distorting the *empirical* picture of sharp moral, political, and social conflict, those who adhere to conventional legal orthodoxy would still ask the following question: who is to judge and where is the line drawn? Equally, those who advocate radical views would decry legal realism as a sell-out because the latter is still seen as being circumscribed by the normativity of law. The simple (but hopefully not simplistic) answer is that the legacy of legal realism rests precisely on political and moral persuasion. It sees the law as *articulated politics*. By rejecting the self-sufficiency of law as radical decontextualization, the legal realist position insists on looking vigorously and empirically at the intricate ways in which law, morality/justice, and politics are inter-implicated. To use Foucauldian parlance, it bears remembering that, in governmentality, the power of law is never conceived of as a total or totalizing sphere (e.g., Foucault's (1980) famous phrase about cutting off the king's head), but as a network implying an intricate interweaving of many micro-events of power and counter-power. At the same time, by rejecting the other version of the self-sufficiency of law as pure radicalism, which is a certain strand of the postmodern politics of a certain endless deconstruction of law, the legal realist position once again returns to the empirical ground of *action and experience* as sites of the strategic but temporary negotiation of what matters. As Rosemary Coombe (1998, p. 35), a scholar of legal anthropology, reminds us, "If law is central to hegemonic processes, it is also a key resource in counterhegemonic struggles."

In the umbrella movement, the legal terrain of civil disobedience, insofar as it is underscored by fundamental struggles over basic rights, exhibited exactly an empirical field or network of dynamic socio-legal entities. Indeed, when we consider civil disobedience as consisting of a set of actions – consciousness-raising, education of relevant laws, journalists' monitoring, the protestors' self-monitoring, provoking police response, or response to the court's intervention – then the whole *system* of rights-associated social laws presents as a critical "apparatus" in the Gramscian sense. This apparatus opens to a multiplicity of overlapping and contradictory spaces, institutions, and even cultural standards of justice. This "extra-legal" apparatus embeds scales (domestic and international), actors (civil society, independent individuals, human rights monitoring groups, and government departments), processes (planned and ad hoc protocols, formation of consensus, debating principles and values, and documentation), and relations (deliberative, legal, and political).

To obey or disobey the law

What becomes of the rule of law under a discursive approach derived from socio-legal realism? What happens to the plain idea that laws are there to be obeyed? If civil disobedience is viewed as a network of socially, culturally, and politically embedded practices (as outlined above), and if these practices follow the normative conventions of lawfulness (i.e., non-violence, proportionality, assumption of legal responsibility, and so on), then the extent to which civil disobedience can challenge law and order is minimal. Benny Tai argues that civil disobedience disrupts the "low levels" of governance-by-law, which require a basic recognition of the law and an absolute obedience to the law. However, it does so in order to exert pressure on governance at the "higher levels". Tai elaborates:

> The higher echelon of governance entails the use of law to restrict power and to achieve justice. The restriction of power by the law is mainly accomplished through decentralization, including the separation of government powers (constitutional restriction), monitoring of the government by the courts (judicial restriction), monitoring by the social body (administrative restriction), popular elections (political restriction), and monitoring by the media and civil society (social restriction) ... At a higher level, the use of law to achieve justice must be responsive in a variety of ways, including ensuring proper legal procedures (procedural justice), offering basic protections (civil rights justice), ensuring equality (political rights justice), maintaining basic provisions of living (social and economic rights justice), and establishing communicative democracy (deliberative justice). (Tai, 2014, A37, author's translation)

The critical point derived from Tai's four-stage schema is that the social realism of civil disobedience is *not* incompatible with the obedience to the law. Nevertheless, neither is civil disobedience willing to disarticulate law from justice or to collapse "is" (that which exists as blackletter doctrines) and "ought" (that which is desirably just as an outcome of political struggle). Put more clearly, civil disobedience is the struggle to press "is" into "ought". To delink law from justice and *realpolitik* would be to assert the obligation and responsibility of each citizen to obey the law unequivocally. At that very instance, the law-and-order system enacts, inevitably and predictably, the repression of freedom.

Civil disobedience challenges repression not only through various forms of citizen actions but also and more crucially by raising important *legal* questions. Should citizens be coerced into obedience to tyranny or unjust laws? Is there an absolute responsibility to obey the law irrespective of the quality of the law (or for Tai, irrespective of the lowly levels of some laws)? Can protest derive a legal legitimacy that can balance the arguments for absolute obedience to the law? The umbrella movement tapped into these vast and timeless questions in legal philosophy, which underpin the notions of duties, rights, and the rule of law.

It is reasonable that in a lawful society citizen grievances can be dealt with through established channels of complaint, such as through working with legislators to formulate objections, through an investigation by specific commissioners, through exerting pressure on the government by the media, or through the ballot box (see Udeh, 2014). However, in the events leading up to the umbrella movement, none of these avenues seemed to yield the desired result, particularly since the protestors were a minority, in the sense that they were not supported by the business hegemony or by the mainstream media, and in the sense that they, as Hong Kongers, were subjugated by a national central political system. The hypothetical question that then arises concerns whether individuals or groups have the right to "disobey the law". The question then arises: in the face of the lack of response from the government to citizens' grievances and the structural lack of restraint on power in the legal system, would the citizens have a duty to express dissent to the law? Legal scholar Collins Udeh (2014, p. 36) reminds us of the following:

> A government true to democratic precepts of representativeness and fairness must be sensitive to demands for change. If it fails in that regard, it is at least arguable that demands for change, while entailing technical breaches of the law, should be accommodated within the constitutional framework... As we have seen in the twenty-first century civil disobedience starting from the Arab Spring up to the Ukrainian

uprising, major social changes of such magnitude would have been impossible without recognition that under certain limited conditions there exists a right of legitimate protest, however inconvenient and uncomfortable this is for governments around the world... [I]t is not necessary to look to such major societal changes brought about by defiance of law in order to refute the law and order model and proclaim some entitlement to dissent.

Hannah Arendt (1972, pp. 83–84) goes further by saying "it would be an event of great significance to find a constitutional niche for civil disobedience – of no less significance, perhaps, than the event of the founding of the *constitution libertatis*, nearly two hundred years ago". In contrast to major liberal thinkers (e.g., John Rawls) who argue that civil disobedience is compatible with a constitutional government that possesses tolerant attitudes, Arendt argues that civilly disobedient citizens should be given access to the very heart of decision-making (Smith, 2010). In the context of the United States, Arendt's proposal includes inviting representatives of civil disobedience movements to "influence and assist Congress by means of persuasion, qualified opinion, and the numbers of their constituents" (Arendt, 1972, p. 101).

Conclusion

William Smith (2010) suggests that Hannah Arendt's proposal to institutionalize civil disobedience, that is, to take it off the streets and into government, is unprecedented within political theory. In the context of the umbrella movement in Hong Kong, where the government was beholden to interests in the central government in Beijing, Arendt's revolutionary spirit may be impractical. Arendt's laudable approach of "politics without ends" does not suit the historical context of only the emerging struggle for constitutional democracy. Instead, my concern, which I have addressed through the perspective of socio-legal realism, is to provoke a discussion regarding whether we may recognize civil disobedience as an action embedded within and qualified for legally valid claims, particularly the following: first, that obedience to law is only *prima facie*; and second, that parallel to the duty to obey the law there exists a duty to express dissent. Civilly disobedient citizens are not enemies of the state and its laws because the social contract outlines only the *prima facie* demand that citizens refrain from breaking the law within the *uncompleted task of democratizing*.[1] It is in this sense that Arendt's proposal to allow civilly disobedient citizens access to legal and constitutional decision-making conjoins with Habermas's striking argument that citizens engaging in civil disobedience may "contrary to their image, prove themselves to be the true patriotic champions of a constitution that is dynamically understood as an ongoing project – the project to exhaust and implement basic rights in changing historical contexts" (Habermas [2004, p. 9]; see also Habermas [1985, 1996, 1998]). By calling these citizens "ambivalent dissidents" (2004, p. 9), Habermas speaks to the legitimacy of thinking about the dual responsibility both to uphold the law and to challenge it. The socio-legal realist view of citizens' actions, thus, is interested only in advancing and guarding an *alternative legal normativity* in the ongoing struggle for liberty.

Disclosure statement

No potential conflict of interest was reported by the author.

Note

1. The view that civil disobedience puts into sharp focus the fact that democracy is an ongoing project is evidenced in the deep divisions that occurred in Hong Kong after the issuance of court injunctions demanding that the protesters clear the streets. After the court injunctions were issued, defiant protesters made public statements of disobedience, refusing to let the law terminate their civil actions. The Hong Kong Bar Association, which had been generally supportive of the movement, criticized the defiance as eroding the rule of law and setting a bad precedent. Similarly, former Chief Justice Andrew Li, a long-time defender of HKSAR's autonomy in the legal arena, also cautioned the organizers not to step over the boundary of the law. Does the stance of the Hong Kong Bar Association and the former Chief Justice nullify the legal validity of civil disobedience as claimed in this commentary? I think not. The courts' role is to maintain the rule of law; this is uncontestable. However, equally undisputed is that courts are not set up to resolve political issues. Thus, when Andrew Li said, "The Occupy movement has lasted such a long time, and the injunctions issued by the court have not yet been obeyed and respected. This will have an adverse effect on our rule of law" *South China Morning Post*, 2014), he clearly wanted to protect the court's judicial authority, while hinting at the prolonged inability of the movement to resolve the political issues at stake. From a socio-legal and realist point of view, this position points precisely at the ambiguity inherent in the lawfulness of civil actions. In other words, these calls for compliance with the law are not the same as the government's blanket claim of the illegality of the movement writ large. For in this sweeping claim, the government shunned away the political dimensions that had animated the movement in the first place in the attempt to reinstall an absolutist view of obedience to the law. Thus, on the one hand, the rule of law, as normatively understood by the Hong Kong Bar Association, judges, and the courts, must be upheld. However, on the other hand, the very same bodies recognize the *realpolitik* at the heart of civil disobedience, which beckons a complex engagement with the rule of law as situated in an (uncomfortable) relation with politics.

References

Arendt, H. (1972). Civil disobedience. In H. Arendt (Ed.), *Crises of the republic* (pp. 49–102). New York: Harcourt Brace Jovanovich.

Coombe, R. (2001). Is there a cultural studies of law? In T. Miller (Ed.), *A companion to cultural studies* (pp. 36–62). Malden, MA: Blackwell.

Coombe, R. J. (1998). Contingent articulations: A critical cultural studies of law. In A. Sarat & T. R. Kearns (Eds.), *Law in the domains of culture* (pp. 21–64). Ann Arbor: University of Michigan Press.

Erni, J. N. (Ed.). (2011). *Cultural studies of rights: Critical articulations*. New York: Routledge.

Erni, J. N. (2012). Who needs human rights? Cultural studies and public institutions. In M. Morris & M. Hjort (Eds.), *Creativity and academic activism: Instituting cultural studies* (pp. 175–190). Hong Kong: Hong Kong University Press.

Foucault, M. (1980). *Power/Knowledge*. New York: Pantheon.

South China Morning Post. (2014, November 17). Ex-chief justice Andrew Li calls on Occupy Central protesters to retreat. Retrieved from http://www.scmp.com/news/hong-kong/article/1642488/ex-chief-justice-andrew-li-calls-occupy-central-protesters-retreat

Habermas, J. (1985). Civil disobedience: Litmus test for the democratic constitutional state. (J. Torpey, Trans.). *Berkeley Journal of Sociology, 30*, 95–116.

Habermas, J. (1996). *Between facts and norms: Contributions to a discourse theory of law and democracy*. (W. Rehg, Trans). Cambridge: Polity.

Habermas, J. (1998). On the internal relation between the rule of law and democracy. In C. Cronin & P. De Greiff (Eds.), *The inclusion of the other: Studies in political theory* (pp. 253–264). Cambridge, MA: MIT Press.

Habermas, J. (2004). Religious tolerance: The pacemaker for cultural rights. *Philosophy, 79*, 5–18.

Holmes, O. W. Jr. (1963). *The common law*. (M. D. Howe Ed.), Boston: Little, Brown.

Kennedy, D. (2002). The international human rights movement: Part of the problem? *The Harvard Human Rights Journal, 15*, 99–125.

Lazar, N. C. (2009). The everyday problem of emergencies. *University of Toronto Law Journal, 59*, 237–249.

R v Jones (Margaret) & Others [2006] UKHL 16.

Sarat, A., & Simon, J. (Eds.). (2003). *Cultural analysis, cultural studies, and the law: Moving beyond legal realism*. Durham, NC: Duke University Press.

Smith, W. (2010). Reclaiming the revolutionary spirit: Arendt on civil disobedience. *European Journal of Political Theory, 9*, 149–166.

Tai, B. (2014, November 12). Reflections on civil disobedience and the rule of law. *Ming Pao.* A37 [in Chinese].

Udeh, C. (2014). Rights, responsibility, law and order in 21st century's civil disobedience. *Journal of Politics and Law, 7*, 32–40.

Von Hayek, F. (1960). *The constitution of liberty*. London: Routlege and Kegan Paul.

Contested news values and media performance during the Umbrella Movement

Chi Kit Chan

Hang Seng Management College, Hong Kong

> Social crises are a huge challenge to the performance of the media. The norms and routines of news making with which journalists comply can become problematic in the context of intensive public sentiment and empathy. News values, including the sacred belief in objective reporting, are questioned in the light of controversies over editorial judgment within and outside the newsroom. I examine the contested news values that manifested in the Umbrella Movement of Hong Kong in 2014. In particular, I focus on the arguments and deliberations regarding news objectivity, which involved several parameters of the performance of the media during this social crisis.

Social crisis and news making

The making of news is embedded in a set of normative practices and organizational routines to which journalists adhere in order to rationalize that what they write is "social fact" (Reese, 1990; Tuchman, 1978). In achieving this goal, the abstract value of objectivity is crucial to news workers. The ideology, however, is a versatile notion that comprises both the normative codes and the field observations of journalistic practices. In his seminal work, Maras (2013) mapped news objectivity according to three dimensions: value, process, and language. Value refers to the codes of practice of what good journalism should be – impartiality, separation between facts and opinions, non-emotive observation and presentation to the course of news events, and so forth – in order to convince the public that the news is non-partisan and does not manipulate social facts (Reese, 1990; Schudson, 2003). Despite complaints about over-reliance on official sources and authoritative testimony to construct social facts (Bennett, 1991, 2005), the normative goal of objectivity is still valued by journalists, news media, and the public in their views of what constitutes quality news.

In addition, objectivity can be understood as the common organizational practices and procedures involved in making news (Reese, 1990; Tuchman, 1978), such as the connection between journalists and their news sources, publishing contrasting views, routinizing unexpected events, and by establishing the system of the news beat, for instance. This dimension focuses on the working efficiency of journalists that are steered by organizational norms and routines. These codes of practice stem from commonsensical and intuitive reactions and mindsets. Robert E. Park coined such knowledge of working standards as "acquaintance with" (1940,

p. 669). In addition to the normative goals described in the previous paragraph, these common organizational practices are also regarded as norms with which journalists should comply (Reese, 1990). Last, objectivity can also imply narrative structure and linguistic discourse, which latently convey news frames as "out there" facts to the audience. Schudson (2000) documented the rise of American journalistic writing styles, which indicated rituals of commercialization and professionalization. Interviews and the "summary lead" format were used to encourage readers to perceive themselves as witnesses of events. The transformation of writing style represented the emerging consciousness of an American press that was independent from partisan patronage, which was the origin of objectivity.

Nevertheless, the understanding of objectivity varies across societies and is subject to local journalistic practices, the structure of the political economy, and other social formations (Maras, 2013). Studies on Hong Kong showed that journalists highly regard the accurate dissemination of reliable facts and information to the public, which they view as their professional role (Leung & Lee, 2014; So & Chan, 2007). These findings are in line with the value of objectivity in which American journalism is embedded. However, the same studies found that news workers in Hong Kong, to varying degrees, recognized other social roles, such as interpretation (discussing and explaining policies), advocacy (promoting reform and public surveillance), adversarialism (questioning and criticizing the government and other stakeholders), and cultural function (educating citizens and entertainment). The versatility of news values indicated that journalists have different (anticipated) social functions, such as watchdogs against authorities (adversarialism), enlightenment (interpretation and cultural function), and social change (advocacy). Although the value of objective reporting is still upheld, the values and organizational norms of quality journalism also matter in the expectations of news workers in the social context.

News values are particularly versatile in times of social crisis. According to the literature on journalism in Hong Kong, because of acute uncertainties, polarized debates, and radicalized collective action arising from social crises, journalists and the public may have multiple expectations of news representation. In particular, advocacy reporting, in which news workers assume the role of commenting and enlightening the public interest instead of being impartial observers, may make inroads into the news ideology of journalists and even the public perception of journalism (So, 1999). Social crises therefore pose questions to routinized practices surrounding the news value of objectivity, and they provoke negotiations among journalists and members of the public, which may redefine accepted definitions of good journalistic practice. For example, during the 1980s, media organizations were not reluctant to take sides during critical moments of the Sino-British talks regarding the 1997 handover in which the future of Hong Kong was decided (Wong, 1999). In 2003, the proposed national security laws provoked a large-scale mass protest in which 500,000 people marched through the main streets of Hong Kong Island, saying "no" to the legislation and the Tung administration (the governing body of Hong Kong at that time). Since the handover of Hong Kong, this large-scale social movement was unprecedented. The subsequent governance crisis also triggered discussion on the involvement of the media in political mobilization (Chan, 2003). In 2012, there was another mega social movement against the proposed curriculum of national education in Hong Kong. In the midst of an enormous public outcry, thousands of people protested and rallied outside government headquarters for days.

Journalists from various media organizations deliberately uploaded their photos of wearing black T-shirts with their arms crossed, which was a political gesture that meant "no" to national education in Hong Kong. This under-discussed phenomenon indicated the negotiation of news values and organizational practices that possibly challenged the priority of objectivity in the representation of the news.

Moreover, the quest for objectivity is also part of the media politics of self-censorship in Hong Kong. As discussed, the notion of objectivity is also conveyed via writing style and narrative format, which indicates news frames and value judgment as "out there" facts. Narrow interpretations of objectivity can be pledged by press organizations in order to avoid taking sides during political controversies (Lee & Lin, 2006). Furthermore, objectivity could be an elusive mask used to cover value judgments by manipulating the representation of "hard facts" (Lee & Lin, 2006, p. 342). Objectivity can also be employed by news managers in the newsroom to justify their questionable editorial decisions and their exercise of informal control over the newsroom (Lee & Chan, 2009). For example, a senior editor may ban a news story because of "bias" or "incomplete information" rather than obvious political considerations. Ironically, it is plausible that the value of objectivity, which is supposed to safeguard the freedom of the press and the quality of the news, could mask the self-censorship of media organizations.

Perceptions and understandings of journalism are rooted in culturally specific norms and practices, not exact science (Lee & Chan, 2009; Patterson & Donsbach, 1996). Therefore, the notion of "objectivity" itself can hardly be "objective." The normative values and organizational practices of objectivity are susceptible to the intensity engendered by social crises, which could trigger conflict among the multi-layered professional roles of journalists. Furthermore, the narrative style of "out there" facts could also be problematized by the doubt incurred by self-censorship. Contestation regarding the content of news objectivity therefore indicates how journalists and the stakeholders on the wider community regard media performance.

The Umbrella Movement of Hong Kong

The Umbrella Movement of Hong Kong in 2014 is an example of the contestation of news values and media performance being provoked by a social crisis. The word "crisis" here does not have negative implications for the movement. It refers to pressing uncertainties that resulted from the unprecedented scale of civil disobedience activities in Hong Kong. The heavy presence of the police force in this democratic movement, and the usage of teargas in late September 2014 led thousands to occupy the main streets in the central business districts of the city – Admiralty, Mongkok, Causeway Bay, and Tsim Sha Tsui. From the beginning of the movement, uncertainties and conflicts were prevalent. No one knew when and how the occupying movement would end. Protesters and the helpers of the movement were steadfast. The affected residents and business owners waited. The political dialogue was interwoven with deadlocks and the "blame game." Even the protest leaders were unable to control the direction of the movement, not to mention the embattled governing leaders.

The intention of this article is not to document all the processes and milestones in the democratization of Hong Kong. However, it does highlight the social sentiment that was manifested overtly in the Umbrella Movement. The former British colony, now a special administrative region of China, has experienced enduring and rising disappointment at the pace of democratization. While thousands of citizens occupied the main roads and pledged civil disobedience for the sake of the democratic vision, the prolonged movement inevitably resulted in divided, if not polarized, social tensions. According to a survey released by the Centre for Communication and Public Opinion Survey of the Chinese University of Hong Kong on 18 December 2014, while 31.1% to 37.8% of Hong Kong people were in favor of the occupying movement from September to December 2014, 35.5% to 46.3% did not support the movement. The results of the survey showed that the younger and more highly educated the interviewees, the more supportive they were of the movement. This cleavage was particularly obvious in people with partisan tendencies. Nearly 7 of 10 "democrats" said "yes" and around 8.5 of 10 "pro-establishment" people said "no" to the movement. Acute social tension and intensive discursive wars among various stakeholders inevitably induced controversies over the news coverage and interpretation of the "social facts." They also plausibly fuelled the media's advocacy of social mobilization and adversarial tendencies against authorities and/or other stakeholders engulfed in the social crisis. Such social circumstances not only reshape the media's strategy in practicing objectivity but also determine the social yardsticks of contested and controversial performances of the media.

Media performance in moments of crisis

On 29 September 2014 – the day after the outbreak of the Umbrella Movement – the narrative format of the headlines of 19 Hong Kong newspapers offered a mixture of objectivity, social advocacy, and cultural reminiscences of public order. Several commercial papers focused on factual descriptions, particularly the firing of tear gas and the occupation of the main roads. For example, the *South China Morning Post* ran the headline "Tear gas fired as thousands join Occupy," and *Ming Pao*'s top news was headlined "Endless teargas from the police, expanding road blockades in Hong Kong island and Kowloon" (警催淚彈放不停 佔領堵路擴港九). However, the headlines of some press organizations were characterized by social empathy and advocacy. *Apple Daily*, a well-known paper that is critical of China, depicted the resistance of protesters against the police as a brave act in the headline "Fearless to suppression, 60,000 people occupied Central and called for Leung [the incumbent head of the government of Hong Kong] to step down" (無懼鎮壓 六萬人佔中叫梁下台). Some papers adopted the metaphors of "crying" and "tears" in the headlines of top news, such as "Hong Kong Cries" (香港哭了) in the *Hong Kong Daily News* and "To move to tears, Hong Kong" (催淚。香港。) in *AM730* (a free local paper). Several commercial papers resorted to cultural reminiscences of public order in their top stories. The word "chaos" (亂) and the phrase "out of control" (失控) were used in the headlines of the *Oriental Daily, The Sun,* the *Hong Kong Economic Times, and Headline Daily*. This echoed the "order" imagery in the discourse of the Hong Kong media, which held that collective action stemming from civil society had been embedded in the social imagination of the public order (Ku, 2007). The "order" imagery represented the social outcry against the Umbrella Movement, which stressed that illegal road blockades disrupted social regularity and livelihoods, and civil disobedience defied the rule of law in Hong Kong. Such hybridized news discourse served to polarize public opinion, indicating the versatility of news values and journalistic practices in social crises. The news discourse about the Umbrella Movement was nevertheless tied to various social empathies beyond the non-emotive construction of social facts (Schudson, 2008), such as sympathy for democratic aspirations as well as the concern for social order in view of the unprecedented, extensive mobilization of civil disobedience.

Despite the varying narrative formats of news headlines at the beginning of the crisis, throughout the Umbrella Movement, the value of objectivity was central in controversies over media performance. Criticism against "media bias," which generally refers to the non-objective presentation of social facts, was blatant. Notably, Television Broadcasts Limited (TVB) was dubbed "CCTVB," the acronym of "Chinese Central Television Broadcasts Limited," to which online comments, some supporters of the movement and even the "Action News" (presenting news by animated melodrama) of *Apple Daily* referred from time to time. Such attacks on the TVB news accelerated when TVB's news controller Mr. Keith Yuen Chi Wai removed the phrase "punches and kicks" (拳打腳踢) from the voiceover describing video excerpt. The scene showed a protester being beaten in a dark corner by seven police officers. The phrase was heard in the voice over, but it was deleted in the later version. This redaction ignited speculations about editorial judgment. The Hong Kong Journalists Association (HKJA) asked TVB news to disclose the reason. Mr. Yuen replied that based on objectivity and impartiality, the coverage of criminal cases has to be prudent and that the people and incidents concerned should be described using words such as "alleged" (涉嫌) and "suspected" (疑犯). However, his explanation failed to satisfy the HKJA (Yuen, 2014). In this case, objectivity was both the ground for public criticism against the questionable editorial decisions of news organizations (removing a phrase that was believed to depict the scene accurately) and the shield used by news executives to defend their judgment (be prudent when narrating a video that could incur a possible criminal charge). Their arguments legitimized the value of objectivity as the benchmark used to evaluate media performance, in spite of the varying interpretation of this abstract construct.

Should journalists take action?

Another controversy surrounding the notion of objectivity and media performance is whether journalists and news organizations may legitimately take action that ostensibly interferes with the course of news events. This is a highly contestable issue, even when journalists assume the social role of a critical watchdog. Direct involvement in news events literally shifts their role from observers who report news to activists who make news. This issue presents a fundamental question in the assessment of media performance: Should journalists remain as objective reporters in times of critical social crises that affect their profession and even the whole society?

On 25 October 2014, "blue-ribbon" supporters, that is, organizations and people who opposed the Umbrella Movement and the occupation of main streets by the protesters, held rallies in Tsim Sha Tsui. The event eventually turned into an outburst against reporters. The "blue-ribbon" people assaulted four journalists. Radio Television Hong Kong, DBC Radio, and the *Apple Daily* decided to boycott the news events organized by the "blue-ribbon" camp. More than 180 journalists pledged to this collective action to condemn violence against newsgathering (RTHK, DBC, and Apple Boycott, 2014). However, the chair of the HKJA, Sham Yee Lan, issued an open letter arguing that the boycott failed to meet the professional requirement of social surveillance and that the selective coverage of news events could hardly be justified (Reporting is the vocation, 2014). This statement was a bitter interrogation of objectivity. When journalists are under attack and deeply involved in bitter conflicts, to what extent does the normative code of being an objective, detached, and neutral reporter still make sense to news workers? The outcry of journalists supporting the boycott demonstrated the overall shift toward a polarized, opinionated, and advocacy-oriented journalistic model. Such contestations of news values arose from the responses of journalists to the intensified self-censorship and other threats against press freedom. In particular, as discussed earlier in this article, even the common belief in objectivity was employed as a discursive tool in exercising "soft" control over newsroom. The tension between objectivity and activism is easily triggered in times of crisis when journalists perceive that their social role and even personal safety are at stake. The conflict between objectivity and advocacy has been largely manifested in occasional debates between managerial and frontline journalists and the practices of some outspoken media, rather than an obvious paradigm shift in the common beliefs and professional codes of journalists. Although we should pay due attention to the multiple facades of news values, it is too early to conclude that objectivity no longer matters in the professional and social assessment of media performance.

Media performance and alternative media

In addition to the debates surrounding the performance of mainstream media, the alternative media have also gained social attention. Alternative media are information agencies that are "deprofessionalized" (less adherence to professional codes such as objectivity), "deinstitutionalized" (less structured organizations allow freelance and volunteering writers to be citizen journalists), and "decapitalized" (much cheaper operational costs based on social media platforms and online resources) (Atton, 2009), which enables them to form a new paradigm of news making. Empowered by the interactivity of social networking sites (SNS), alternative media assumed a significant role in shaping public opinion and collective action during the Umbrella Movement. Notable examples are *Inmedia, SocRED* (the content is mainly contributed by citizen journalists who are social activists), *Passion Times* (which is generally regarded as a media organization supporting politician Wong Yeung Tat), and *Hong Kong Golden Forum* (a highly popular online forum in Hong Kong).

Because alternative media are often closely tied to social movements, they go beyond the social roles of objective reporting and critical watchdog to become part of the movement by mobilizing rallies and promoting collective action. According to an anonymous broadcast journalist who covered news about the Umbrella Movement, the *Passion Times*, which is spearheaded by a political group called *Civic Passion*, gradually became the major source of news about the "occupying zone" of Mong Kok. The anonymous journalist said that members of the *Passion Times* were stationed in the zone day and night. They broadcast updates on the situation in Mong Kok via an online platform in real time. Another example is the *Hong Kong Golden Forum*. A protester who was engaged in confrontations with the police told me that he kept checking the *Hong Kong Golden forum* for calls for mobilization. Alternative media obviously redefined the role of media in this social movement, as well as the parameters of media performance.

Furthermore, the alternative media that were active during the Umbrella Revolution were striking in their stance toward objectivity in attacking the mainstream media. A noteworthy comment posted in *Inmedia* illustrates this paradox. The author criticized TVB news by saying that the news channels offered by other paid television stations (excluding those of TVB) were more neutral and claimed that the neutrality of TVB news was nothing more than a cunning cover-up of its hidden agenda (Wai, 2014, October 2). Similar criticisms of TVB news were common among those who supported the Umbrella Movement. Given the proactive involvement of alternative media in the movement, they could hardly pledge themselves to the values, organizational practices, and narrative format of the conventional understanding of objectivity. However, they used this contested notion to criticize the performance of mainstream media.

Conclusion

The assessment of media performance depends on how we define journalistic values and the organizational and discursive practices of news making. Whether news is conceived as trustworthy social facts depends on journalistic values and practices meeting public expectations. The abstract idea of objectivity, however contested, has long been the imagined standard providing normative values, direction of practices, and narrative format for the production and dissemination of quality news. Nevertheless, the professional roles of journalists constitute a set of multi-dimensional constructs that are sensitive to the contextual dynamics underlying this common belief. Social crises elicit the following question: What kind(s) of news does the community expect in times of social crisis? Undoubtedly, objective reporting is still highly regarded by both journalists and the public. Uncertainties arising from social crises usually increase the social demand for information. Thus, the supply of reliable news that reports social facts is imperative. However, social crises may also challenge core values and provoke unjust subjugation. On such occasions, the public (including some journalists) expects journalists to take sides, favoring advocacy on the one hand and on the other still valuing objective journalism. The repercussions are that not only does objectivity become a kind of media strategy but also the yardsticks used to measure the media's performance could be contradictory. Situations such as the Umbrella Movement of 2014 problematize the long-standing definition of quality journalism as valuing objectivity. The problem is particularly pronounced when objectivity itself also becomes a contested, multi-layered and problematic discourse articulated by various stakeholders. Such negotiations of the news paradigm imply plausible shifts in and further controversies over the benchmark of media performance.

Finally, how will the news media of Hong Kong cover the political and socio-cultural uneasiness between China and Hong Kong in the future? The Umbrella Movement clearly showed the accumulated and entrenched confrontation between the Chinese government and the people of Hong Kong regarding democratization and core values, such as social freedom and national identity. The social crisis expressed by the movement may fade, but the divisions remain. In particular, how will the news media of Hong Kong continue to uphold the primacy of local interest (Chan

& Lee, 2011)? The news coverage of confrontations between China and Hong Kong is thus a litmus test of the enduring concerns about media performance in the context of the shrinking freedom of expression and rising self-censorship in the media.

Disclosure statement

No potential conflict of interest was reported by the author.

References

Atton, C. (2009). Alternative and citizen journalism. In K. Wahl-Jorgensen & T. Hanitzsch (Eds.), *The handbook of journalism studies* (pp. 265–278). New York, NY: Routledge.

Bennett, W. L. (1991). Toward a theory of press-state relations. *Journal of Communication, 40*, 103–125.

Bennett, W. L. (2005). *News: The politics of illusion* (6th ed.). New York, NY: Pearson Education.

Chan, J. M. (2003). Xiang Gang Jia Shu: Chuan Mei Ying Fou Jie Ru Zheng Zhi? (Letter to Hong Kong: Should media intervene in politics?). In J. M. Chan (Ed.), *Qi Yi Jie Du (Interpreting 1st July Rally)* (pp. 115–118). Hong Kong: Ming Pao Publishing.

Chan, J. M., & Lee, F. L. F. (2011). The primacy of local interest and press freedom in Hong Kong: A survey study of journalists. *Journalism, 12*, 89–105.

Ku, A. S. M. (2007). Constructing and contesting the "order" imagery in media discourse: Implications for civil society in Hong Kong. *Asian Journal of Communication, 17*, 186–200.

Lee, F. L. F., & Chan, J. M. (2009). Organizational production of self-censorship in the Hong Kong media. *The International Journal of Press/Politics, 14*, 112–133.

Lee, F. L. F., & Lin, A. M. Y. (2006). Newspaper editorial discourse and the politics of self-censorship in Hong Kong. *Discourse & Society, 17*, 331–358.

Leung, D. K. K., & Lee, F. L. F. (2014). How journalists value positive news: The influence of professional beliefs, market considerations, and political attitudes. *Journalism Studies, 16*, 289–304.

Maras, S. (2013). *Objectivity in journalism*. Cambridge: Polity Press.

Park, R. E. (1940). News as a form of knowledge: A chapter in the sociology of knowledge. *American Journal of Sociology, 45*, 669–686.

Patterson, T. E., & Donsbach, W. (1996). News decisions: Journalists as partisan actors. *Political Communication, 13*, 455–468.

Reese, S. D. (1990). The news paradigm and the ideology of objectivity: A socialist at the Wall Street Journal. *Critical Studies in Mass Communication, 7*, 390–409.

Reporting is the vocation of journalists which cannot be boycotted easily. (2014, October 26). *Ming Pao*. Retrieved from http://goo.gl/IL7DDJ

RTHK, DBC, and Apple boycott pro-police groups. (2014, October 27). *Apple Daily*. Retrieved from http://hk.apple.nextmedia.com/news/art/20141027/18914189

Schudson, M. (2000). *The good citizen: A history of American civic life* (2nd ed.). Cambridge, MA: Harvard University Press.

Schudson, M. (2003). *The sociology of news*. New York, NY: W.W. Norton & Company.
Schudson, M. (2008). *Why democracies need an unlovable press*. Cambridge: Polity Press.
So, C. Y. K. (1999). Dialectic of journalistic orientation: A study of the treatment of government news by the Hong Kong Press. In C. Y. K. So & J. M. Chan (Eds.), *Press and politics in Hong Kong: Case studies from 1967 to 1997* (pp. 95–136). Hong Kong: Hong Kong Institute of Asia-Pacific Studies, Chinese University of Hong Kong.
So, C. Y. K., & Chan, J. M. (2007). Professionalism, politics, and market force: Survey studies of Hong Kong journalists 1996-2006. *Asian Journal of Communication, 17*, 148–158.
Tuchman, G. (1978). *Making news: A study in the construction of reality*. New York, NY: Free Press.
Wai, T. (2014, October 2). No more interviews from CCTVB, okay? *Inmedia*. Retrieved from http://www.inmediahk.net/cctvb-0
Wong, F. L. K. (1999). Sino-British Talks on 1997: A case study of political communication. In C. Y. K. So & J. M. Chan (Eds.), *Press and politics in Hong Kong: Case studies from 1967 to 1997* (pp. 179–232). Hong Kong: Hong Kong Institute of Asia-Pacific Studies, Chinese University of Hong Kong.
Yuen, K. (2014, October 15). Improper words of punches and kicks. *Hong Kong Economic Journal*. Retrieved from http://www2.hkej.com/instantnews/current/article/916996/%E8%A2%81%E5%BF%97%E5%81%89%3A%E6%8B%B3%E6%89%93%E8%85%B3%E8%B8%A2%E7%94%A8%E5%AD%97%E4%B8%8D%E7%95%B6

Business as usual: the UK national daily press and the Occupy Central movement

Colin Sparks

Hong Kong Baptist University, Hong Kong

> This essay reviews the coverage of the Occupy Central movement in the UK national daily press from the first notice of the growing movement in July 2013 to the time of writing in January 2015. This is a relatively small subset of the total mentions of Hong Kong in the UK press, which cover a wide range of cultural, leisure, sport, and business stories. Hong Kong is very far from invisible to the UK press in "normal" times but, given that the UK is the former colonial power in Hong Kong, and that the terms under which the territory was returned to China were formalized in an inter-state agreement between the UK and China (the Joint Declaration, ratified in 1985), it is reasonable to assume that developments in the constitutional situation would attract very considerable attention on the part of the UK government. Studies of foreign news suggest that nationally specific factors tend to influence news salience so we would concomitantly expect that the UK newspaper press would devote substantial amounts of space to reporting and discussing the issues raised by these developments.

Introduction

This essay reviews the coverage of the Occupy Central movement in the 10 UK "national" daily newspapers from the first notice of the growing movement in *The Guardian* on 2 July 2013 to the time of writing on 23 January 2015. This material constitutes a relatively small part of the total coverage of Hong Kong in the UK media during the period, which reported a wide range of topics including business, culture, and sport. The papers analysed are published in London six days a week and circulate throughout the country. Some of them have very substantial web presences which are visited by readers from around the world, but their online hard news material tends in most cases to be identical with their printed editions. In this study, only unique stories from the printed editions were considered; duplicates appearing in other outlets were disregarded. Newspapers appearing on Sundays were ignored, even when they are closely related to the daily titles, since the structure of the Sunday newspaper market is distinct from that of the dailies.

This is not a scholarly article resting upon an extensive review of the literature, the formulation of hypotheses, and the deployment of elaborate research methods in order to test them. Rather, as an essay, it uses established findings in order to offer a first assessment of the contemporary performance of part of the mass media. The main bearings of this essay are taken from four relatively well-explored areas of news reporting: the determinants of foreign news; the issue of framing; the attribution of agency in discursive structures; and the influence of advertising upon media.

The coverage of foreign affairs is an established field in the analysis of news reporting, dating back at least to Galtung and Ruge's seminal article (Galtung & Ruge, 1965). There have subsequently been many revisions of their work, some of them substantial, but they still remain a favourite starting point for analyses (Harcup & O'Neil, 2001). More recently, authors have been concerned with the mechanisms by which foreign news gains salience through various kinds of proximity – geographical, cultural, political, ethnic, etc. (Joye, 2010; Nossek, 2004; Wilke, Heimprecht, & Cohen, 2012). Hong Kong is very far from invisible to the UK press in "normal" times, but, given that the UK is the former colonial power in Hong Kong and that the terms under which the territory was returned to China were formalized in an inter-state agreement between the UK and China (the Joint Declaration, ratified in 1985), it is reasonable to assume that developments in the constitutional situation would attract very considerable attention on the part of the UK government. The above studies suggest that nationally specific factors tend to influence news salience, so we would concomitantly expect that UK newspaper coverage of the Occupy movement would be reasonably extensive and that it would represent the situation in Hong Kong as an issue of particular importance to the UK government.

On other hand, while there is a substantial community of Hong Kong origin in the UK, this has not yet emerged as an organized political pressure group of any scale. There is therefore little internal pressure either on the UK government or the UK media to pay detailed attention to Hong Kong issues or to make any attempt at active intervention. While imperial memories continue to play a disproportionate, and deeply objectionable, role in the British consciousness, the material impotence of the UK government with respect to Hong Kong has been clear to the whole world at least since Deng Xiaoping informed Mrs Thatcher that he could repossess the colony in an afternoon should he so choose. While the press might cover Occupy Central is some detail, we would expect that it would almost certainly restrict itself to factual reporting and commentary of the hand-wringing kind, rather than any direct appeal for government intervention.

Issues of framing and the discursive analysis of newspaper reporting are similarly well established topics in the analysis of news reporting. This essay is not concerned with whether the framing of news stories results in any determinant audience response to news, so we can adopt the simple and uncontentious definition advanced by Entman, which is that framing is "selecting and highlighting some facets of events or issues, and making connections among them so as to promote a particular interpretation, evaluation and/or solution" (Entman, 2004, p. 5). Following this lead, in any study of a case in which there were strongly contested conflicting views, for example on the impact of street occupations, we were interested in what was selected and highlighted and how these choices produced specific ways of reporting the movements.

Discursive analysis, as well, has long been concerned with the ways in which processes are represented, and in particular with lexical choices and transitivity (Fowler, 1991, pp. 70–71). More recently, Richardson argues that "given that transitivity forms the very basis of representation, transitive choice cannot be overlooked in any linguistic analysis of journalism" (Richardson, 2007, p. 57). In the case in point, there were a number of events in which issues of transitivity – who was the active party in a particular process – were of central importance, and in which a range of lexical choices as the characterization of particular participants were available, so we were interested in examining how these factors contributed to the overall representations that were articulated.

The final issue with which this essay is concerned is very well known, but not usually explored in contexts analogous to the one under investigation. It is commonplace amongst many competing schools of thought about media economics to argue that advertising has an important influence on the character of news reporting (Baker, 1994; Curran, 2002; Hamilton, 2004; Herman & Chomsky, 2008; Picard & Brody, 1997). While there is general agreement that dependence upon advertising as a whole influences journalism in various ways, there is much less investigation of the relationship between newspaper journalism and particular advertisers, partly because most large newspapers do not commonly depend upon any small group of advertiser, still less any single firm. For reasons we will explore below, specific features of the case in point raised the relationship between a general dependence upon advertising and the influence of a particular advertiser, which we explore so far as is possible on the basis of the material available.

We have, therefore, presented a sketch of UK press coverage which rests upon the above well-known approaches to news analysis. The article begins with a descriptive account of the scope of the coverage. This is followed by a discussion of the dominant frames used in the reporting, the extent to which the situation in Hong Kong was interpreted through UK concerns, and the balance and tone of the coverage. The issue of the way the relationship between the UK press and different large corporations was handled is considered in general and a special case of alleged capitulation to advertising pressure is examined in more detail. Finally, the general lessons of the essay are reviewed in the conclusion.

The scope of the coverage

As was anticipated, coverage was reasonably extensive. A search was conducted using the Factiva database of UK national newspapers.[1] It was found that there were 156 unique articles reporting or discussing the Occupy movement and/or the Umbrella Revolution during this period. As can be clearly seen from Figure 1, the distribution of these articles follows the predictable patterns of news coverage: it is primarily driven by events, and in particular dramatic events. The coverage is concentrated around the peak of the opening period of Occupy Central in late September and early October. Twelve of the stories ran on the front page, nine of these on 29 and 30 September, at the height of demonstrations, and 123 of the articles dealt with civil disruption. Before and after the major events there is very little, or no, coverage of the developing situation.

The "quality" newspapers all devoted resources to original reporting rather than relying purely on agency copy. The vast majority of the reports were by named journalists employed by the newspapers in question, and the five titles of the "quality press" had their own correspondents in Hong Kong for at least part of the time. Only three of the news articles, all of them brief, did not have an author attribution, and none of the articles was attributed to one or more news agency. *The Financial Times*

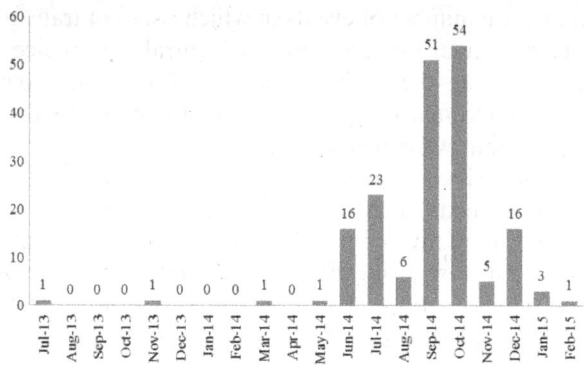

Figure 1. Number of stories per month. Source: Factiva.

and *the Guardian* have China bureaus, and the former at least has a permanent Hong Kong office. The other three titles had articles attributed to reporters in Hong Kong, but these were apparent only in the September–October phase of the movement and it is likely that these were the work either of stringers or staff journalists parachuted in for the crisis. Most of the journalism was reporting, although there were a number of editorials, as well as opinion pieces and letters, written by both individuals from the newspapers in question and outside experts.

This picture of detailed attention to events in Hong Kong, although not to underlying causes and trends, must immediately be qualified by noting the distribution of the articles across the 10 titles in question. The penetration rate of national newspapers into the adult (15 +) population of the UK during this period was around 30%, so the majority of UK citizens were not exposed to this sort of coverage: to the extent that they were made aware of events in Hong Kong, it would have been through other sources, most likely television news. Within that section of the population who did get information from newspapers, there was a distinct social profile. As Table 1 demonstrates, the articles were overwhelmingly in the five titles of the "quality" press. These have relatively small circulations, predominantly amongst relatively well-educated and wealthy members of the population. The five mass circulation popular papers, with predominantly manual and white-collar working-class readers, barely covered the issues. Taken together, the quality titles reached about 27% of the newspaper-reading population and around 8% of the total adult population. The readership of the titles that could reasonably be claimed to have offered substantial coverage of the situation (*The Financial Times* and *The Guardian*) taken together constitute an even smaller proportion of the population. This finding fits very well with previous studies of UK press coverage of China: outside of these two titles it is fitful at best, and responds primarily only to the most dramatic events (Sparks, 2010).

The two titles with the most coverage have a very extensive global audience through their online presences, so their coverage was available to a much larger group of people, including in the UK. Of the other titles, *The Daily Mail* has a huge online presence (it is searched on Google several times more frequently than *The New York Times*, for example) but the majority of its online coverage is celebrity gossip and human interest, so while its coverage of Occupy Central may

Table 1. Distribution of coverage in the UK press.

Title	Number of articles	Readership
The Financial Times	48	150,000*
The Guardian	30	748,000
The Times	18	1,110,000
The Daily Telegraph	17	1,261,000
The Independent	11	845,000
The Daily Mirror	3	2,893,000
The Daily Mail	1	3,866,000
The Daily Express	1	1,097,000
The Sun	0	5,508,000
The Daily Star	0	1,039,000
Total	129	

Sources: Numbers of articles from Factiva database. Readership from the National Readership Survey, June 2013–June 2014.[2]
Notes: *The National Readership survey does not gather figures for the *Financial Times*. I have estimated the figure for this title on the basis of a paid UK circulation of around 50,000 (http://www.theguardian.com/media/2014/feb/14/the-sun-post-christmas-sales-bounce).
The figures given refer only to the printed editions of the newspapers.

have been more widely diffused, it was so minimal as not to affect the overall picture.

Of these articles, seven were short pieces of less than 100 words each and 17 were substantial articles of more than 1000 words. Table 2 gives the distribution of these articles by length across the various titles. As is clearly evident, there is a close relationship between quantity of articles and the length of articles: in other words, those titles that covered the movement most regularly also covered it most extensively. *The Financial Times* stands out as providing by far the most coverage, with the largest numbers of both longer reports and more substantial analytic pieces. Of the other titles, only *The Guardian* can be said to have provided both regular and substantial coverage. It is reasonable to conclude that only the readers of these two papers, either online or offline, would have the opportunity to encounter anything

Table 2. Distribution of attention to Occupy Central across titles.

Title	Brief (< 100 words)	Medium (100–500 words)	Long (500–1000 words)	Substantial
The Financial Times	0	12	30	6
The Guardian	0	8	20	2
The Times	1	8	7	2
The Daily Telegraph	0	10	7	0
The Independent	1	3	4	3
The Daily Mirror	2	1	0	0
The Daily Mail	0	0	1	0
The Daily Express	0	1	0	0

like a full and detailed record of the events and debates. Readers of the other quality titles would have fitful, but sometimes quite substantial, accounts of developments in Hong Kong, while the readers of the popular press would have little other than a fleeting picture of the most dramatic events.

This evidence confirms that the normative claims made about the function of the press in securing a democratic order are not appropriate with regard to the actual performance of the bulk of the UK press. The issue of the struggle for democracy in Hong Kong was not, as we shall see below, framed solely in terms of foreign affairs. On the contrary, the elite press discussed British responsibility towards the people of the former colony and argued that it was also an internal political issue for the UK. At best, we might say that less than 10% of the population would, if they relied on the newspaper press, have any idea at all of the existence of any problem. An even smaller proportion of those, primarily the tiny and elite minority that reads *The Financial Times*, but perhaps also the less elite and socially liberal readers of *The Guardian*, would have any substantive basis for understanding the issues at stake. On any reasonable account, the British newspaper press did not play the role ascribed to it by most theories of democracy.

Framing the issue

The national newspaper press of the UK is notoriously partisan. Although it does not display most of the elements of "political parallelism" that have been argued to characterize the press in Southern Europe, neither does it correspond to the non-partisan model of the US press. UK national newspapers are fairly clearly aligned with political parties, although none of them are owned by parties, and their coverage of many issues tends to reflect their different ideological stances. We might therefore expect to find these factors produced significant differences in coverage of the Occupy Central movement, but in fact we could find no firm evidence of this. The overall frame within which the coverage is cast was shared by all of the titles, and it was that of the struggle for democracy between, on the one side, largely young demonstrators and, on the other, both the Hong Kong local government and the Chinese national government. *The Financial Times* of 27 September (*Financial Times*, 2014a), for example, headlined its story "Pro-democracy leader held after mass student protest". The issue of democracy was mentioned in 147 of the articles and the same number mentioned the PRC government. *The Guardian* of 7 March (*Guardian*, 2014a) began its report with a clear identification of the issue:

> Importing a western-style democratic system to Hong Kong would be "disastrous", a senior Chinese leader warned yesterday, in a sign of Beijing's hardening stance ahead of a planned direct election in 2017.
>
> Zhang Dejiang, who heads the leading group on Hong Kong affairs, told a closed door meeting that copying a foreign electoral system could "become a democracy trap... and possibly bring a disastrous result, one delegate, Ma Fung-kwok, told Reuters. His comments came as activists in Hong Kong prepare for Occupy Central, a pro-reform civil disobedience campaign that wants to see thousands take over Hong Kong's financial district – much to Beijing's alarm.

The focus on the mainland government did not mean that the role of the Hong Kong government was neglected, however. The same article went on to quote Hong Kong Chief Secretary Carrie Lam making a statement agreeing with the main thrust of the

Beijing government's view and other articles carried extensive reports of Chief Executive C.Y. Leung's views on the movement.

Perhaps surprisingly, the issue was not primarily couched in terms of an ideological concern with communism, which was in the past a pervasive frame in Western coverage of China. This element was certainly present, but it was generally used in the form "communist", referring to the mainland's ruling party, rather than in the form "communism" referring to a social system. This is, of course, partly because it increasingly lacks credibility to use the latter term in the case of the mainland China, given the nature of the economic and social system actually operating there. It is also partly because anti-communism, although certainly strongly present in the UK, does not have the status of "national religion" in that country which some commentators have identified in the US. There is, however, another aspect to this elision to which we will return below.

The UK's special responsibility

Within the general frame of a struggle for democracy, the situation was placed within an international framework in which the UK, as we expected, was presented as a major actor. The context of reporting was that Hong Kong issues were clearly identified with China but also as matters that were of concern to the UK. The major theme of this link with the United Kingdom was in terms of a debate over whether this country had any historic responsibility for the situation in Hong Kong and how far this continued to be the case in the present. The first occurrence of this theme was in an opinion piece by Isabel Hilton, a well-known China expert, writing in *The Guardian* on 2 July (*Guardian*, 2014b). In an article titled "A great power we can't trust: as democracy protests in Hong Kong gain strength, China must honour its commitment to liberty", Hilton wrote that although the British had refused to allow democracy in Hong Kong during their rule, the Joint Declaration made a promise of progress towards democratic elections which Beijing was now reneging upon:

> As a British colony, Hong Kong never enjoyed universal suffrage, but this was subsequently promised in elections for both the chief executive and the legislature – half of whose members are elected by elite special interest groups that include bankers and lawyers. Beijing has repeatedly delayed the introduction of a fully democratic system and, critics say, steadily expanded its influence in Hong Kong's affairs. This creeping control has provoked increasingly frequent confrontations on the streets. The issue has come to a head over the conditions for the next legislative elections in 2016, and elections for chief executive in 2017. Beijing wants to allow only approved candidates who "love China" to stand.

This article, and others like it – for example, that in *The Financial Times* three days later – invariably begin with a reference to the last British governor, Christopher Patten, leaving Hong Kong in tears 17 years earlier and the commitment to eventual democratic elections as being part of the deal over the future of Hong Kong agreed with Deng Xiaoping as a condition for the handover of sovereignty (*Financial Times*, 2014b).

The contemporary responsibilities of the British government towards Hong Kong became more and more of a salient issue as the crisis developed. When the prime minister, David Cameron, refused to meet Anson Chan and Martin Lee in London in July 2014, Philip Stephens, an associate editor of *The Financial Times*, noted the sharp contrast between this frosty reception and the enthusiasm with which the same David Cameron, then in opposition, greeted the same two prominent pro-democrats on their previous visit. On that occasion, Cameron launched a sterling defence of Hong Kong's rights as guaranteed by his Conservative predecessor Margaret Thatcher, who was the British signatory to the joint declaration. On 18 July Stephens wrote:

> That was before Mr Cameron took office; and, more saliently, before the punitive freeze in bilateral relations imposed by Beijing after he had the temerity to meet the Dalai Lama, Tibet's spiritual leader. The prime minister yielded, offering tribute to Xi Jinping, China's president, during a trade mission to Beijing last year. The message disseminated through Whitehall this week was that he did not want to find himself back on the naughty step. Mr Clegg was left to wonder how it now falls to the Liberal Democrats to defend an agreement signed by Thatcher and ratified by John Major, her Conservative successor ...
>
> I suppose it was possible, if only just, to argue that Mr Cameron's crouch in Beijing was embarrassing, but ultimately inconsequential. Mr Xi's administration has made it clear that it sees Britain as a small power – a "historical relic" as the state-backed media likes to say.
>
> Neutrality over Hong Kong, however, is different. Even if one puts aside the profound moral obligation to the citizens of the formerly British territory, the Joint Declaration imposes a legal duty on the British government. Registered as an international treaty with the UN, it confers responsibility on both signatories. (*Financial Times*, 2014c)

These twin themes of British interest in not offending China in order to gain trading advantages and the moral, and possibly legal, duty entailed by the terms of the handover agreement formed an enduring frame for coverage of the developing crisis. It was also a frame which was echoed in reporting of the views of Hong Kong activists. *The Guardian* of 1 October 2014 reported that Martin Lee had accused "David Cameron of selling out activists in the territory 'for 30 pieces of silver,'" and said that the British prime minister has not been strong enough in his criticism of Beijing's response to the crackdown on protesters" (*Guardian*, 2014c).

This frame came to a head when the Chinese government refused a delegation from the House of Commons entry in to Hong Kong. The delegation from the Foreign Affairs Committee proposed to travel to Hong Kong to meet with the government and with leaders of Occupy Central. Reports gave prominence to the statements of the chair of the Committee, Conservative MP Peter Ottaway, that China was breaching the terms of the Joint Declaration and that the UK had a legal duty to observe the implementation of the measures it contained. *The Financial Times* also quoted the government minister responsible for Hong Kong affairs, Hugo Swire (a member of *that* Swire family), to the effect that "'As a cosignatory, the United Kingdom has both a legal obligation and a moral duty to see it is upheld' (3 December 2015). It went on to report that "Beijing is showing no signs of backing down. Speaking before the debate began Hua Chunying, a spokesman for the Chinese foreign ministry, said: 'If some people from the UK want to continue to nag, it is irrational and useless. They will only end up crushing their own foot while trying to throw a rock'" (*Financial Times*, 2014d).

Overall, the coverage reported the political argument in the UK over the special historical responsibilities of the former colonial power, and noted with disapproval that the government placed a higher value on trading relationships with China than on either democracy in Hong Kong or its commitments under international law.

The balance and tone of coverage

A major question that arises from the evident sense in the government and elite press that the UK has some sort of responsibility to Hong Kong, albeit one that it lacks any power to enforce against the wishes of China, is whether this perception influenced press coverage. It is certainly true that Beijing's case was given a reasonably fair hearing: *The Financial Times*, for example, ran an article by the Chinese Ambassador, Liu Xiaoming on 9 of July 2014, where he set out in detail the reasons for his country's stance and defended it in terms of international standards (*Financial Times*, 2014e). Pro-Beijing commentator Martin Jacques was allowed 1200 words in *The Guardian* on 1 October to set the Occupy movement in the context of recent Hong Kong history and argue that its fundamental motivation was that:

> Understandably, many Hong Kong Chinese are struggling to come to terms with these new realities. They are experiencing a crisis of identity and a sense of displacement. They know their future is inextricably bound up with China but that is very different from embracing the fact. Yet there is no alternative: China is the future of Hong Kong. (*The Guardian*, 2014d)

Hong Kong politicians were also frequently quoted making the case against Occupy Central. *The Financial Times* ran a story on 16 August 2014 that detailed C. Y. Leung's opposition to the movement and recorded some of the support he had obtained from local businesses (*Financial Times*, 2014f). Similarly, Beijing's allegation that the protests had been stirred up by foreign governments was frequently mentioned, although the complete absence of any evidence for this meant that it could not be discussed in detail and was treated in a very dismissive fashion. For example, *The Daily Telegraph* on 1 October 2014 reported that the issue had been raised on Russian television and quoting allegations by *Wen Wei Po* that Joshua Wong, a leader of the school student's movement *Scholarism*, had a close relationship with the US government (*Daily Telegraph*, 2014).

A more difficult question is the tone of the reporting of conflicts between demonstrators and the police, particularly those on the night of 28 September 2014. As we have seen, the events during these few days were the source of most of the coverage in the UK press, and this is in accord with the well-established tendency to concentrate reporting on dramatic, and particularly violent, events. *The Daily Express's* article on Occupy Central, a 124-word piece headlined "Freedom riot in Hong Kong" published on 29 September (*Daily Express*, 2014), is a good example of this, as was *The Daily Mail's* article, a 592-word piece headlined "100,000 protesters paralyze Hong Kong: banks shut after worst violence since handover," published on 30 September (*Daily Mail*, 2014).

While only reporting on the most dramatic incidents is hardly surprising for these semi-tabloid newspapers, the tone of their coverage was more remarkable. *The Daily Express* reported that "riot squads in gas masks fired tear gas and pepper spray and baton charged demonstrators" and *The Daily Mail* noted that "Defiant residents joined activists on the streets to express anger at the use of baton charges and tear gas by riot police during clashes with students at the weekend," although in fairness it should be noted that the latter also reported that "Police said they were forced to respond after protesters charged barricades, adding that 12 officers were among the injured." *The Daily Mirror*, for its part, began a report on 30 September with the line "Thousands of brolly-wielding demonstrators defied brutal riot police to continue their pro-democracy protest" (*Daily Mirror*, 2014a). On 1 October 2014, it continued in the same vein with the headline "Riot police poised to smash peaceful democracy demo" (*Daily Mirror*, 2014b).

The elite press reported these events in a similar way. *The Guardian*'s report on 29 September (*The Guardian*, 2014e) began with "Hong Kong police fired teargas grenades and launched baton charges as tens of thousands of protesters brought a central area of the city to a standstill last night." *The Times* on the same date began with an almost identical sentence, writing "Hong Kong police fired tear gas yesterday to quell one of the biggest prodemocracy protests in the former British colony as an estimated 80,000 people demanding a free vote brought the city's financial district to a standstill" (*Times*, 2014a), and on the next day it referred to "brave protesters" facing down Beijing who "were not scared away by tear gas or the threat that the Chinese army would be deployed to clear the streets" (*Times*, 2014b).

From a discursive point of view, these reports are both interesting and revealing in that, in what might be argued to be a rather unusual fashion for the UK media, the agency of violence is generally represented as the police. It was the police who used "baton charges" and "fired tear gas" and were "poised to smash" the demonstrators. The latter, on the other hand, are portrayed as "brave" and "peaceful" crowds who "brought the city's financial district to a standstill" and expressed "anger" at the police. The claim that the demonstrators used any form of violence is not reported as an independently witnessed fact but as an opinion attributed to the police. This tendency to represent the protestors as the victims of police action, and potentially as victims of another Tiananmen-style massacre by the PLA, is evidence of a framing of the Occupy movement in terms of legitimate opposition to an oppressive situation.

This interpretation is reinforced by the attention given to the self-organization of the protesters. The extent to which the occupations were orderly, well run and supplied by the voluntary efforts of ordinary Hong Kongers was repeatedly noted in reports. The establishment and maintenance of the three protest sites and their persistence in the face of attacks from organized thugs were all positively reported, sometimes at considerable length. *The Guardian*, for example, wrote on 30 September 2014 about:

> A cluster of young women in smart office clothes, clutching bulging plastic bags, appeared to be on a post-work shopping spree. But they stopped at a hardware store to buy goggles in case of a teargas attack. They were not the only ones. The hardware store sold dozens of pairs of goggles in just 15 minutes.
>
> The marketing employees, who had bags full of crackers, plastic ponchos and water for protesters, had not planned to become involved, but said they felt they had to support them after seeing the scenes of billowing teargas on television. "Not everyone goes to the frontline. They need people to support them with resources," said Helen Ng. (*Guardian*, 2014f)

The Independent took as similar line, publishing a long article on 2 October 2014 which discussed the high level of organization, the complete absence of litter, the politeness of the occupiers, and their readiness to engage in friendly discussion about the movement. "Despite more than four days of continuous occupation by tens of thousands," it reported, "you could just about eat your chow mein off the tarmac:

volunteer rubbish collectors with black sacks patrolled constantly" (*Independent*, 2014a)

The evidence suggests very strongly that the reporting in the UK press was cast within a frame that saw the movement as a legitimate one which took to the streets in protest at unreasonable restrictions on their democratic rights by an authoritarian government both in Hong Kong and Beijing. In terms of both the lexical choices and transitivity, the reporting was marked by a pattern that attributed violence to the police and thugs rather than to demonstrators. The crowds were young people, at first mostly students but later joined by many other ordinary people, who were well-organized, determined, and above all peaceful in the face of violence from the police and thugs and the perceived threat of bloody suppression by the PLA.

Newspapers and business interests

This sense that the fundamental frame employed by the UK national press was pro-democracy and pro-Occupy is reinforced by their handling of the support given to Beijing and the Hong Kong government by local and international capitalism. The advertisement against Occupy placed by the "Big Four" accountancy firms was reported, but so too were the protests by Amnesty International and others. *The Independent* of 2 July 2014 quoted Richard Murphy, founder of the Tax Justice Network, who said: "These companies have shown by placing these adverts the world they live in – one in which protest is seen as a threat to business. In the meantime, their work continues to reduce the tax income of democratic governments" (*Independent*, 2014b) *The Financial Times* reported the advertisement, but also ran a reader's letter sharply critical of the action, while its associate editor, Michael Skapinker, commented at length on 10 July 2014 as to what is properly meant by the phrase "the rule of law" and criticized the firms sharply for putting their business relations with Beijing before those of democracy:

> The Hong Kong Big Four have every right to be alarmed if people plan to invade premises and disrupt business. That is a crime in any society. But if that were their concern, they should have combined it with a recognition that people do have the right to protest peacefully, as tens of thousands did in Hong Kong last week.
>
> They should also have supported the independence of the judiciary as a cornerstone of citizens' and companies' security. But while they talked about a "law-based society" and called on people to "follow the law", they had nothing to say, in their advertisement, about how law is made and judged.
>
> It may be that they have accepted that China plans to exert greater control and that they would like to retain Beijing's favour.
>
> There are businesses in other parts of the world that make the same deal, that accept the protection of a government's strong arm in return for the chance to make money without disturbance.
>
> That is fine when things go well. Businesses need to think how they would fare if they did not. In China, GlaxoSmithKline officials have been accused of corruption. Hong Kong business leaders who wish Lord Patten and the democracy campaigners would pipe down should ask themselves this: if something similar happened to them, who would they prefer to appear before – China's judges or Hong Kong's? (*Financial Times*, 2014g)

A similar hostile attitude towards collaboration between big business and the Chinese government was expressed over the publication of a report by HSBC that linked its downgrading of the outlook for Hong Kong stocks to the rise of Occupy Central and its subsequent revision in the face of criticism. *The Financial Times* headlined its report on 8 July 2014: "HSBC Hong Kong report altered to downgrade democracy group fears" (*Financial Times*, 2014h). On the same day it published a critical, albeit satirical, comment by City Editor Jonathan Guthrie on the turnaround (*Financial Times*, 2014i), and four days later they detailed the back-down by HSBC, linking it both to the accountancy firms' advertisement and to earlier reports that the bank had refused to advertise in the pro-democracy Hong Kong paper *Apple Daily* (*Financial Times*, 2014j). *The Times* of 9 July 2014 published a similar report, linking the decision with wider opposition to the Occupy movement on the part of businesses: "Tycoons, financiers and other members of Hong Kong's elite fear that the movement's civil disobedience activities could so infuriate China's leaders that the territory might be punished in a way that would cause growth to sputter" (*Times*, 2014c)

Given that these newspapers, and *The Financial Times* in particular, are in general the reverse of hostile to big business, this sharply negative coverage of the actions of some of the most prominent international companies active in Hong Kong requires further comment. In the first place, the evident and open collaboration of both local and international capitalists with Beijing and the Hong Kong government is at least part of the reason why it was relatively difficult to fall back upon the staple anti-communist framework that has marked UK press coverage of China in the past. Secondly, the close relations between large media corporations and other big businesses does not necessarily imply that the former will applaud every decision taken by every company all of the time. One of the functions of elite newspapers, particularly a newspaper like *The Financial Time*, is to provide a strategic perspective for businesses as whole, and it is quite possible for them to argue that, in this or that case, particular businesses are pursuing an incorrect strategy that may damage either themselves or the general climate for business. We should also, in charity, accept that, in most cases at least, the journalistic staff in question, who have spent all or most of their lives in a relatively comfortable environment where business and democracy are thought to be reasonably compatible, have internalized a commitment to the democratic political system which is reflected in their coverage.

These latter points, about the importance of distinguishing between a pro-business general outlook one the one hand and a positive view of any particular business on the other, not to mention the personal beliefs of an individual journalist, are well illustrated by the recent furore over the very public resignation of the former chief political correspondent of *The Daily Telegraph*, Peter Oborne, which happens to relate to the issue of UK press coverage of the democracy movement in Hong Kong. In a long article published on Opendemocracy.net on 17 January 2015, he claims that his former employer has systematically downplayed coverage of HSBC in order to win back advertising which the company had withdrawn as a result of critical reporting of its activities (Oborne, 2015). Specifically with regard to his paper's coverage of the Occupy movement, he wrote:

> The paper's comment on last year's protests in Hong Kong was bizarre. One would have expected the Telegraph of all papers to have taken a keen interest and adopted a robust position. Yet (in sharp contrast to competitors like the Times) I could not find a single leader on the subject.

At the start of December the Financial Times, the Times and the Guardian all wrote powerful leaders on the refusal by the Chinese government to allow a committee of British MPs into Hong Kong. The Telegraph remained silent. I can think of few subjects which anger and concern Telegraph readers more.

On 15 September the Telegraph published a commentary by the Chinese ambassador, just before the lucrative China Watch supplement. The headline of the ambassador's article was beyond parody: "Let's not allow Hong Kong to come between us".

There is certainly some evidence for this charge. None of the articles published in this newspaper during the period mentions HSBC, despite the prominence of its activities in Hong Kong in other quality papers. It is harder to establish the other points in his article. The commentary by Ambassador Liu Xiaoming does not refer to Occupy Central, and thus was not included in this analysis, but while one might wish to reject its arguments, it is not substantially any different from the article by same author in *The Financial Times*. It does not, therefore, constitute evidence of slipping editorial standards, since any editor could reasonably argue that, since the fate of Hong Kong will be determined by China, the remarks of its ambassador represents an important view which should, in the interests of balance, be made available to readers. The paid editorial content of the 'China Watch' supplement is another matter, but the production of such material either for direct payment or in search of advertising revenue, however undesirable, is neither a new journalistic practice nor unique to *The Daily Telegraph*. The newspaper did cover (on 1 December 2014), even if it did not editorially comment upon, China's refusal to allow the UK Parliamentary Group to enter Hong Kong. *The Daily Telegraph* did not, on the figures presented in Table 2, devote substantially less coverage to Hong Kong than did *The Times*, although whether that amount of coverage is adequate is an entirely subjective question. Whether Hong Kong was a cause of "anger and concern" to the paper's readers is impossible to say, although since Oborne's rather Trollopian idea of who those people are is "country solicitors, struggling small businessmen, harassed second secretaries in foreign embassies, schoolteachers, military folk, farmers", one has grounds for wondering whether his vision of the world is entirely in line with the realities of contemporary Britain.

Whatever the truth of Oborne's allegations, and they have been vigorously denied by *The Daily Telegraph*, it is the fact that they are so unusual that is interesting. Senior journalists resigning their lucrative posts on issues of principle are not everyday events and informed insiders denouncing the role of this or that advertiser are equally rare. It may be that in the straitened business circumstances of newspapers, faced with the flight of their advertising staple to the Internet, they will become more and more open to such pressures, but at the moment all that we can reliably claim is that while there is ample evidence for the integration of the newspaper press in to the capitalist system as a whole, they are relatively independent of this or that company, however large. The evidence from UK press coverage of the Occupy movement tends to support this view.

Conclusions

Overall, the findings of this article confirm a number of well-established observations about the nature of foreign news. Coverage of the Occupy movement tended to focus on major, dramatic, and confrontational events. The character of the coverage was given a strong "national" flavour through the frequent recurrence of reports and discussions of the history of British rule in Hong Kong, the agreement which facilitated its return to China, the capitulation of the British government to Chinese economic pressure, and the general inability of the UK actually to exercise what were seen as its moral and legal duties. News about Hong Kong is particularly easy to "'domesticate" because of this legacy from the imperial past.

In the narrower context of the UK press, the findings reproduced those of earlier investigations which demonstrated that Chinese news only finds extensive coverage in the quality press, and thus is only available to a relatively small number of elite readers. The large majority of the UK population either do not read newspapers or read titles that, at the most, give extremely cursory coverage even to relatively dramatic stories from China. Within the elite press, one could make a further distinction and argue that *The Financial Times* and, perhaps, *The Guardian* are the only titles in which there is any attempt to provide systematic and analytic coverage of the issues involved. Put crudely: if one wishes to learn about China through reading the UK press, then only these two titles come anywhere near close to providing the necessary coverage. Interestingly, although UK newspapers are notoriously partisan in their handling of domestic affairs, there is no evidence of a party political bias in their reporting of Occupy Central.

The main frame within which the coverage was cast was that of a struggle between democrats, seen predominantly as youthful, and the anti-democratic government, nationally in Beijing and locally in Hong Kong. Perhaps surprisingly, the struggle was not framed in terms of a conflict between democracy and communism: the fact that the ruling party in China calls itself the Communist Party meant that this category was frequently deployed, but it was not used to suggest any form of systemic opposition between the two forces. Coverage of the major events tended to frame the protestors as the actual victims of violence by the Hong Kong police and as potential victims of violence by the PLA. The actions of the protesters were generally reported in neutral or positive terms. Taken together, these factors suggest that the UK press framed the movement in generally positive terms and cast the authorities in a negative and repressive light. Whether this framing constitutes something that could be termed "bias" is another, and much more subjective, question upon which judgements will inevitably differ.

One distinctive feature of the conflict allows us to reflect on a general question about the social role of the media and to relate it to a topical issue in the UK. The Occupy movement might be characterized in practice as student-led, but attracting support from large numbers of ordinary Hong Kong residents, particularly in Mong Kok. Its most prominent elite backers were the three original leaders, who were marginalized in the course of the development of the movement, and Jimmy Lai. Ranged against it were the Beijing Communist Party government, the predominantly very wealthy local governing class, pro-Beijing organizations with some popular following, a majority of local businesses, the leaders of assorted transport companies, triad gangsters, and very large international firms like HSBC. These constellations meant that it was impossible to frame the issue in terms of "communism" versus "capitalism" or even "communism" versus "democracy". By adopting a "pro-democracy" frame, the UK media were positioning themselves critically with regard both to the Communist Party and to those capitalists who offered them aid and succour in one way or another. This was reflected in the sharp criticisms made of

HSBC and Big Four accountancy firms when they came out publically with statements and advertisements that sided with the anti-democratic forces.

All of the newspapers in question except *The Guardian* are owned by large corporations. *The Guardian* is owned by a limited company called The Scott Trust whose "core purpose" is "to secure the financial and editorial independence of the Guardian in perpetuity" but which is obliged to operate in the same way as any other corporation in order to survive (Scott Trust, 2015). These newspapers are primarily run as businesses rather than as the expression of the views of rich individuals or political organizations, and they and their senior journalists are thoroughly integrated in to the political and economic elite of the UK. This form of integration into capitalism does not imply that newspapers are unable to criticize particular businesses. Their main source of revenue is, still today, from advertising, and that comes from a large number of different companies. Other things being equal, their senior staff see their responsibilities as being to the system as a whole rather than to any particular constituent element of the system, and thus an individual company, or individual politician, can be subjected to criticism if their activities are seen as damaging overall.

Peter Oborne's (2015) criticisms of *The Daily Telegraph*, however one judges them, do not contradict this general point. His claim is, in substance, that other things are no longer equal. Financial difficulties have made this newspaper particularly sensitive to the attitudes of a major client and, when their journalism was seen to have led to the withdrawal of significant advertising, he claims that they moderated their coverage in an attempt to win back the business. The evidence available for this article is inconclusive with regard to *The Daily Telegraph*, and there is no evidence that any of the other newspapers moderated their reporting of major companies for these sorts of reasons. To the extent that Oborne's claims turn out to be well-founded, they are a symptom of a possible future in which newspapers are more dependent upon single businesses, either as advertisers or as struggling corporations, than they are at the moment.

In sum, the coverage of the Occupy movement in the UK press contains much interesting material but few surprises. Most, if not all, of the findings reported here can be accommodated within established theories of the media without too much modification. There is, perhaps, a hint that a central tenet concerning business influence will need to be revised, but any necessary revision is still a task for the future.

Disclosure statement

No potential conflict of interest was reported by the author.

Notes

1. *Factiva*, Dow Jones. https://global-factiva-com.lib-ezproxy.hkbu.edu.hk/sb/Simple-Search.aspx?NAPC = p. Accessed 3 September 2015.
2. NRS Ltd. *National Readership Survey*. http://www.nrs.co.uk/. Accessed 3 September 2015.

References

Baker, E. (1994). *Advertising and a democratic press*. Princeton, NJ: Princeton University Press.
Curran, J. (2002). Capitalism and control of the press. In J. Curran (Ed.), *Media and power* (pp. 79–103). London: Routledge.
Daily Express. (2014). Freedom riot in Hong Kong, September 29. *The Daily Express*. Retrieved from https://global-factiva-com.lib-ezproxy.hkbu.edu.hk/ha/default.aspx#./!?&_suid=14412663736630636874108808115l
Daily Mail. (2014). 100,000 protestors paralyse Hong Kong; Banks shut after worst violence since handover, September 30. *The Daily Mail*. Retrieved from https://global-factiva-com.lib-ezproxy.hkbu.edu.hk/ha/default.aspx#./!?&_suid=144126308245707829831175040454
Daily Mirror. (2014a). Umbrella revolution, September 30. Retrieved from https://global-factiva-com.lib-ezproxy.hkbu.edu.hk/ha/default.aspx#./!?&_suid=144126353172408439525256399
Daily Mirror. (2014b). Hong Kong on brink as biggest protest looms. Riot police poised to small peaceful democracy demo, October 1. Retrieved from https://global-factiva-com.lib-ezproxy.hkbu.edu.hk/ha/default.aspx#./!?&_suid=14412636512580987160177901387 2
Daily Telegraph. (2014). Demonstrations orchestrated by America and Britain, says Moscow, October 1. Retrieved from https://global-factiva-com.lib-ezproxy.hkbu.edu.hk/ha/default.aspx#./!?&_suid=144126274818301906471080l4673
Entman, R. (2004). *Projections of power: Framing news, public opinion and US foreign policy*. Chicago, IL: University of Chicago Press.
Financial Times. (2014a). Pro-democracy leader held after mass student protest, September 27. Retrieved from https://global-factiva-com.lib-ezproxy.hkbu.edu.hk/ha/default.aspx#./!?&_suid=14412586741610829417207743972 5
Financial Times. (2014b). Patten backs Hong Kong judges against Beijing, July 5. Retrieved from https://global-factiva-com.lib-ezproxy.hkbu.edu.hk/ha/default.aspx#./!?&_suid=144125895381808385816137306392
Financial Times. (2014c). Britain slams the door on Hong Kong's freedoms, July 11. Retrieved from https://global-factiva-com.lib-ezproxy.hkbu.edu.hk/ha/default.aspx#./!?&_suid=144125922078305154355985578l5
Financial Times. (2014d). MPs attach China over Hong Kong travel ban: Commons committee, December 3. Retrieved from https://global-factiva-com.lib-ezproxy.hkbu.edu.hk/ha/default.aspx#./!?&_suid=144125948220508388792688492686
Financial Times. (2014e). Reform in Hong Kong must follow the Basic Law, July 11. Retrieved from https://global-factiva-com.lib-ezproxy.hkbu.edu.hk/ha/default.aspx#./!?&_suid=144125967316902707798974588513 4
Financial Times. (2014f). HK chief opposed Occupy Central campaign. (2014, August 16). *The Financial Times*. Retrieved from https://global-factiva-com.lib-ezproxy.hkbu.edu.hk/ha/default.aspx#./!?&_suid=144125985333808438240780960768
Financial Times. (2014g). Hong Kong Big Four get rule of law wrong, July 10. Retrieved from https://global-factiva-com.lib-ezproxy.hkbu.edu.hk/ha/default.aspx#./!?&_suid=144126002538100442293398082256 3
Financial Times. (2014h). HSBC Hong Kong report altered to downgrade democracy group fears, July 8. Retrieved from https://global-factiva-com.lib-ezproxy.hkbu.edu.hk/ha/default.aspx#./!?&_suid=144126020722700632196692749857 9

Financial Times. (2014i). HSBC's HK sell note raises red flags over political bias, July 8. Retrieved from https://global-factiva-com.lib-ezproxy.hkbu.edu.hk/ha/default.aspx#./!?&_suid = 14412602072270063219669 27498579

Financial Times. (2014j). HSBC modifies tone on Hong Kong downgrade: Banks, July 12. Retrieved from https://global-factiva-com.lib-ezproxy.hkbu.edu.hk/ha/default.aspx#./!?&_suid = 14412604968560776004972 4020064

Fowler, R. (1991). *Language in the news: Discourse and ideology in the press*. London: Routledge.

Galtung, J., & Ruge, M. (1965). The structure of foreign news. *Journal of Peace Research, 2*(1), 64–91.

Guardian. (2014a). Occupy protest threatened in downtown Hong Kong: Democracy campaigners put occupation plan to test: Beijing signals disapproval of western-style system, March 7. Retrieved from https://global-factiva-com.lib-ezproxy.hkbu.edu.hk/ha/default.aspx#./!?&_suid = 14412611226460750639942009002

Guardian. (2014b). Comment: A great power we can't trust: As democracy protests in Hong Kong gain strength, China must honour its commitment to liberty, July 2. Retrieved from https://global-factiva-com.lib-ezproxy.hkbu.edu.hk/ha/default.aspx#./!?&_suid = 14412613648330527224803 8090765

Guardian. (2014c). Cameron has failed to back us, says Hong Kong democracy campaigner: Thousands of protesters pack city's down area. Demonstrators give chief deadline to change rules, October 1. Retrieved from https://global-factiva-com.lib-ezproxy.hkbu.edu.hk/ha/default.aspx#./!?&_suid = 14412614831330501369378 2966584

Guardian. (2014d). China is Hong Kong's future - not its enemy Martin Jacques: Protestors cry democracy but most are driven by dislocation and resentment at mainlander's success. (2014, October 1). *The Guardian*. Retrieved from https://global-factiva-com.lib-ezproxy.hkbu.edu.hk/ha/default.aspx#./!?&_suid = 14412617034680427784195 4026371

Guardian. (2014e). Hong Kong at a standstill as thousands of pro-democracy protesters flood streets: Police charge with batons and fire teargas grenades. Activists rally against plan to limit electoral changes, September 29. Retrieved from https://global-factiva-com.lib-ezproxy.hkbu.edu.hk/ha/default.aspx#./!?&_suid = 14412618659700863453057 5945973

Guardian. (2014f). Protests swell for "umbrella revolution" in Hong Kong: Protests swell for "umbrella revolution. (2014, September 30). *The Guardian*. Retrieved from https://global-factiva-com.lib-ezproxy.hkbu.edu.hk/ha/default.aspx#./!?&_suid = 1441262099721016438239021226764

Hamilton, J. (2004). *All the news that's fit to sell*. Princeton, NJ: Princeton University Press.

Harcup, T., & O'Neil, D. (2001). What is new? Galtung and Ruge revisited. *Journalism Studies, 2*(2), 261–280.

Herman, E., & Chomsky, N. (2008). *Manufacturing consent: The political economy of the mass media* (2nd ed.). London: Bodley Head.

Independent. (2014a). 'This is the opposite of looting. They are giving stuff away', October 2. Retrieved from https://global-factiva-com.lib-ezproxy.hkbu.edu.hk/ha/default.aspx#./!?&_suid = 14412638996370390055657 36442804

Independent. (2014b). 'Big Four' audit firms under fire for opposing Hong Kong democracy, July 2. Retrieved from https://global-factiva-com.lib-ezproxy.hkbu.edu.hk/ha/default.aspx#./!?&_suid = 14412640197570351088349 70742464

Joye, S. (2010). News media and the (de)construction of risk: How Flemish newspaper select and cover international disasters. *Catalan Journal of Communication, 2*(2), 253–266.

Nossek, H. (2004). Our news and their news: The role of national identity in the coverage of foreign news. *Journalism, 5*(3), 343–368.

Oborne, P. (2015). Why I have resigned from the Telegraph. Retrieved from https://www.opendemocracy.net/ourkingdom/peter-oborne/why-i-have-resigned-from-telegraph

Picard, R., & Brody, J. (1997). *The newspaper publishing industry*. Needham Heights, MA: Allyn & Bacon.
Richardson, J. (2007). *Analysing newspapers: An approach from critical discours analysis*. Basingstoke: Palgrave Macmillan.
Scott Trust. (2015). *The Purpose of the Scott Trust*. Retrieved from http://www.theguardian.com/the-scott-trust/2015/jul/23/the-purpose-of-the-scott-trust
Sparks, C. (2010). Coverage of China in the UK national press. *Chinese Journal of Communication, 3*(3), 337–352.
Times. (2014a). Hong Kong rises up as tens of thousands take on Beijing, September 29. Retrieved from https://global-factiva-com.lib-ezproxy.hkbu.edu.hk/ha/default.aspx#./!?&_suid=144126428858809453821068163961
Times. (2014b). Red Alert, September 30. Retrieved from https://global-factiva-com.lib-ezproxy.hkbu.edu.hk/ha/default.aspx#./!?&_suid=14412644449070975912329275161
Times. (2014c). Hong Kong protests force HSBC to change its tune on downgrade, July 9. Retrieved from https://global-factiva-com.lib-ezproxy.hkbu.edu.hk/ha/default.aspx#./!?&_suid=1441264591529017539037275128067
Wilke, J., Heimprecht, C., & Cohen, A. (2012). The geography of foreign news on televsion: A comparative study of 17 countries. *International Communication Gazette, 74*(4), 301–322.

The coming colonization of Hong Kong cyberspace: government responses to the use of new technologies by the umbrella movement

Lokman Tsui

The Chinese University of Hong Kong, Hong Kong

> Governments are increasingly playing catch-up and sometimes even leapfrogging ahead of social movements in the use of digital tactics; government responses to new technologies include surveillance, censorship and demonization of foreign influence. This development has implications for the emancipatory potential of new technologies, in particular for the anonymous, decentralized and autonomous character of the Internet.

On 30 October 2014, Regina Ip, the former secretary of security and current member of the Legislative Council, highlighted the use of smartphone apps, including Twitter, Google Maps, Firechat, Telegram and Zello Walkie Talkie, citing these apps as proof that Occupy Central was a comprehensive campaign aided and supported by foreign powers.[1] A video of this went viral on social media, with people making fun of her, cheekily asking whether she still relied on traditional telegram or pigeons for communication.

Ip's story raises the question: what role did the Internet play in the umbrella movement? Her ominous warning for the powers of new technologies rides on an established narrative of how the common people have been using new and often Western technologies to confront and challenge oppressive regimes. However, the story of the umbrella movement did not quite follow this narrative: yes, the movement was able to leverage new technologies; but no, the movement has yet to achieve its goal, true universal suffrage. This article is an exploration of the emancipatory role of the open Internet in the umbrella movement, with an emphasis on the government's capacity to resist, respond to and counter these new technologies. Its purpose is to analyze, grounded on observation, the changing potential of new technologies for advocacy by social movements.

I argue that the government was able to play catch-up with the social movement: it not only neutralized the various challenges the Internet posed to its authority, but in certain cases was even able to leapfrog the movement in the use of new technologies. This is somewhat surprising. After all, in contrast to the mainland, the Internet in Hong Kong is supposed to be open and free; the government has little to no track record of online censorship. Hong Kong also has two of the highest rates of mobile phone () and household broadband penetration (241.7% and 83.2% respectively) in the world (Office of the Communications Authority [OFCA], 2015). Various scholars have documented how new technologies empower social movements (Castells, 2013; Shirky 2011), offering new forms of connective action (Bennett & Segerberg, 2012) or allowing it to go transnational, broaden its set of allies and tap into new resources (Keck & Sikkink, 1998; Tarrow, 2005).

For this article, I am interested specifically in the government response to the umbrella movement and its use of new technologies. Governments around the world have employed a wide variety of tactics and strategies to control the Internet (Deibert, Zittrain, Palfrey, & Rohinski, 2011; Freedom House, 2014; Goldsmith & Wu, 2006; MacKinnon, 2012; Morozov, 2012). However, research on how governments respond specifically to social movements is relatively sparse. The broader literature on new technologies and social movements can be separated into two camps: the optimists who argue that new technologies are effective for mobilization, coordination and the organization of social movements (Castells, 2013; Shirky, 2011); whereas the pessimists take a more critical or cautionary stance. Some warn us against naive optimism, that technologies might not be as powerful for social movements as we sometimes believe (van Laer & van Aelst, 2010). Others argue that "clicktivism" or "slacktivism" even might be harmful to social movements, because it leads people to erroneously believe that they have made a significant contribution to the movement (Gladwell, 2010; Morozov, 2012). In terms of research that specifically looks at government response, perhaps the most attention has been given to the disconnect or shutdown of the Internet, suggesting that governments have very limited means to respond besides the "nuclear" option of blacking out the entire communication networks (Gohdes, 2015; Howard, 2011). But governments also increasingly realize that the shutdown of the Internet is a crude or even desperate last resort. For example, Tufecki (2014) suggests that governments are starting to adopt a multi-pronged strategy to address the challenges of the online public sphere, including tactics of legal pushback, flooding the online public sphere with paid "trolls", or increasing the cost of accessing what the government deems undesirable information. In addition, King, Pan, and Roberts (2013) argue that the Chinese government relies on a sophisticated combination of technology, human censors, and traditional propaganda to prevent citizens from organizing and coordinating. But while the Chinese government's capacity to regulate and control the Internet is well documented, we have barely started to understand how it extends this regime of control to Hong Kong, which lies outside the Great Firewall and has a separate legal jurisdiction. Thus, an exploration of the attack vectors on the Internet during the umbrella movement might provide pointers for future research into how the Chinese government is looking to extend its battle for "Internet sovereignty" to Hong Kong or even the global stage.

The use of new technologies by the umbrella movement

The Internet offered the movement an alternative channel for public communication, it helped them evade censorship, and it was instrumental in assisting them with group formation, coordination, and mobilization. In this regard, the story of the umbrella movement follows a fairly typical script of the use of new technologies by social movements.

To start with, the Internet and social media played an important role in the coordination and organization of protesters. Take, for example, the high level of flexibility and resilience the umbrella movement demonstrated immediately after police attacked the protests with tear gas on 28 September 2014; the movement not only survived the attack, but adapted and split up into three independent but connected Occupy areas, all whilst drawing in more members to its cause. Similar uses of new technologies in crisis response have been documented elsewhere (Brafman & Beckstrom, 2006; Coyle & Meier, 2009). The umbrella movement not only relied on the Internet for coordination or organization, but also to mobilize larger groups of people by lowering the cost of participation, widening the range of contentious activities, and allowing the movement to go transnational. Consider the "Add Oil" machine: an on-site installation that projected a giant-sized message board on a wall at the center of the Occupy site; anyone around the world could submit a message and show support for the protesters. The Add Oil machine is eye-catching and a good example of using technology to mobilize people and to widen the range of contentious activities; it was particularly useful for people from around the world who were unable to physically participate but still wanted to support the movement, including supporters from mainland China, who had to "jump" the great firewall to do so.

In addition, the movement made use of the Internet as a critical channel for communication with the public. For example, Glacier Kwong, a student at the University of Hong Kong, uploaded a video on YouTube on 28 September 2014, in which she pleaded to the world to pay attention to what was happening in Hong Kong. This video was widely watched and received over a million views. Social media in general play an important role for people in Hong Kong: the overwhelming majority of people in Hong Kong (91%) use Facebook (Lam, 2014) and rely on it for political news, especially so during the movement (Lee, 2014).

Government responses to the use of new technologies by the umbrella movement

Even though Hong Kong enjoys a wide diffusion of social media, a high penetration of mobile phones, broadband, and a largely open Internet, I argue that the government has been able to effectively respond to and defend itself against the umbrella movement's use of new technologies; in certain cases the government was even able to go on the offensive using these digital tactics against the movement. Its response is based on a mix of surveillance, censorship, and the demonization of foreign influence.

Surveillance

The government increasingly has been turning to surveillance to counter and control the umbrella movement. Physical surveillance of key people in the movement has been on the rise (Lague, Torode & Pomfret, 2014), but online surveillance is not far behind. Perhaps not surprisingly, emails of Occupy leader Benny Tai have been hacked and leaked to the press. In Hong Kong, it appears that online communication has less legal protection than communication via telephone, fax, or postal mail, thanks to serious loopholes in the legal framework that regulates surveillance, the Interceptions for Communications and Surveillance Ordinance (ICSO).[2] According to ICSO, if law enforcement wants to wiretap citizens using telephone, fax, or postal mail, they need to prove to a judge reasonable suspicion of the target and the necessity of wiretapping to prevent or detect serious crimes or protect public security.

In practice, the review process resembles a rubber stamp process: of the total of 1372 written applications for interception made in 2013, only seven applications were rejected (The Commissioner on Interception of Communications and Surveillance, 2014). ICSO covers telephone, fax, and postal mail only, but not online communications. Asked on several occasions, the government has refused to confirm whether ICSO covers email and chat applications such as WhatsApp (Global Voices Advocacy, 2015; Hong Kong Government Press Release, 2015).

In addition to ICSO, law enforcement is increasingly relying on another regulation to arrest citizens, Crimes Ordinance section 161.[3] Originally designed to combat crimes like online fraud, Section 161 allows law enforcement to arrest citizens on the basis of "access to computer with criminal or dishonest intent". One of the more problematic arrests made under Section 161 includes charging a 23-year-old from Mongkok with "access to computer with criminal or dishonest intent" and "unlawful assembly" for allegedly messaging folks on an online discussion forum to join him in a protest in Mongkok. The overly broad scope of Section 161 has led to criticism from Legislative Council member Charles Mok, calling it a "catch-all cyber law [that] threatens Hong Kong's freedom of speech" (Mok, 2014) and from Andrew Raffell, a barrister and consultant at the law faculty of Chinese University of Hong Kong, stating that "the police and the prosecution have been allowed to artificially extend to the point of distortion the law" (Zhang, 2014).

Censorship

In addition to surveillance, censorship is also on the rise, especially self-censorship. Consider how TVB, the major public television channel in Hong Kong, broke the news in the early hours of 15 October 2014, showing a video of seven cops dragging a protester into a dark corner, proceeding to punch and kick him while he was on the ground. However, by mid-morning, TVB senior management intervened and demanded the removal of the commentary that the "protester was punched and kicked"; in their explanation, a "necessary" edit because of the "subjective nature" of the words. In response, more than 140 TVB employees signed a public letter to senior management to protest their editorial decision (Levin & Lee, 2014). It is important to note that the public knows about this news story not only because of the fortunate timing of when it broke, but also because social media kept it alive once it was published. Unfortunately, this story of self-censorship is not an outlier: traditional press freedom has been on a dramatic decline in the past several years (Hong Kong Journalists Association [HKJA], 2014; PEN America, 2015). Hong Kong occupies the 70th place in a ranking of 180 countries in the Reporters Without Borders Press Freedom Index, down from the 61st place in 2013.[4] It is sobering to note that Hong Kong used to occupy the 18th place in 2002 (Reporters Without Borders 2002).

The decline of press freedom not only further highlights the important role of the Internet, but also underscores the necessity of not taking the Internet for granted, to pay attention to how the government is seeking to control and regulate online speech. It is why it is worrying that law enforcement has significantly stepped up its efforts to remove and delete content online: the number of requests for content removal in the four months of October 2014 until February 2015 exceeds the number of requests made in the previous four years combined (Harris, 2015). But law is not the only means to regulate speech; technology continues to play a critical role as well.

Take, for example, the distributed denial of service (DDoS) attack, a digital variation on the classic sit-in; the idea is to make a website inaccessible by having large numbers of people visit at the same time (Coleman, 2014; Sauter, 2013). For example, the activist group Anonymous announced a DDoS attack on several pro-government websites, rendering them inaccessible for short moments of time (Blum, 2014). But is the DDoS effective as a tactic, and how do governments respond to it? I argue that DDoS is a prime example of a digital tactic where the pro-government side has not only caught up, but is able to use new technologies more effectively than the social movement. The pro-government side was able to hit a series of critical websites with an unprecedented amount of junk traffic (500 Gigabytes per second), including the website of the *Apple Daily*, a pro-democracy newspaper in Hong Kong, and PopVote, Hong Kong University's online voting platform, leading Matthew Prince, the CEO of a hosting company that specializes in DDoS protection, to call it the "largest cyber attack in history" (Olson, 2014). The objective of these attacks is twofold: to bring the website down at a critical time, such as during the announced referendum in the case of the online voting platform, or simply to raise the cost of maintaining the website, a cost that is often significant for otherwise already marginal and under-resourced civil society organizations. Last but not least, the Internet might lower the cost of participation, allowing more people to join or support the movement, but this does not mean the movement has a natural advantage over the government. Similar to the DDoS tactic, the government can bring overwhelming resources to bear to respond to and counter the movement. Governments elsewhere have been known to flood the online space using "paid trolls" (Tufecki, 2014). Perhaps not surprisingly, signs of the "50 cents army" have also been appearing in Hong Kong cyberspace, so called because of the 50 cents people get paid to post a pro-government message, and a tried and trusted tactic of the Chinese government (Sterbenz, 2014; Wang, 2010).

Demonization of foreign influence

In the opening to this article, I mention how Regina Ip is admonishing her colleagues for the dangers of Western new technologies. The story suggests that the government understood very well that new technologies can play a powerful role in enabling a social movement to take its activism transnational, allowing it to broaden its set of allies and tap into new resources (Keck & Sikkink, 1998; Tarrow, 2005). The government countered this threat by pushing a narrative of "foreign interference", a xenophobic narrative that accuses civil society organizations of being inauthentic, that they are being used and funded by foreign governments, especially the United States government, who seek to undermine and weaken China by fomenting revolution in the name of "democracy". This is a typical play by Beijing; more surprising is how readily and how far Hong Kong, that bills itself "Asia's world city", was willing to go along with this narrative, at the risk of losing credibility with the international community. Even Chief Executive Leung, Hong Kong's top government official, gave it his stamp of approval: "there is obviously participation by people, organizations from outside of Hong Kong". He promised to disclose conclusive evidence of "foreign influence", although despite repeated prompting, he has so far failed to do so (So, 2015).

At this point, it is useful to clarify the use of the term "the government" in this article. Under "One Country, Two Systems", the Basic Law promises and guarantees

Hong Kong citizens a "high level of autonomy", raising the questions of where this autonomy ends and of when Beijing can step in and take over. On top of this, the anonymous character of the Internet further complicates the problem of defining "the government". For example, take the DDoS attacks: it is hard to say who was directly responsible for this, although this does not mean it is impossible to say anything about these attacks (Healey, 2012). While it is impossible to make direct attribution, or even to say that the Hong Kong government encouraged or supported these attacks, is it possible to argue that the Hong Kong government allowed or tolerated them? If it turns out that the attacks were state sponsored by Beijing, which many believe is the case, what actions, if any, would the Hong Kong government pursue? Will the Hong Kong government continue to protect the high level of autonomy of Hong Kong, including the autonomy of its online space?

Conclusion

Hong Kong and the Internet share one similarity: both have been able to thrive because of a relatively high level of autonomy, but in both cases its autonomy is also under threat. Will the Internet in Hong Kong remain a space of autonomy for civil society or will it end up becoming colonized and used as a tool for government surveillance and suppression? Two developments are important to keep in mind. First, the government is learning how to anticipate and respond to the challenges of new technologies and social movements. It can apply preemptive strategies, such as neutering the movement from going transnational; or it can take existing digital tactics and allow them to be used/use them against the movement, such as DDoS attacks. Access to resources, not new technologies, is what makes a critical difference in many of these cases. Second, "the Internet", situated at the nexus between governments and markets, continues to undergo massive structural changes, with serious implications for its emancipatory potential. Much of the research on new technologies and social movements accepts "the Internet" as a constant, as if the Internet we have now is the same Internet from two, five or even ten years ago. A lot of work remains to be done to examine to what extent political economy drives changes in the values that together form the heart and soul of the Internet's emancipatory potential; values such as autonomy, anonymity, and decentralization. In terms of autonomy or decentralization, the Internet has long ceased to be a "sovereign" space where corporations and governments are no longer welcome. Instead, powerful institutions continue to colonize the online space. In the process, the Internet is becoming more centralized, to the extent that millions of people using Facebook have no idea that they are even using the Internet (Mirani, 2015). In terms of its anonymity, one would be naive to assume that participants in social movements or even law-abiding citizens are safe from government surveillance, especially post-Snowden. In general, surveillance technology is improving, governments are willing to invest significant resources in it, and existing laws offer little transparency, accountability, let alone much protection.

The Internet still has the potential to empower social movements; they might even allow temporary gaps of freedom. But the umbrella movement suggests that both the Internet and Hong Kong are at a crossroads, that both cannot take its freedoms for granted. This is not to say that spaces of autonomy and freedom no longer exist online or in Hong Kong; however, they are increasingly being marginalized and, at this point in time, are best understood as the exceptions rather than the norm.

Acknowledgements

I'd like to thank Francis Lee, Jason Li, and Vincent Huang for their helpful suggestions and feedback on this article.

Disclosure statement

No potential conflict of interest was reported by the author.

Notes

1. See video https://www.youtube.com/watch?v = ct9TbXXzFls.
2. Ordinance can be found at http://www.legislation.gov.hk/blis_pdf.nsf/6799165D2FEE3FA94825755E0033E532/DDA393C36B7FE4BA482575EF001FD1A4/$FILE/CAP_589_e_b5.pdf.
3. Ordinance can be found at http://www.legislation.gov.hk/blis_ind.nsf/fb2d3fd8a4e2a3264825647c0030a9e1/aabf383866751ea5c8256483003222823?OpenDocument.
4. See https://index.rsf.org/#!/.

References

Bennett, W. L., & Segerberg, A. (2012). The logic of connective action: Digital media and the personalization of contentious politics. *Information, Communication & Society*, *15*(5), 739–768.

Blum, J. (2014, October 18). 'Anonymous' hacker group declares cyber war on Hong Kong government, police. *South China Morning Post*. Retrieved from http://www.scmp.com/news/hong-kong/article/1607579/anonymous-hacker-group-declares-cyber-war-hong-kong?pageall

Brafman, O., & Beckstrom, R. A. (2006). *The starfish and the spider: The unstoppable power of leaderless organizations*. New York: Penguin.

Castells, M. (2013). *Networks of outrage and hope: Social movements in the Internet age*. Hoboken, NJ: John Wiley.

Coleman, G. (2014). *Hacker, hoaxer, whistleblower, spy: The many faces of Anonymous*. London: Verso.

Commissioner on Interception of Communications and Surveillance. (2014). Annual report 2013 to the chief executive. Retrieved from http://www.info.gov.hk/info/sciocs/eng/pdf/Annual_Report_2013.pdf

Coyle, D., & Meier, P. (2009). *New technologies in emergencies and conflicts: The role of information and social networks*. Washington, DC: UN Foundation-Vodafone Foundation Partnership.

Deibert, R., Zittrain, J. L., Palfrey, J., & Rohozinski, R. (2011). *Access contested: Security, identity, and resistance in Asian cyberspace*. Cambridge, MA: MIT Press.

Freedom House. (2014). Freedom on the Net 2014. Retrieved from https://freedomhouse.org/report/freedom-net/freedom-net-2014

Gladwell, M. (2010). Small change. *The New Yorker*, *4*(2010), 42–49.

Global Voices Advocacy. (2015). Hong Kong civic groups demand legal protections against mobile app surveillance. Retrieved from https://globalvoicesonline.org/2015/05/04/hong-kong-civic-groups-demand-legal-protections-against-mobile-app-surveillance/

Gohdes, A. R. (2015). Pulling the plug: Network disruptions and violence in the Syrian conflict. *Journal of Peace Research*, *52*(3), 352–367.

Goldsmith, J. L., & Wu, T. (2006). *Who controls the Internet? Illusions of a borderless world*. New York: Oxford University Press.

Harris, B. (2015, February 15). Surge in web posts taken down by Hong Kong police sparks censorship fears. *South China Morning Post*. Retrieved from http://www.scmp.com/news/hong-kong/article/1713551/hong-kong-police-pulled-down-more-web-content-last-four-months?pageall

Healey, J. (2012). Beyond attribution: Seeking national responsibility for cyber attacks. Retrieved from http://www.atlanticcouncil.org/images/files/publication_pdfs/403/022212_ACUS_NatlResponsibilityCyber.PDF

Hong Kong Government Press Release. (2015). LCQ15: Interception of communications and surveillance ordinance. Retrieved from http://www.info.gov.hk/gia/general/201504/29/P201504290534.htm

Hong Kong Journalists Association. (2014). Press freedom under siege: Threats to freedom of expression in Hong Kong. Retrieved from http://www.hkja.org.hk/site/Host/hkja/UserFiles/file/annual_report_2014_Final.pdf

Howard, P. (2011). When do states disconnect their digital networks? Regime responses to the political uses of social media. *The Communication Review*, *14*(3), 216–232.

Keck, M. E., & Sikkink, K. (1998). *Activists beyond borders: Advocacy networks in international politics* (6). Cambridge: Cambridge University Press.

King, G., Pan, J., & Roberts, M. E. (2013). How censorship in China allows government criticism but silences collective expression. *American Political Science Review*, *107*(02), 326–343. Retrieved from http://journalistsresource.org/wp-content/uploads/2012/10/China_KingStudy.pdf

Lague, D., Torode, G., & Pomfret, J. (2014, December 14). Special report: How China spies on Hong Kong's democrats. Reuters. Retrieved from http://www.reuters.com/article/2014/12/15/us-hong-kong-surveillance-special-report-idUSKBN0JT00120141215

Lam, L. (2014, August 22). Facebook is Hong Kong's top digital platform in survey commissioned by company. *South China Morning Post*. Retrieved from http://www.scmp.com/news/hong-kong/article/1578755/facebook-citys-top-digital-platform-survey-commissioned-company

Lee, F. (2014, December 4). An overview of Hong Kong citizens' new media use during the Occupy movement. *Ming Pao*. p. A40. Retrieved from http://news.mingpao.com/pns/%E8%A7%80%E9%BB%9E/web_tc/section/20141204/s00012

Levin, N. A. L., & Lee, Y. (2014, October 22). Hong Kong protests reveal chasm in media outlets' visions for city's future. *The Wall Street Journal*. Retrieved from http://www.wsj.com/articles/hong-kong-protests-expose-differences-in-local-media-1413977464

MacKinnon, R. (2012). *Consent of the networked: the world-wide struggle for Internet freedom*. New York: Basic Books.

McChesney, R. W. (2013). *Digital disconnect: How capitalism is turning the Internet against democracy*. New York: The New Press.

Mirani, L. (2015). Millions of Facebook users have no idea they're using the Internet. *Quartz*. Retrieved from http://qz.com/333313/milliions-of-facebook-users-have-no-idea-theyre-using-the-internet/

Mok, C. (2014). Catch-all cyber law threatens Hong Kong's freedom of speech. Retrieved from http://charlesmok.blogspot.hk/2014/12/catch-all-cyber-law-threatens-hong.html?m1

Morozov, E. (2012). *The net delusion: The dark side of Internet freedom.* New York: Public Affairs.

Office of the Communications Authority (OFCA). (2015). Key communications statistics. Retrieved from http://www.ofca.gov.hk/en/media_focus/data_statistics/key_stat/

Olson, P. (2014). The largest cyber attack in history has been hitting Hong Kong sites. *Forbes.* Retrieved from http://www.forbes.com/sites/parmyolson/2014/11/20/the-largest-cyber-attack-in-history-has-been-hitting-hong-kong-sites/

PEN America. (2015). Threatened harbor: Encroachments on press freedom in Hong Kong. Retrieved from http://www.pen.org/sites/default/files/PEN-HK-report_1.16_lowres.pdf

Reporters Without Border. (2002). Press freedom index 2002. Retrieved from https://en.rsf.org/press-freedom-index-2002,297.html

Sauter, M. (2013). 'LOIC will tear us apart': The impact of tool design and media portrayals in the success of activist DDOS attacks. *American Behavioral Scientist, 57*(7), 983–1007.

Shirky, C. (2011). The political power of social media: Technology, the public sphere, and political change. *Foreign affairs, 90*(1), 28–41.

So, P. (2015, January 14). CY Leung repeats claim of 'external forces' influencing Occupy – but provides no evidence. *South China Morning Post.* Retrieved from http://www.scmp.com/news/hong-kong/article/1679392/cy-leung-reiterates-claim-external-forces-influencing-occupy-provides?pageall

Sterbenz, C. (2014). China hires as many as 300,000 Internet trolls to make the Communist Party look good. Retrieved from http://www.businessinsider.in/China-Hires-As-Many-As-300000-Internet-Trolls-To-Make-The-Communist-Party-Look-Good/articleshow/44859392.cms

Tarrow, S. (2005). *The new transnational activism.* Cambridge: Cambridge University Press.

Tufekci, Z. (2014). Social movements and governments in the digital age: Evaluating a complex landscape. *Journal of International Affairs, 68*(1), 1–18. Retrieved from http://jia.sipa.columbia.edu/social-movements-governments-digital-age-evaluating-complex-landscape/

Van Laer, J., & Van Aelst, P. (2010). Internet and social movement action repertoires: Opportunities and limitations. *Information, Communication & Society, 13*(8), 1146–1171.

Wang, C. (2010). Concerning the development and administration of our country's Internet. Retrieved from http://www.hrichina.org/en/content/3241

Zhang, J. (2014). Police are using Hong Kong's computer crime law to crack down on pro-democracy organizers. *Quartz.* Retrieved from http://qz.com/285998/police-are-using-hong-kongs-computer-crime-law-to-crack-down-on-pro-democracy-organizers/

Yellow or blue ribbons: analysing discourses in conflict in the televized government-student meeting during the Occupy Movement in Hong Kong

Yiqi Liu

The University of Hong Kong, Hong Kong

> In this commentary, the legal discourses in conflict evolving around the 2014 Occupy Movement in Hong Kong are analysed with Lemke's theorization of textual semantics and Goffman's participation framework. Specifically, I analyse the thematic patterns of "democracy" and "rule of law" in the televized meeting between the HKSAR Government officials and the representatives of Hong Kong Federation of Students on constitutional reform on 21 October2014. It is revealed that both sides not only construct dramatically different representation of "democracy" and "rule of law" but also show different orientational stances towards Hong Kong and China. I then propose a more plural understanding of each other and exploration of the other's discourse histories as one strategy and the first step to going beyond binarism on the road of constitutional development in Hong Kong.

In this article, I aim to deconstruct the social and political relations that led to social cleavage during and after the Occupy Movement by mapping out the thematic patterns about the hotly debated notions of "democracy" and "rule of law" as argued by different social communities. Central to our discussion is to find out how what appears to be the common ground (i.e., striving for democracy under the rule of law) led to fierce social controversy and divided the Hong Kong society into radically opposing social groups. To this end, I analyse the televized meeting between the Hong Kong Special Administrative Region (HKSAR) government officials and the representatives of Hong Kong Federation of Students (HKFS) on constitutional reform on 21 October2014 (accessed at https://www.youtube.com/watch?v=Xx9I5E4Ve24).[1] drawing on Lemke's (1995) theorization of text semantics to tease out the major conflicts between the "yellow-ribbons" leaders (i.e., the proponents of the movement) and the "blue-ribbons" (i.e., the opponents of the movement). Excerpts of the meeting related to democracy and the rule of law are chosen as representative data showcasing competing tensions in the movement. My analysis shows essentialist binaries in opinions arise from thematic patterns and value orientations of their discourses, leaving little space for voices of the middle. I then propose a more plural understanding of each other and exploration of the other's discourse histories as one strategy and the first step to go beyond binarism on the road of constitutional development in Hong Kong.

Text semantics and participation framework

How can we understand the meaning of discourses? Based on Lemke's (1995) theorization of text semantics, meaning of texts can be understood in three interrelated dimensions: (i) the presentational meaning or the thematic pattern, which is "the construction of how things are in natural and social world"; (ii) the orientational meaning, i.e., the construction of stances toward the present and the potential addresses and the content of the discourses; and (iii) the organizational meaning, which refers to "the construction of relations between elements of discourse" (p. 41). However, the meaning of interaction is also related to the context of communication, e.g., who speaks to whom under what circumstances. In order to gain a contextualized understanding of the meeting, I will make reference to Goffman's (1981) participation framework or participation structure to understand the roles of students and government officials in the meeting. Specifically, there are three production roles for a speaker, i.e., the animator who speaks others' words in the capacity of a "sounding box" (Goffman, 1981, p. 226), the author who scripts the lines and the principal whose position is established by the utterances, and there are addressed and unaddressed ratified and unratified listeners.

As "rule of law" and "democracy" have been the centre of heated discussion about the Occupy Movement, it is important to analyse its diverse implicit precepts when used by different parties with a view to understanding their ideological divides. My analysis will show the text semantics, i.e., the thematic patterns, the value orientations and how one side internally constructs its heteroglossical relations to the other, and the possible effect of the participation structure. What should be noted, however, is that the larger community of the movement activists and the anti-Occupy Movement citizens may have a very wide range of views in relation to the excerpts presented.

The socio–historical context: Hong Kong's national identity

Before I move on to examine the televized meeting in question, one most relevant dimension of the broader socio–historical context must be outlined in order to situate the discursive conflicts engendered by the constitutional development debate: discourses of Hong Kong's national identity following China's resumption of sovereignty over Hong Kong in 1997. It has been argued by sociolinguists that Hong Kong's national identity has been much influenced by tensions between oppositional cultural traditions and values. For example, Flowerdew (2012) suggests that Hong Kong's political identity is a result of jostling between the utilitarian (Western influenced) and the Confucian public discourses which are typically regarded as Chinese. Ku (2015), in enunciating Hong Kong's postcolonial cultural trends, proceeds to maintain that the discourses about the postcolonial Hong Kong are characterized by hybridity and between-ness, i.e., remaining critical about imperialism/global capitalism as well as Chinese nationalism.

In addition to cultural differences between the East and the West, Hong Kong's national/political identity is also forged by educational policies during the colonial and postcolonial eras. For example, it is considered that Hong Kong's lack of emotional attachment to contemporary China is much ascribed to the Hong Kong secondary curriculum during the colonial rule which deliberately avoided topics related to contemporary China (Deng, 2009; Morris, 1997) and emphasized the virtues of ancient China that were described as unlearned and forgotten in modern China (Morris & Vickers, 2015), resulting in a vague national identity as Luk (1991, p. 668) describes

Thus generations of Hong Kong Chinese pupils grew up, learning from the Chinese culture subjects to identify themselves as Chinese but relating that Chineseness to neither contemporary China nor the local Hong Kong landscape. It was a Chinese identity in the abstract ... because it was not connected to tangible reality.

In reviewing Hong Kong's citizenship education, Lee (2008) and Jackson (2014) summarize the two cultural trends in Hong Kong which may undermine development and implementation of multicultural and intercultural citizenship education in the HKSAR, i.e., delocalized nationalization and localized internationalization. According to Lee (2008) and Jackson (2014), "delocalized nationalization" refers to the approach to citizenship education which deemphasizes local distinction in favour of national commonality and underscores the cultural and ethnic connection with mainland China while "localized internationalization" denotes the process to identify with a global level of citizenship favouring the connection with values and legal/economic systems perceived as more global than mainland Chinese. Jackson (2014) critiques such binary orientations and maintains that identification with one level (i.e., the local, the national, or the global) should not be made at the expense of another in citizenship education in order to foster mutual understanding and mutual recognition in the Hong Kong society. These two notions are relevant in the context of the televized meeting in that the government officials' utterances during the televized talk were homogeneous with the "delocalized nationalization" (Jackson, 2014; Lee, 2008) approach, whereas the student representatives advocated deviation from the political norms in mainland China to cater for Hong Kong local circumstances. Inspired by Lee (2008) and Jackson (2014), I therefore maintain that the government officials embodied "delocalized nationalism". However, as the student representatives did not explicitly refer to the international or Western legal tradition during the televized meeting, I adapt the notion of "localized internationalization" in Lee (2008) and Jackson (2014) and instead suggest that the HKFS representatives embodied "localized isolationism". I will further elaborate these ideas in the next section.

The legal discourses in the televized student–government meeting

At 18:00 on 21 October 2014, the government representatives and the leaders of HKFS met for a two-hour talk to formally discuss constitutional development after the commencement of the Occupy Movement. Specifically, the talk was the first face-to-face meeting between the top government officials and the representatives of student activists to discuss the issues which sparked off the Occupy Movement, and was therefore regarded as a critical juncture of the event. The meeting, mediated by President Leonard K Cheng of Lingnan University, was attended by five top government officials, i.e., Chief Secretary for Administration Carrie Lam, Director of the Chief Executive's Office Edward Yau, Secretary for Justice Rimsky Yuen, the Secretary for Constitutional and Mainland Affairs Raymond Tam, and Under-secretary for Constitutional and Mainland Affairs Lau Kong-wah, and five representatives of the HKFS at that time, i.e., Secretary-general Alex Chow, Deputy Secretary-general Lester Shum, General Secretary Eason Chung, and Council members Yvonne Leung and Nathan Law. The talk was broadcast by overseas and mainland media as well as Hong Kong local TV stations. Excerpts related to the rule of law and democracy are transcribed and translated from Cantonese Chinese to English by the author (see Appendix).

Diagrams of the intertexual thematic formations and their relations about legal discourses made by the government officials and the HKFS representatives respectively are given in Figures 1 and 2, based on the excerpts. What can be seen from the diagrams

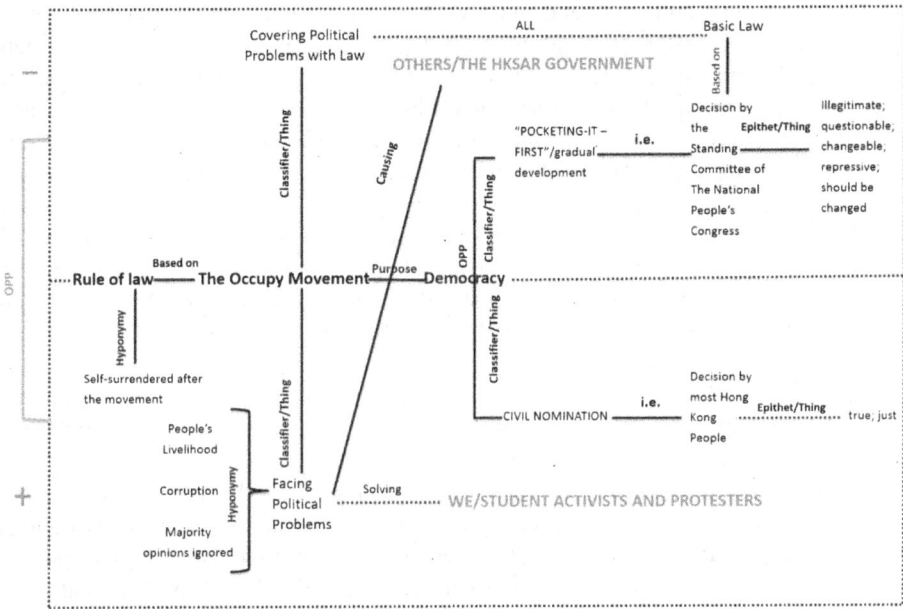

Figure 1. Major thematic formation in students' legal discourses.
Note: The solid line: what is explicitly mentioned; the dashed line: the implied presentational or orientational meaning; –: negative orientational meaning; +: positive orientation meaning

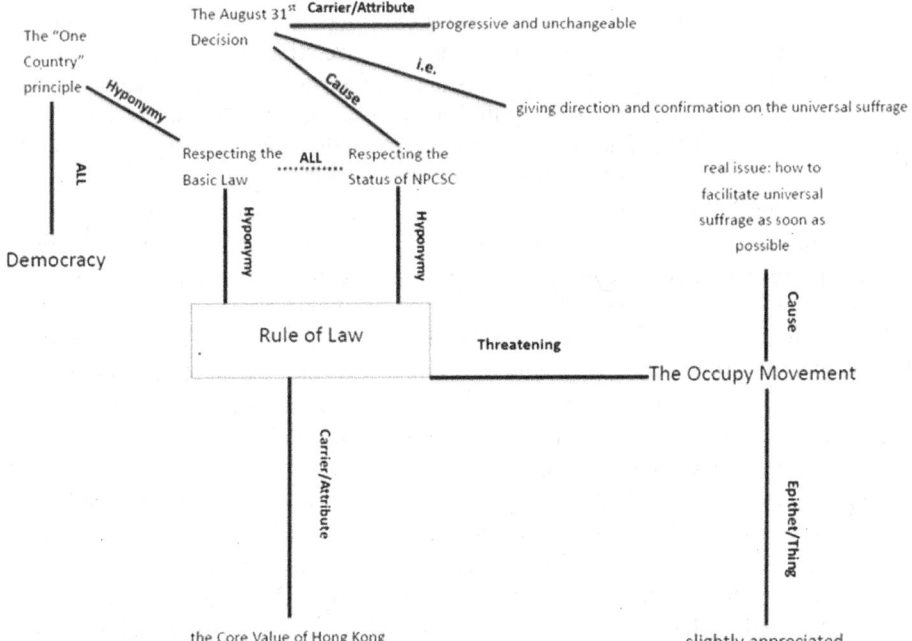

Figure 2. Major thematic formation in the government officials' legal discourses.

is that the proponents and opponents of the Occupy Movement mobilize different lexical choices to construct different moral orders and storylines, and construe different orientations of each other. Specifically, both the government officials' and students representatives' responses are marked by essentialist binaries and negative evaluation towards each other. In addition, the government officials tend to adopt an animator's role in constantly referring to the canonical texts such as the Basic Law and the Decision of the Standing Committee of the National People's Congress, while the student representatives often take the author's role. The students also constantly address the ratified unaddressed listeners (i.e., the TV audience) by constantly referring to the audience in front of the TV and invoke negative, essentialist judgements about the HKSAR government and the 31 August decision promulgated by the Standing Committee of the National People's Congress.

Taking a closer look at the government officials' rhetoric of rule of law, we find the notion is semantically closely related to the ideological identification with mainland China and therefore the rhetoric is intended to emphasize loyalty to China. For example, from 33:55 to 39:42, Chief Secretary Carrie Lam has constructed the thematic proposition that Hong Kong is a special administrative region of China, but not an independent political system, and affirmed the constitutional power of the Central Government. Her point is echoed by Secretary for Justice Rimsky Yuen's remark during 46:22 to 51:53 that "Alex said the law should be for the protection of people not for the restriction of people. I totally agree with this. Under the 'one country' regime, the Hong Kong Basic Law, including Article 45, is to secure the stable, long-term development of Hong Kong."

Additionally, in response to students' interrogation about Article 45 and the possibility of amendment of the Basic Law, the government officials' language is marked by opaque legal terms and thematic condensation which is difficult to understand for the TV audience without legal training. Thematic condensation refers to the discursive structures in which "the number of unexpressed thematic items and relations that are needed to make sense of those that are expressed, is much greater than for other discourse types" (Lemke, 1995, p. 62). For example, in clarifying the correct understanding of "democratic procedures" ([1:47:28–1:50:13]) and the exact Chinese wording for "confirmation" ([46:22–51:53]), Secretary for Justice Yuen does not offer detailed explanation, but instead only mentions foreign laws and Professor Chen Hung-yee's viewpoints as references. While thematic condensation lends technicality and authority of the account, the government's legal discourses can hardly be understood by most of the general audience. The lack of local sensitivity again is evidenced by Chief Secretary Lam's remark about the impossibility of changing the Basic Law during 1:44:05 and 1:44:40, that the real problem facing Hong Kong is how to implement the universal suffrage. As the student representatives have repeatedly raised the problem of widening socioeconomic disparity in Hong Kong in the preceding turns, a lack of discussion about Hong Kong people's livelihood can render the officials unsympathetic to the needs and wants of the underprivileged local people. As such, a strong emphasis on the national belongingness of Hong Kong is evidently constructed, while the local sentiment is relatively seldom attended to, which indicates the "delocalized nationalist" orientation (Jackson, 2014; Lee, 2008). "Delocalized nationalization" refers to advocacy for "allegiance from the local/regional level of Hong Kong to a nation-state level, deemphasizing local distinction, in favor of national commonality (although mainland China is hardly homogeneous in reality, itself)" (Jackson, 2014, p. 39).

What should be noted, however, is that in reinforcing Hong Kong's national identity, the HKFS is assumed to be in opposition to the patriotic or politically correct stance, evidenced in Chief Secretary Lam's remark "Alex said he could not accept (these/this)" before her re-statement of the principles of Basic Law after Alex Chow's opening statement. However, the scope of the above-mentioned principles, including the status of Hong Kong, and the "one country two systems" policy, is semantically larger than that of the major proposition by the HKFS representatives, i.e., civil nomination. In other words, the HKFS has not explicitly objected to the "one country" policy. In positioning the HKFS representative in opposition to all the mentioned Basic Law principles, the discourses of the officials have essentialized HKFS as resistant and blasphemous to the regime of China and thus unpatriotic, because Hong Kong is perceived as a local government exercising a high degree of autonomy within a unitary country (not a federal country) in which sovereignty is firmly vested with Mainland China, not Hong Kong (e.g. Cooray, Lin, Law, Littlewood, & Zafrullah, 2010).

On the other hand, students' account of rule of law is construed in the Western liberal democracy legal tradition, i.e., local people's civil and political rights – a class of rights which protect citizens' freedom from infringement by governments and which ensure one's freedom to participate in the civil and political life of the state without repression, conflated with strong resentment towards the HKSAR government and relatively little attention to the political procedures at the national level in China, as evidenced in the words of Lester Sum, Alex Chow and Yvonne Leung. Although the thematic patterns of HKFS representatives' discourses have not clearly defined the "people" or the "people's wills", it can be inferred that the people the students mention are the Hong Kong local residents (in Nathan Law's words during 42:26 to 44:43). From 42:26–44:43, Nathan Law's comments are not only addressed to the government officials but also addressed to the general public (i.e., the ratified unaddressed audience of the interaction). He has explained in detail the social problems such as the rich–poor discrepancies and ascribed all the social problems to the HKSAR government. Additionally the student representatives also show a lack of attention to the national legislation procedures. For example, from 40:07 to 42:21, Yvonne has problematized and challenged the legitimacy of the 31 August decision by the Standing Committee of the National People's Congress, and committed high degree of certainty for the government to negotiate with the National People Congress, without substantially evaluating the feasibility of doing so.

Linguistic strategies are also mobilized to signal strong negative stances towards the Government's decision. For example, Eason Chung sets up a thematic contrast between participation in the movement and the government's reform proposal, and describes the activists' form of participation in democracy as more progressive. Also, Lester Sum has used parallel structures to condemn the government and maintain that Hong Kong's democracy and Hong Kong's future have been terminated by the 31 August decision of the Standing Committee of the National People's Congress and the HKSAR government ([1:54:59–1:55:13]). It can be seen that in the value system of the student representatives, the liberal democracy in the common law tradition is the necessary condition for Hong Kong's future, without the necessity to explicate the possible influences on the rest of China after adopting an election system radically different from that in the Standing Committee of the National people's Congress, which can be understood as localized isolationism from mainland China.

Coda

As seen from the analysis, the televized student–government meeting is ostensibly about constitutional development. In effect, it is also the negotiation and contestation of the ideological binary between delocalized nationalism and localized isolationism and expression of identity crisis, i.e., uncertainties about whether or how to identify with mainland China and the Communist Party of China, towards which many Hong Kong people show negative attitudes, and how to redefine the position of Hong Kong in China after the 1997 handover. As Lemke (1995, p. 99) points out, "human organisms and human communities must be defined by their developmental trajectories as temporally extended constructions, rather than as present-moment structures", which means human subjectivities, emotions and desires are constituted by previous exposure to various discourses. By the same token, the ideological disparities between the proponents of the movement, aka the yellow ribbons, and the proponents of the movement, aka the blue ribbons, are not formed overnight, but by years or even decades of socialization into distinct discourses.

Given the intense tensions between the "blue" and the "yellow", a good starting point may be attending to ideological rifts with alternate, more diverse understanding about the other in the place of the dominant binary categories. For example, the "blue" and the "yellow" can put aside the grand narratives or dominant stereotypes about each other to understand each other's critiques in situ, and explore each other's sociocultural and political status quo and histories of discourses and trajectory of practices. More importantly, they can reflect on the limitations of their own perspectives. Such a contextualized, multi-perspective approach to differences can be metaphorically termed as "going green", i.e., mixing the "blue" and the "yellow". It is our hope that dialogical encounters and shared histories and value commitments can be promoted for the purpose of facilitating peaceful integration between the two camps in such a politically challenging epoch in Hong Kong's history.

Acknowledgements

I truly thank Professor Angel Lin and Mr Anson Sinn for their extremely helpful advice. I would also like to extend sincere gratitude to the anonymous reviewers and editors for their insightful comments on earlier versions of this article.

Disclosure statement

No potential conflict of interest was reported by the author.

References

Cooray, M. J. A., Lin, F., Law, A., Littlewood, M., & Zafrullah, H. (2010). *Constitutional law in Hong Kong*. Alphen aan den Rijn: Kluwer Law International.
Deng, Z. (2009). The formation of a school subject and the nature of curriculum content: an analysis of liberal studies in Hong Kong. *Journal of Curriculum Studies, 41*(5), 585–604.
Flowerdew, J. (2012). *Critical discourse analysis in historiography: The case of Hong Kong's evolving political identity*. Houndmills: Palgrave Macmillan.
Goffman, E. (1981). *Forms of talk*. Philadelphia: University of Pennsylvania Press.
Jackson, E. J. (2014). Who belongs in what Hong Kong? Citizenship education in the special administrative region. *Citizenship Education around the World: Local Contexts and Global Possibilities, 22*–42.

Ku, A. S.-m. (2015). *Post-colonial cultural trends in Hong Kong – imagining the local, the national, and the global*. Paper presented at the Siting Postcoloniality: Colloquium and Workshop, School of English, The University of Hong Kong (25–27 June 2015).

Lee, W. O. (2008). The Development Of Citizenship Education Curriculum in Hong Kong after 1997: Tensions between national identity and global citizenship. In David L. Grossman, Wing On Lee, & Kerry J. Kennedy (Eds.), *Citizenship curriculum in Asia and the Pacific* (pp. 29–42). Hong Kong: Springer/ Comparative Education Research Centre, The University of Hong Kong.

Lemke, J. L. (1995). *Textual politics: Discourse and social dynamics*. London: Taylor & Francis.

Luk, B. H. K. (1991). Chinese culture in the Hong Kong curriculum, heritage and colonialism. *Comparative Education Review, 34*(4), 650–658.

Morris, P. (1997). School knowledge, the state and the market: An analysis of the Hong Kong secondary school curriculum. *Journal of Curriculum Studies, 29*(3), 329–349.

Morris, P., & Vickers, E. (2015). Schooling, politics and the construction of identity in Hong Kong: The 2012 'Moral and National Education' crisis in historical context. *Comparative Education,*. doi: http://dx.doi.org/10.1080/03050068.2015.1033169

Appendix 1. Excerpts of the televized government–student meeting

[33:55–39:42]

Carrie Lam:

I hope every student understands that we should also obey the law. The Basic Law has regulated how the political system of Hong Kong should be developed ... This is an important constitutional basis ... Hong Kong is a special administrative region, not an independent country or political system. We cannot decide our own political system all by ourselves. The Central Government has significant constitutional power and responsibility in the political system of the special administrative region of Hong Kong ... We need to remember some basic principles in the Basic Law when designing the system of universal suffrage, which Alex said he could not accept. These principles include: firstly, the reality that Hong Kong is not an independent regime, and we must know that we are only a special administrative region in the country; secondly, the principle of "one country, two systems" must be obeyed; the third principle is equal participation so that the chief executive can be found with balanced participation from all walks of life in Hong Kong, which is based on the interests of all, instead of just one particular sector. The fourth is gradual development ... The decision on August 31st is a big step forward towards democracy. Now that we have already had a legal framework, after including the discussion in the coming second public consultation, we can let the five million electorates elect the chief executive in 2017 with one person, one vote. I totally cannot understand why you said it was not a significant progress towards democracy ... Of course, we slightly appreciate the peaceful, ordered, and civil manner of students' protest. But after all, it is an illegal act. It is hoped that in striving for democracy, students can also stick with the rule of law. The rule of law is the core value of Hong Kong. I'm afraid absence of rule of law will only put Hong Kong's future in danger.

[40:07–42:21]

Yvonne Leung:

The officials have repeated many times that the August 31st decision by the Standing Committee of NPC is unchangeable. But the constitutional basis of the August 31st decision needs further interrogation. The decisions by the Standing Committee of NPC in 2004 and 2007 have clearly stated that the chief executive must submit a proposal or a report regarding the universal suffrage to the standing committee. And the Standing Committee is only responsible for the confirmation (in Chinese, *que ren*確認) of the content of the report, i.e., to approve or disapprove it ... Pursuant to Article 62, Paragraph 11 in the Constitutional Law of PRC, when the NPC knows the Standing Committee's decision is inappropriate, NPC is vested with absolute power to alter or annual the decision. So is the August 31st decision unchangeable? Can the presupposition of today's dialogue blind the changes in recent months for the government? I hope the officials will not confuse Hong Kong people and make them think the August 31st decision equals everything.

[42:26–44:43]

Nathan Law:

We are very glad to hear the principal officials say that the purpose for us to be here today is to facilitate the well being of the Hong Kong people. But we hope the principal officials and friends in the government not to blur the focus: this is not just a constitutional, legal issue, but also a political issue. The August 31st framework by the Standing Committee of NPC is based on a political decision. Ultimately, this is a political problem we have to face right now. Why are there so many people on the street? This is exactly because this political issue had led to a serious problem about conscience and even people's livelihood. We can see one million people living under the poverty line and some elderly have to make a living by collecting debris, despite the 2,000 Hong Kong dollars monthly living allowance. We also see lots of corruption scandals of high-ranking officials, and even the police using violence and tear gas to expel the protesters. The cause of these problems is the undemocratic political system ... Conscience and people's livelihood have forced us to go out to face this problem. We would like to work with the government to solve this political problem of binaries and political disputes. We must recognize the cause of these political problems is the August 31st decision by the Standing Committee of NPC. Taking a step backward, it comes from the report submitted by the HKSAR government in the first phase. We also see that the report is not an objective and comprehensive as the secretary described. According to the survey done by Asia-Pacific Studies Institute, The Chinese University of Hong Kong on March 11 to 21, 2014, 76.2% of the interviewees don't accept that only establishmentarians, including pro-Beijing and government officials can become the candidates for the chief executive. And in the consultation report, this point was never mentioned. As we see after the August 31st framework comes out, only pro-establishment candidates can be nominated.

[46:22–51:53]

Rimsky Yuen:

Maybe I'll try to answer the question by Yvonne. We all know NPC is the highest power structure in China and NPCSC is the standing committee of the highest power structure. In the explanation on April 6th 2004, the word used by NPCSC is "confirming" (in Chinese, *que ding*確定) not "deciding" (in Chinese, *jue ding*決定) or other words. We have done lots of research on the question raised by Yvonne. We think that the word "confirming" (in Chinese, *que ding*確定) has allowed NPCSC to give directional guidance in addition to the decision on whether or not it should be revised. There are many reasons for this. Put simply, the noun "confirmation" (in Chinese, *que ding* 確定) should not have such a narrow deduction as offered by Yvonne. Secondly, in deciding the direction, when we refer to other common law systems or other countries' laws, often when government departments have the power to do something, they can list some directional guidance or even some requirements. This point is echoed by Professor Chen Hung-yee in Hong Kong. We internally have done research about this and we think in this situation NPCSC is vested with absolute power [Lester Sum looks the other way] to give some clauses which Alex briefly discussed in the opening statement in addition to the August 31st Decision ... This is understandable and effective because in the five steps of constitutional reform ... the second step needs the NPCSC to make a decision, and in the fifth step the NPCSC will be involved. If the NPCSC can give some directions in the second step, it will be only helpful and will not exert any negative influence ... As repeated by the government many times ... Hong Kong is a special administrative region so the Central Government has the responsibility and the duty to handle this and it must be involved. If in the last step it is disapproved, please use your common sense to consider, the constitutional crisis faced by Hong Kong and mainland China will be larger. So giving directional guidance in the August 31st decision ... is legitimate, totally understandable and conducive for the constitutional reform under the current situation ... So in my response to your question, Yvone, there's no need to be any doubt about this [Yvonne Leung shifts her eyes from Rimsky Yuen and looks down].

[52:54–53:39]

Yvonne Leung:

Under this premise, the Hong Kong government should shoulder the constitutional responsibility and strive for biggest democracy for Hong Kong citizens in the proposal for methods in universal suffrage, and then submit the proposal to the Legislative Council for approval before submitting it to the NPC for confirmation ... The government should not let go its responsibility because of the NPC's gatekeeping role ... We should not focus our discussion on whether the NPCSC's decision is changeable or not, because the Constitution of PRC has clearly stated it can be changed. So I'll let Eason ask the government about how to solve this political problem.

[53:48–56:08]

Eason Chung

I agree that democracy is an attitude ... This is exactly because their wills are ignored that they protest and tell the government about their dissatisfaction today ... If we have any common sense, as in the secretary's words, we can see our democratic rights are severely damaged after the NCPSC's August 31st decision ... So this is not a big progress towards democracy ... We have promised to surrender ourselves to the court after the movement, which also demonstrates the spirit of rule of law and the biggest resistance within the rule of law.

[1:04:48–1:06:50]

Lester Sum:

Why are we protesting on the streets? Why are we willing to be charged? ... It is for the hope that the HKSAR government can secure Hong Kong people's basic rights ... including democratic rights to vote, to be voted and to nominate. These are all basic rights which we believe should be protected by the rule of law. The secretaries have mentioned many times that the rule of law is the core value of Hong Kong. We certainly respect the rule of law ... However, the law essentially is used to secure the basic rights of the people and it is written for the people. It should not become a political apparatus for the privileged few and some government officials to trample our political rights. Politics is our biggest problem right now. This is the political will of the Hong Kong government. This is the political will of the NPC. This is a political problem packaged with legal means by the government officials.

[1:37:02–1:37:30]
Alex Chow:

The rule of law is to protect, but not to restrict civil rights. Do all the rights belong to the nominating committee or Hong Kong people under the current law? ... Secretary for Justice mentioned that the Basic Law has regulated the nomination, but can the Basic Law be changed, when the Basic Law is unjust and not constitutional?

[1:44:05–1:44:40]
Carrie Lam:

Can we amend the Basic Law? It has been promulgated for over 24 years and run for 17 years after the handover. It has safeguarded our different rights. Such a solemn constitutional document cannot be changed randomly. Additionally, any amendment of the Basic Law cannot solve the problem Hong Kong is facing today. The problem right now is how to facilitate the democratic development and implement universal suffrage in 2017.

[1:47:28–1:50:13]
Rimsky Yuen:

I want to clarify two points. Firstly, just now Yvonne just mentioned the democratic procedures. I'd like to point out that some people say because Article 45 says there are democratic procedures, so Article 45 can be understood as securing civil nomination. We don't agree with this understanding of Article 45. This understanding is wrong. Democratic procedures refer to the procedures to nominate members of the nominating committee. We cannot overthrow the nominating committee. This is impossible and also violates Article 45. As Secretary for Constitutional and Mainland Affairs Raymond Tam just mentioned, only the nominating committee has the substantial power to nominate candidates. Secondly, Alex said the law should be for the protection of people, not for the restriction of people. I totally agree with this. Under the "one country" regime, the Hong Kong Basic Law, including Article 45, is to secure the stable, long-term development of Hong Kong. We have decided to adopt Article 45. Some people, probably including Alex and Lester, may have different opinions about Article 45. I can understand, because different people can have different opinions about a law, which leads to the suggestion of amending the Basic Law. Chief Secretary Lam has just responded to this, so I will not talk more about this. I only wish you could refer to the relevant provisions about amending the Basic Law, i.e., Article 159 of the Basic Law, the requirements of which is higher than Clause 7 of Annex I to the Basic Law, or the five-step approach. In other words, it is harder to amend the Basic Law pursuant to Article 159 given the diversity of opinions in Hong Kong. So it is impossible to change the Basic Law by 2017. So, if we can satisfy most Hong Kong people's will to implement universal suffrage in 2017, it is not a practical idea to amend the Basic Law.

[1:53:38–1:54:22]
Eason Chung:

It is exactly because the government officials have excluded many other opinions that many citizens come out and refuse accept the government … Democracy is a decision made by the majority, not by the elites. In the movement, people of different social strata are practising democracy in the streets despite differences in opinions and this is more progressive than the "pocketing-it-first" democracy mentioned by the principal officials.

[1:54:59–1:55:13]
Lester Sum:

There is only one reason that leads to the movement today: the Hong Kong government and the decision by NPCSC have killed Hong Kong people's future and the dream for democracy that Hong Kong people have fought for three decades.

Index

accountancy firms 107, 108, 111
Add Oil machine 117
advertising: influence on media 98, 99, 107, 108–9, 111
advocacy reporting 89–90, 91, 92–3, 94
agents of mediatization *see* media and information praxis of young activists
Alexander, J. 69
Allam, N. 63
Altheide, D.L. 46
Amnesty International 107
Anonymous 119
anti-establishment discourses 39
Anti-Express Rail Link (Anti-XRL) Movement 51, 56
anti-globalization protests 8
Anti-Moral and National Education Movement 49, 51, 52, 56
anti-nuclear movements 20
anti-WTO protests (Seattle, 1999) 8
Apple Daily 7, 11, 12, 14, 32, 37; 51, 68, 91, 92, 108, 119
Arab Spring 38, 50, 84–5
Arditi, B. 24, 28
Arendt, H. 82, 85
arrests: access to computer with criminal or dishonest intent 118
Asen, R. 38
Atton, C. 93
autonomy 120–1
awareness, shared 29, 57, 58

Baby Boomers+ 31, 32–8
Baggott, C. 25
Baker, E. 99
Bakker, T.P. 27
Barzilai-Nahon, K. 25
Baumgartner, J.C. 27, 68
Beam, C. 52
Beck, U. 25
Beech, H. 26
Benkler, Y. 27
Bennett, W.L. 1, 3, 24–5, 26, 28, 38, 46, 66, 88, 116

between-ness and hybridity 125
bias 74, 90, 92, 110; structural 8, 66
big data 39
Biggs, M. 63
Bimber, B. 25
Blum, J. 119
Boudreau, C. 63
Bourdieu, P. 8
boycott of news events 92–3
Brafman, O. 117
business interests and newspapers 99, 107–9, 110–11

Cameron, David 103–4
Cammaerts, B. 44, 46
Carr, W. 48
Castells, M. 1, 2, 24, 26, 27, 28, 38, 39, 46, 57, 116
censorship 39, 118; online 115, 116, 118–19; self- 90, 93, 95, 118
Chaim, G. 65, 69
Chan, Anson 103–4
Chan, C.K. 11
Chan, D.K. 53
Chan, J.M. 3, 4, 45, 46, 55, 56, 57, 66, 74, 89, 94–5
Chan, K.M. 15, 61
Chan, M. 6, 8, 11
Chen Hung-yee 128
Cheng, L.K. 126
Childs, R. 25, 26
Chile 24, 29
Chow, Agnes 55
Chow, Alex 126, 129, 134
Chu Yiu-ming 61
Chung, Eason 126, 129, 133, 135
citizenship education 126
Civic Passion 93
civil disobedience 4, 61–76, 90; analysis and findings 68–73; concluding discussion 73–6; data and method 66–8; definition 65, 68–9; duty to express dissent 85; future research 76; legal realist view: citizens' actions in 4, 80–5; levels of understanding of 68–71; motivation,

INDEX

ability and opportunity 65, 74; predictors of understanding of 71–3; repertoire of contentious actions and oppositional political knowledge 62–4; research questions and hypotheses 64–6
civil society organizations 119
Clare, C. 25
clicktivism 116
Cohen, J. 65
Coleman, G. 119
collaboration, learning through 63
Colom, Alvaro 29
communication and political learning 65–6, 68, 71–3, 74–5
communicative mobilization 49, 55–6
communism 103, 110
conceptual knowledge 66, 74
connectivity among young activists and Movement participants 48–9, 52–3
consumer politics 25
contested news values and media performance 4–5, 88–95; media performance and alternative media 93–4; media performance in moments of crisis 91–2; should journalists take action? 92–3; social crisis and news making 88–90
Coombe, R. 81, 83
Cooray, M.J.A. 129
corporations 7–8, 39, 120; business interests and newspapers 99, 107–9, 110–11
Costanza-Chock, S. 45, 54
counterpublics 28, 38, 39–40
court injunctions 76
Coyle, D. 117
critical discourse moment 75
critical legal studies 81
cross promotion 54
culture-consuming public 28
Curran, J. 99

The Daily Express 105
The Daily Mail 100–1, 105–6
The Daily Mirror 106
The Daily Telegraph 105, 108–9, 111
Dalton, R. 38
Dash 50, 53, 54
DBC Radio 92
De Fazio, G. 63
Deacon, D. 44, 46, 47
Dean, J. 40
decentralization 120
Deibert, R. 116
Delli Carpini, M.X. 63, 65, 73
delocalized nationalization 126, 128, 129–30
DeLuca, K.M. 8–9, 20
demonization of foreign influence 119–20
Deng Xiaoping 98, 103
Deng, Z. 125

determinism, technological 7
diffusion 63
digital natives 25, 31, 44, 45, 54, 57
discourse dissemination 49, 53–5
discursive analysis 98–9, 106–7
dissent, duty to express 85
distributed denial of service (DDoS) attacks 119, 120
Dorizas, A. 25
Downing, J. 28

e-tactics 63
Earl, J. 39, 63
echo chamber effect 39
education and identity 125–6
education, social movement as civic *see* civil disobedience
Egypt 24, 29
Ekiert, G. 62
elections: district board 58
Ellison, N. 38
email chatrooms 52
email and Interceptions for Communications and Surveillance Ordinance (ICSO) 117–18
emails hacked 117
Entman, R. 98
environmental protests 63
Erni, J.N. 81
Eveland, Jr, W.P. 65
expression, freedom of 95, 118

face-to-face meetings 52
Facebook 26, 27, 29, 31–2, 33–8, 39, 45–6, 50, 117, 120; Scholarism 50, 51, 52, 53–4, 55–6, 57
Facebook generation 25
The Financial Times 99–100, 101–5, 107–8, 109, 110
Firechat 115
Fiske, J. 8
Flowerdew, J. 125
Fominaya, C.F. 45
foreign influence, demonization of 119–20
foreign news coverage: UK national daily press 5, 97–111
Fortune magazine 57
Foucault, M. 83
Fowler, R. 98
Fraile, M. 63
framing in UK national daily press 98, 102–3, 106–7, 108, 110
France 63
Fraser, N. 28
Friedman, T.L. 45

Galtung, J. 98
Gamson, W.A. 62, 75
Garrett, R. 39

INDEX

Generation X 31, 32–8
Generation Y 25
Generation Z 25
Gerbner, G. 7
Gil de Zúñiga, H. 27, 30, 38, 68
Gladwell, M. 47, 57, 116
Goffman, E. 125
Gohdes, A.R. 116
Goldsmith, J.L. 116
Google Maps 115
government: televized government–student meeting 5, 124–30
government responses to use of new technologies 5, 115–21
governmentality 83
grievances: television and mediated instant grievances 4, 6–21
The Guardian 97, 100, 101–3, 104, 105, 106, 110, 111
Guatemala 24, 29
Guthrie, J. 108

Habermas, J. 28, 85
hacking of emails 117
Hamilton, J. 99
Hampson, R. 58
Harcup, T. 98
Harlow, S. 29
Harris, B. 118
Hartley, J. 8
Hayes, G. 63, 75
Headline Daily 91
Healey, J. 120
Herman, E.S. 8, 99
Hilton, I. 103
Hogan, J. 25
Holmes, O.W., Jr 81
Hong Kong Bar Association 76
Hong Kong Daily News 91
Hong Kong Economic Times 91
Hong Kong Federation of Students (HKFS) 45, 50, 55, 56; televized government–student meeting 5, 124–30
Hong Kong Golden Forum 93
Hong Kong Inmedia 50, 93, 94
Hong Kong Journalists Association (HKJA) 92–3, 118
Hong Kong University: PopVote 119
Howard, P. 116
HSBC 107–9, 110–11
hunger strikes 55, 56, 61
hybridity 125

iCable News 51
identity: national 125–6, 128–30; personal and group 38
images live on TV of police firing tear gas *see* television and mediated instant grievances

The Independent 106–7
information aggregation and verification 48, 50–2, 56
information literacy *see* media and information praxis of young activists
information sharing 38–9
injunctions 76
Inmedia 50, 93, 94
Instagram 26, 50, 52
insurgent public sphere: social media 4, 24–40; discussion and conclusion 38–40; hypotheses 29–31; identities, personal and group 38; individuated networked structure 28; information sharing 38–9; insurgent nature of SNS 27–9; method 31–2; networked media and Net Geners (18- to 29-year-olds) 26; new form of mobilization 24–5; results and analysis 32–8; SNS and political participation 26–7
Interceptions for Communications and Surveillance Ordinance (ICSO) 117–18
Internet 6, 25, 26, 27, 31, 39, 45, 46, 47, 50; advertising 109; government responses to use of new technologies 5, 115–21; Scholarism 51; Web 2.0 29
interviews, press 55
Ip, Regina 115, 119
Iyengar, S. 63

Jackson, E.J. 126, 128
Jacques, Martin 105
Jenkins, H. 27
Jenkins, J.C. 63
Johann, D. 63
Joye, S. 98
Juris, J. 24, 28

Kaufhold, K. 63
Keck, M.E. 116, 119
Kern, A. 9
Kim, Y.M. 63
King, G. 116
Klinger, U. 46, 47
Kohut, A. 26
Koopmans, R. 20
Ku, A.S. 21, 64, 76, 91, 125
Kushin, M. 27
Kwong, Glacier 117

Lague, D. 117
Lai, Y.K. 57
Lam, Carrie 102–3, 126, 128–9, 131, 134
Lam, L. 117
Lash, S. 57
Lau Kong-wah 126
Law, Nathan 126, 129, 132
Lazar, N.C. 81
lazybones picture packages 54

INDEX

Leadbeater, C. 27
Lee, A.Y.L. 47
Lee, F. 117
Lee, F.L.F. 3, 4, 11, 13, 19, 21, 62, 63, 64, 66, 71, 74, 75, 76, 90
Lee, Martin 103–4
Lee, W.O. 126, 128
legal essentialism 82
legal interpretivism 81–2
legal positivism 81–2
legal realism 4, 80–5
Lemke, J.L. 124, 125, 128, 130
Lenhart, A. 26
Lester, L. 46, 55
Leung, C.Y. 103, 105, 119
Leung, D.K.K. 11, 38, 89
Leung, L. 64
Leung, Yvonne 126, 129, 131–2, 133
Levin, N.A.L. 118
Lewis, J. 63
Li, X.X. 26
LinkedIn 26
Liu Xiaoming 105, 109
Livingstone, S. 25
Loader, B. 26, 38, 39
localized internationalization 126
localized isolationism 126, 129–30
Lovink, G. 46, 54
Lui, T.L. 64
Luk, B.H.K. 125
Luk, Y.C. 11
Luskin, R. 65

Ma, E.K.W. 6
Ma, N. 3, 10
Ma, W.K. 26
McCausland, C. 69
McKee, A. 28
MacKinnon, R. 116
McLeod, D.M. 8, 38
Mansbridge, J. 63
Maras, S. 88, 89
Marx, K. 56
mass/mainstream media 3, 25, 29, 36, 37, 38, 39, 40, 56, 57–8; alternative media: criticism of 94; bypass 46, 54; civil disobedience, understanding of 66, 68, 71–2, 74; contested news values and media performance 4–5, 88–95; integrating information from various sources 51, 52; oppositional knowledge 66, 74; public sphere 28; reframing stories 54–5; Scholarism 51, 54–5, 57; UK national daily press 5, 97–111; *see also* television
Mattoni, A. 44
Mazzoleni, G. 46
media and information praxis of young activists 4, 44–58; communicative mobilization 49, 55–6; conclusion and discussion 56–8; connectivity among young activists and Movement participants 48–9, 52–3; definition of media and information literacy 47; digital youth and social movements 45–6; discourse dissemination 49, 53–5; information aggregation and verification 48, 50–2, 56; mediatization of social movements 46–7; research methods 49–50; Scholarism and Umbrella Movement 49
media logic 46–7, 55, 58
media performance and contested news values 4–5, 88–95
mediated instant grievances and television 4, 6–21; analysis and findings 14–19; discussion 19–21; empirical analysis 10–13; method and measurements 13–14
Meirick, P.C. 66
Mexico 24
Millennials 25
Ming Pao Daily 21, 51, 68, 91
Mirani, L. 120
mobile phones/networks 25, 26, 56, 57, 115–16, 117
Mok, C. 118
Morozov, E. 47, 57, 116
Morris, P. 125
Mubarak, Hosni 29
Murphy, Richard 107
Mutz, D. 66
MySpace 26, 27

national identity 125–6, 128–30
natives, digital 25, 31, 44, 45, 54, 57
Negt, O. 28
neoliberal economics 25
net generation 25–6, 31, 45; insurgent public sphere: social media 4, 24–40; *see also* Scholarism
networked social movement 46, 57
news values and media performance, contested 4–5, 88–95; media performance and alternative media 93–4; media performance in moments of crisis 91–2; should journalists take action? 92–3; social crisis and news making 88–90
newspapers 26, 55, 68, 71–2, 74, 91–2; UK national daily press 5, 97–111
Norris, P. 65
Nossek, H. 98
Now TV News 32, 37, 51

objective reporting 88–90, 91–2, 94–5; alternative media 93–4; should journalists take action? 92–3
Oblinger, D. 25
Oborne, P. 108–9, 111
oligopoly 7–8

INDEX

Ollis, T. 62
Olson, P. 119
oppositional political knowledge 62, 65–6, 71, 74, 75; repertoire of contentious actions and 62–4
Oriental Daily 32, 91
Ostman, J. 63
Ottaway, Peter 104
Owens, L. 39

Palczewski, C. 38
Palfrey, J. 25
pamphlet distribution 54, 57
Papacharissi, Z. 39
Pariser, E. 39
Park, R.E. 88
participation framework 125
party politics 25, 110
Passion Times 93
Pateman, C. 28
Patterson, T.E. 90
peer-to-peer learning 45
Picard, R. 99
political knowledge, oppositional 62, 65–6, 71, 74, 75; repertoire of contentious actions and 62–4
political parallelism 102
politics, consumer 25
Postman, N. 7
postmodernism 83
power relations 27, 38
Prensky, M. 25
press conferences 55
press releases 55
Price, V. 65
Prince, Matthew 119
privatization 25
promotional pamphlets 54, 57
prosumers 57
protest paradigm 55; television news 8
public screen *see* television and mediated instant grievances
public sphere(s) 28; insurgent public sphere: social media 4, 24–40; multiple 28
Putnam, R. 38

Quill, L. 65, 69
Quintelier, E. 27, 30

R v Jones (Margaret) & Others (2006) 80–1
radio 32, 51, 55, 92
Radio Television Hong Kong (RTHK) 51, 92
Raffell, Andrew 118
Raine, L. 26
Rawls, J. 65, 85
Reese, S.D. 88, 89
Reporters Without Borders Press Freedom Index 118

Richardson, J. 98
Rosenberg, Rodrigo 29
Rovira Sancho, G. 24, 28, 29

Sarat, A. 81
Sauter, M. 119
Scholarism 6, 14, 26, 105; media and information praxis of young activists *see separate entry*
Schudson, M. 88, 89, 92
Schulz, W. 46
security of information 56
Sham Yee Lan 92–3
shared awareness 29, 57, 58
Shirky, C. 29, 57, 116
Shum, Lester 126
Simmons, E. 9
Simons, N. 25
Skapinker, M. 107
slacktivism 47, 57, 116
smartphones 56, 57, 115
Smith, A. 27
Smith, M.K. 48, 56
Smith, W. 85
So, A. 3
So, C.Y.K. 45, 89
So, P. 119
social capital 26, 27, 38
social contract 85
social crisis and news making 88–90, 94–5; media performance and alternative media 93–4; media performance in moments of crisis 91–2; should journalists take action? 92–3; Umbrella Movement 90–1
social fragmentation 25
social media 9, 11, 16, 19, 20, 93–4, 115; Add Oil machine 117; coordination 29, 116–17; government surveillance 117–18; insurgent public sphere 4, 24–40; media and information praxis of young activists 4, 44–58; shared awareness 29, 57, 58; understanding of civil disobedience and political use of 66, 68, 71–3, 74
socialization 130
SocRED 93
South China Morning Post 91
Spain 24
Sparks, C. 100
Squires, C. 28
Stephens, P. 103–4
Sterbenz, C. 119
Stiegler, B. 26
Strange, M. 63
street booths 54, 57
Sum, Lester 129, 133–4, 135
The Sun 91
surveillance 39, 117–18, 120; information verification by young activists 52, 56

INDEX

Tai, B.Y.T. 61–2, 64, 68–9, 75, 82, 83–4, 117
Tam, Raymond 126
Tang, G.K.Y. 27, 30, 38, 74
Tapscott, D. 25, 45
Tarrow, S. 116, 119
tear gas 2, 3, 24, 50, 56, 57, 91, 105, 106, 117, 132; live TV images *see* television and mediated instant grievances
Telegram 51, 52, 53, 56, 57, 115
television 26, 32, 51, 92, 100; censorship 118; civil disobedience, understanding of 68, 71–2, 74; mediated instant grievances 4, 6–21; Television Broadcasts Ltd (TVB) 11, 12, 14, 16, 19, 20, 32, 37, 92, 94, 118; televized government–student meeting 5, 124–35
television and mediated instant grievances 4, 6–21; analysis and findings 14–19; discussion 19–21; empirical analysis 10–13; media beliefs 11–12, 14, 16, 19; methods and measurements 13–14; political attitude 10–11, 13–14, 16, 19; reasons for participation 12, 14, 16, 19; time of participation decision 13, 14–16, 19; view on self-mobilized action 12–13, 14, 16, 19
televized government–student meeting 5, 124–30; excerpts 131–5; legal discourses in 126–9; socio–historical context: Hong Kong's national identity 125–6; text semantics and participation framework 125
text semantics 124; participation framework and 125
Thatcher, Margaret 98, 104
Theocharis, Y. 27
Tilly, C. 62
Time magazine 55
The Times 106, 108, 109
Ting, K.W. 56
trolls, paid 116, 119
Tsang, H.W. 13
Tuchman, G. 88
Tufekci, Z. 7, 24, 28, 29, 116, 119
Tulgan, B. 25
Turkey 24
Twitter 29, 50, 51, 115
Tworzecki, H. 66

Udeh, C. 84–5
UK national daily press 5, 97–111; balance and tone of coverage 105–7; business interests and newspapers 107–9; framing the issue 102–3; scope of coverage 99–102; special responsibility of UK 103–5
Ukraine 84–5
UNESCO 47
United States 24, 26, 27, 29, 85, 102, 103, 119

Valenzuela, S. 7, 24, 29, 38
Van de Donk, W. 44, 46
Van Dijck, J. 47
Van Laer, J. 116
Van Zoonen, L. 28
visual images: lazybones picture packages 54
Von Hayek, F. 81

Wada, T. 62
Wai, T. 94
Walsh, E.J. 9, 20
Wang, C. 119
Wang, D.J. 63
Wang, J. 56
Warner, M. 38
Weslund, O. 45
WhatsApp 26, 46, 50, 51, 52, 55, 56, 57; Interceptions for Communications and Surveillance Ordinance (ICSO) and 118
Wicks, R.H. 66
Wilke, J. 98
Willnat, L. 40
Wilson, B. 25
wiretapping 117–18
Wong, F.L.K. 89
Wong, J.C.F. 26, 49, 50, 51, 53, 55–6, 57, 105
Wong, M.L. 13
Wong Yeung Tat 93
WTO Conference (Seattle, 1999) 8
Wu, A. 26

xenophobic narrative 119
Xi Jinping 104

Yau, Edward 126
Yim, C.H. 51
young activists *see* media and information praxis of young activists
YouTube 26, 50, 51, 117
Yuen, K. 92
Yuen, Rimsky 126, 128, 132, 134–5

Zello Walkie Talkie 115
Zhang, J. 118
Zhang, W. 27